Sea Gypsy

To Russell –

May your sails of <u>hope</u>
always be trimmed in
gentle tradewinds.

May the stars in the heavens
above always guide and protect
you –

And always – on your horizon –
a patch of blue.

Merry Christmas

December – 1966

SEA
GYPSY

Peter Tangvald

E. P. DUTTON & CO., INC.
New York / 1966

TO SIMONNE

TO SIMONNE

Contents

Illustrations

All maps have been drawn by the author

1

Dorothea Ahoy

PRESENTING my passport to the English immigration officer I was startled to hear him say: 'Coming back for another boat, I suppose?'

'Well, yes . . . but how did you know?' I stammered.

'Don't you remember? I am the one who cleared you last time. When I asked the purpose of your visit in England you told me that you had come to buy a yacht which you wanted to sail back to California. Now, how much money are you bringing into the country?'

'Just over eleven thousand dollars.'

'That's about one thousand more than last time, then. Here is a three-month visa. Hope you'll enjoy your visit.'

I looked at him with awe. What a memory! I could not remember his face even after he reminded me who he was, yet I had only been in contact with a couple of dozen custom and immigration officers, while there must have been many thousand men walking past this officer. Two years before I had indeed bought a yacht in England—*Windflower*—and sailed her to America. Two years will make a lot of changes, sometimes. I found out to my sorrow that prices had gone up tremendously since my last visit and I began to regret having sold the *Windflower*. Yachtbrokers were very helpful, but I found out once more that the boats that I could afford I did not like and the boats I liked I could not afford. I lost a lot of time waiting for buses and trains, so I finally bought a second-hand scooter with a double seat for eighty pounds. It was early spring. It was biting cold riding on the scooter, but it gave me a wonderful sense of independence and saved a lot of time.

After a month of riding around on my faithful scooter, I came to a lovely little yacht harbour called Birdham Pool. Walking along the berths and then over a miniature lock gate I saw a nice, husky cutter in beautiful shape —the *Dorothea*. I remembered her from two years before, when I almost bought her instead of the more elegant *Windflower*. But it is with boats like it is with women—the most beautiful girl will not necessarily make the best wife. Many a time had I thought regretfully about the more seaworthy

Dorothea when I was in rough weather and when so many things went wrong aboard *Windflower*. Now I had found her again; this time there was no 'For Sale' sign on her, but then you never know unless you ask.

'Ahoy! The *Dorothea*! Anybody on board?' I shouted.

A distinguished-looking man in his fifties, with a friendly smile, came up out of the hatch.

'Would you by any chance consider selling your yacht? I am looking for one just like yours.'

He looked a bit surprised and before he had time to answer I added: 'If we should agree, I can pay cash, and I'll do my own survey in a few hours.'

He laughed and said she was not really for sale, but would I come on board for a cup of tea?

Next day we met at the bank. I gave him the money and he gave me the papers and the key. That very day I moved on board. My long search for a boat was over. 'You can have everything in her,' the owner had said, 'except the big clock. That was a present from my father, so I wouldn't feel right to let it go.'

I considered that was fair enough, as most owners strip their ships almost completely before handing them over.

On the way back to the boat I bought some bread, meat, vegetables and fruit, so I could set up housekeeping right away. Lying in my bunk for the first time, I was reading a magazine when I saw an advertisement which gave me a brilliant idea. It read: '22-year-old girl desires to go sailing at week-ends and holidays.' I mailed a letter next morning and two days later I met her at the station. We drove to the boat and had lunch together. She was cute and she just loved boats. She looked over every detail of the ship and asked a thousand questions. We sympathised immediately and I said to her: 'Listen, let's not beat about the bush. You tell me what you expect out of me and I'll tell you what I expect out of you.'

'I only know that I like to sail. You tell me what you've got in mind,' she said.

'You told me you are looking for a new job and that you would like to go sailing on week-ends when you will be free. I propose that you forget about that job. When I've fitted out the ship and it's ready for sea we'll leave together for the south. I don't promise you any special destination, as you might get seasick and fed up about sailing the very first day out, but that's the chance you take. While you stay with me you don't need an income, for even if I can't give you too much you will not be in need of anything and I'll pay all the bills. If all should go well you might stay with me till the French Riviera, the West Indies or, who knows, farther yet. One thing you should realise, though: if I were satisfied to sleep all by myself in that quarter bunk I would have looked for a man crew.'

But it was not to be—we are not always master of our destiny. I went right to work on the boat, looking forward to her arrival and making all the changes I felt were necessary for a long sea voyage. Among the most important jobs was to take out the engine, as I believe this spoils all the fun and romance of sailing, besides the fact that they are a continual nuisance, take up a lot of room, give a bad smell in the boat and require continuous maintenance. Lifting the thing out of the boat was rather more than I could handle even with block and tackle, so I thought about Scotty, a friend of mine, who is always willing to lend a hand. I drove over to Emsworth and Scotty was amazed when I asked him if he could help me to get my motor ashore.

'My God! It's only a week ago that you had no boat and here you are with fitting-out problems!'

An hour later the engine was ashore with a big 'For Sale' sign on it. Scotty would come often for a visit after that day and each time I had to drive to Southampton for purchases I would stop at Emsworth for a chat with him.

I took out the cockpit and made the deck flush, so I got more storage room below and also avoided the danger of a deep cockpit full of water in a gale. I reinforced the rigging, and made a few changes in the accommodation down below. I made a large chart table and shelves for the navigation books and for my sextant. I rearranged the galley and installed a stainless steel sink for making it easier to do the dishes. I overhauled the W.C., or 'head' as a seaman is supposed to call the thing, and hoped it would never break down.

A couple of days later on a grey rainy morning I opened the hatch and saw an elegant woman walking toward the *Dorothea*. There was something strangely familiar about her. Then I realised it was my wife. An instant later she stood by the ship and gave me a sour-sweet smile: 'May I come on board, dear?'

It was rather inconvenient, but I am raised as a gentleman, so how could I refuse hospitality to a woman on a rainy day, especially if she happens to be my wife?

I soon discovered that Lillemor had come to stay, and I prefer not to recall the half-hour when I had to break the news to my prospective crew. I can truthfully say that at the time I wished that I had been born a woman-hater, so that this awkward situation would not have arisen.

The days went by, and when the most important work was done I decided to do the rest in Brixham. That would give us the double advantage of a trial sail and a change of routine. The last couple of days were spent in getting all the food on board and stowing everything securely for sea. I don't care too much for tinned food, so I tried the ways of the old square

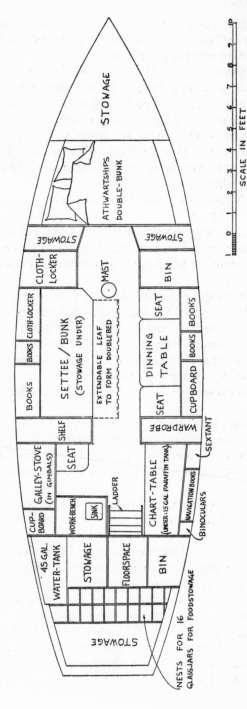

NOTES :
1. LADDER HINGES UP TO GIVE ACCESS AFT.
2. STOWAGE UNDER ALL 3 SEATS & UNDER BOTH BUNKS

STOWAGE

ATHWARTSHIPS DOUBLE-BUNK

STOWAGE

STOWAGE

CLOTH-LOCKER

BIN

CLOTH-LOCKER

BOOKS

SETTEE / BUNK
(STOWAGE UNDER)

EXTENDABLE LEAF TO FORM DOUBLEBED

MAST

SEAT

BOOKS

DINNING TABLE

BOOKS

BOOKS

SHELF

SEAT

SEAT

CUPBOARD

GALLEY-STOVE
(IN GIMBALS)

WARDROBE

CUPBOARD

SEXTANT

CUP-BOARD

WORK-BENCH

SINK

LADDER

CHART-TABLE
(UNDER-15 GAL PARAFFIN TANK)

NAVIGATION BOOKS

BINOCULAR'S

45 GAL. WATER-TANK

STOWAGE

FLOORSPACE

BIN

STOWAGE

NESTS FOR 16 GLASSJARS FOR FOODSTOWAGE

ACCOMMODATION PLAN OF DOROTHEA

SCALE IN FEET
0 1 2 3 4 5 6 7 8 9

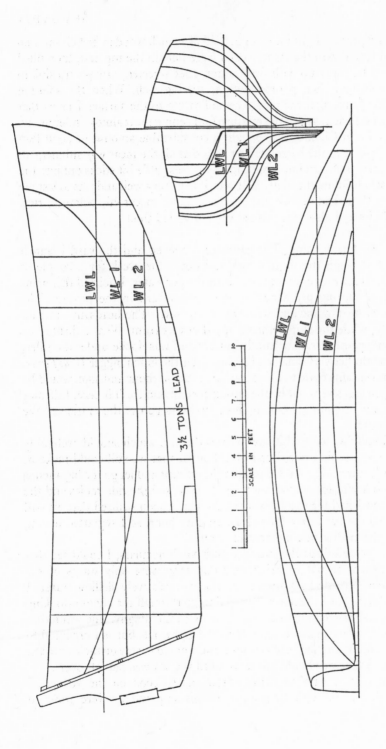

LINES OF DOROTHEA

Designed by Dr. Harrison Butler. Built in 1934 at Whitstable, England.

Dimensions: 11 tons T.M. Overall length: 32 ft. Waterline length: 29 ft. Beam: 9 ft. 10 in. Draught: 6 ft. Sail area 660 sq. ft. Outside lead keel of 3½ tons.
Materials: Oak frames, pitchpine planking, teak interior, solid Norwegian pine mast, copper fastenings.

rigger and prepared salt meat. I got hold of a small wooden barrel, sat it on end and lashed it to the mast. I cut a large hole in the top end, then filled the barrel half-way up with fresh water. I let a peeled, raw potato sink to the bottom and then poured salt in, stirring well. When the solution became so heavy that the potato came floating to the surface I knew that there was sufficient salt in the mixture for keeping meat almost indefinitely. In the store in Chichester I bought a considerable amount of good lean beef and put it in the barrel, taking care that all the meat was submerged. This I knew was very important, for if the least little bit sticks out into the air, the whole lot might spoil. As it was, it kept very well and was to last me until the West Indies. We also stored a lot of macaroni, potatoes, rice, sugar, fruits and also some tinned cans of varied food.

The day finally came. The gates were opened and the yard's launch towed us through the narrow lock and down the creek for a couple of hundred yards, where we were in a little deeper water. I hoisted the mainsail, almost cutting my hands on the thin halyard in the process. The launch cast off my line and we were on our own. The headsails came up hesitantly, while the ship gathered speed downstream. What a thrill to be under sail again! *Dorothea* handled nicely and was docile under the tiller, but I thought her very small and stubby after the much bigger *Windflower*.

When we came close to the extremity of the harbour and soon would be in the open sea, swept out by the strong current and fresh breeze, Lillemor shouted out in panic: 'Look at those breakers across the entrance! We can't go out!'

Admittedly we were a bit late to cross the bar, which should preferably be done around high tide, but I had thought that we still could make it. As it was, I hurriedly rounded up into the current and let go the big anchor over the side and lowered all the sails. I rechecked the tide-tables and the information I had for the crossing of the bar. I soon realised that we still could cross the bar safely for at least another hour, so I regretted having dropped the anchor in a moment of panic.

Looking carefully at the entrance with my binoculars, I could see that the breakers were not breaking, but that they were only waves of the peculiar shape made by a strong current over relatively shallow water. I explained this, but Lillemor was scared to go through the choppy-looking entrance, and begged me to take her ashore in the dinghy. She wanted to join up in Brixham again, where she would go by bus, but as I prepared to lower the dinghy she changed her mind and wanted to stay on the *Dorothea*. She insisted that we should not leave until the sea was flat 'all over'.

Exasperated to have so many arguments so soon on the voyage, I declared that I was the only skipper on this ship and we were going to leave right now with no further delays. I must have tried to let off my anger on the anchor winch and attacked it with too much vigour, for on the very first stroke I hit my thumb-nail so cruelly that I thought at first that I had smashed the bone. All thought about getting under way vanished. I decided to stay right where we were, even if the water was not too protected. At nightfall we hung a paraffin light in the rigging, so that no boat would run us down.

The next day, when the tide was right, we finally sailed out of Chichester Waters. I was thrilled to be at sea again. On the way from Birdham I tried all the tricks I knew of to get the ship to keep her course without anyone on the tiller, like the *Windflower* had done half-way around the world. But if it had worked on my previous ship, it certainly didn't on the *Dorothea*, for no matter what I tried she would either luff up into the wind or fall off completely until she gybed. I therefore decided to copy the self-steering gear of Bernard Moitessier, a Frenchman I had met in Trinidad while the *Windflower* lay next to his boat, the *Marie-Therese II*. He had built the boat himself to replace the boat he had just lost on a reef in the Chagos Archipelago. He then sailed the new boat across the South Atlantic to Trinidad, where he explained to me how his ingenious windvane worked. The basic idea was that a relatively small vane would actuate a tiny auxiliary rudder which trailed behind the locked main rudder. Thus we avoided the need of a huge vane, powerful enough to move the big rudder, for very little effort was needed to actuate the small rudder. Of course, the ship had to be well balanced and the sails well adjusted, for the small rudder did not have much power. Bernard had claimed that the device was so reliable that he could sleep safely all through the nights in the trades while the ship took care of herself.

The fact that Bernard lost his boat a few weeks after we talked about the vane does not show that it was no good; sailing between the islands of the Caribbean he had adjusted the vane for St. Vincent Island, set the alarm clock so he would wake up safely before arriving there and gone to sleep. He did not wake up until the ship was in the breakers off St. Vincent. The boat was a total loss and Bernard was lucky to escape with his life. It was a brilliant demonstration of how accurately the automatic pilot worked, though at the same time it showed that his alarm clock was somewhat unreliable. I therefore decided to make the same arrangement, keeping only in mind not to sleep too soundly near land.

At Brixham the port captain gave me permission to lie alongside the wall in the inner harbour, where the ship would alternately float level with the dock or stand on the dried-out harbour bottom as the tide went out. With the help of a crane the heavy rudder was lifted on the dock so I could install the little auxiliary rudder needed for the self-steering arrangement.

I laid by that dock for several weeks, for when one job was done another followed. I reinforced the rigging, cleaned and painted the bottom, made a chart table, waterproofed the decks which were leaking, stowed more provisions, made a gravity outlet on the old petrol tank so I could use it as a paraffin storage for my lamps and for the cooking stoves.

While all this work went on several journalists came down and made long articles about our voyage to Tahiti. We even got an offer to go on television, which I declined, as I thought it all most embarrassing to be made so much fuss of, before having done anything. For all I knew, the trip could end in disaster by fire, by going aground, by collision or any other reason, even before leaving England, in which case I would feel rather silly having ever talked about sailing to the other side of the world.

As a result of all the newspapers, many people got to know about us, and often we could hear their remarks about us through the open portholes while we were down below. From inside a boat we can hear surprisingly well all conversation on the dock, a fact which is certainly not realised by most people. Sometimes I would hear men who sounded genuinely in love with the sea and really seemed to wish nothing more than to be able to go on a similar cruise. Sometimes I would get amused by the complete ignorance of some people: 'Wonder what they'll do in the middle of the Atlantic at night? Will they anchor every night, do you suppose?'

But sometimes I would also get annoyed, as when I heard a woman's high voice lament: 'Yes! It's incredible, but this is the boat! It says *Dorothea* on its rear end! How can a man dare to take his wife on such a tiny boat! If he wants to commit suicide, he should do it alone and not drag his wife along. And they say that he does not even have a motor and not even a wireless to call for help when he gets in trouble!'

Lillemor's reproachful eyes resting on me told me that she had also heard the woman.

Many yachts came and went while we were in Brixham. Some were day-sailing along the south coast of England, but some were long-distance boats like the *Wanderer III* with the Hiscocks on board. Unfortunately I did not spot them until they were ready to leave. They were just breaking out the anchor when I came alongside, so we could only exchange a few words before they motored out. I was very disappointed, as I would have liked to have had a long talk with them. They are the most well-known cruising couple in England and having already been around the world they could have given me much valuable advice. Eric's parting words with a friendly smile were: 'We are going towards Panama also, we are bound to run into each other again.' Unfortunately they travelled too fast for me and I never caught up with them.

A few days before our departure the old owner of *Dorothea*, Raymond

Taylor, came by car all the way from London to say good-bye and wish me a happy voyage. He brought a package with him and I was deeply touched when I saw it was the ship's clock which was not included in the sale.

'I thought that you would have more use for it than me, so I asked father if he would mind if I gave it you; he said he would be glad to hear that the clock had crossed a few oceans. So here you are.'

The clock was a real ship's clock, and looked nice in the saloon. Throughout the voyage it proved very handy, as its large size made it easy to read even from the galley, about twelve feet away, and more than once did I send Ray my thankful thoughts.

Once it is known that a ship is preparing for a long voyage we get to hear the constant question: 'When are you going to leave?' We'll try for a long time to avoid a direct answer by saying: 'Soon', or 'As soon as we get the ship ready', but sooner or later we feel that we have to set a date of departure. Once we have done that, the point of no return has been reached, for as the said day arrives friends will show up on the dock to take pictures and wave good-bye. The ship is, of course, far from ready, as it always seems to take a lot longer to fit out a boat for the sea than we expect, but we still have to go unless we have the courage to face everybody and tell them to come back with their good-bye gifts some other time.

So on the chosen day, despite the flat calm and half a dozen undone jobs, I hoisted the sails, got the anchors on board and waved good-bye. But the waving soon threatened to last a long time, as the ship did not move, and we felt rather silly just sitting in the same spot fifty yards from shore waving and waving. I finally took out my long sweep and started to scull the heavy ship away. I hardly got her to move more than half a knot or so, but little by little our friends faded in the distance.

As we rounded the outer breakwater one of the Torquay-Brixham ferries passed close to us and gave us the three traditional blasts on his whistle to mark our departure, while the skipper waved to us. Thus started our departure from England to Tahiti.

As so often happens with things we dream about for a long time, they do not always materialise the way we want them to. The flat calm soon changed to a strong south-westerly wind which for us was a direct head-wind and made progress very slow and painful. When the night came heavy rain blinded us and made us shiver with cold and seasickness. Lillemor cried and begged me to turn back. I soon decided to turn towards Falmouth, where we could wait for good weather.

Daylight finally came, but the rain and the strong wind had not abated, the clouds still raced close to the surface and I could not take a sight for my navigation. Had I had a radio direction-finder it would have been easy to find my way into Falmouth, but as it was I had just to try to trust my dead reckoning, a most foolhardy thing to do along the coast of England for a foreigner who does not fully understand the complicated sets of its strong currents and is not even yet really familiar with his own ship. But seasickness, cold, tiredness and a nagging wife are not the best advisers.

I steered straight for where I estimated the invisible harbour entrance to be, but time passed while I peered into the rain. Then all of a sudden the ship was rocked by such a vicious sea that books, pots and pans which I had considered safely stowed flew from their shelves, the heavy entrance hatch opened and closed, back and forth like a ramrod, water cascaded on deck and down the hatchway, Lillemor screamed and I thought we were in the breakers and would go aground any second. Yet on deck I could still not see land and the lead which I hurriedly threw over the side showed deep water! I then realised that we were in one of the many races which surround the English coast under certain stages of wind and tide. I threw the tiller over and turned the ship to get out of the race the way we had come.

When the motion had again reached more normal proportions I studied the chart, glanced over the sailing directions and soon found the only likely race it could have been. It was a little north-east of the entrance to Falmouth harbour, so the course was set on that assumption, and it proved to be correct, for I soon saw land through the rain a few hundred yards away, which proved to be the entrance to our port. It felt wonderful to be in smooth water again and a great relief to get the anchor over the side and the sails safely stowed. We were dead tired and soon fell asleep, but I thought it was indeed a long way to Tahiti.

Next morning our neighbour, in a modern French ocean racer, came over for a visit. He complimented us on our manoeuvre under sail the previous evening and added that the modern radio direction-finders were indeed wonderful inventions, as without them it would have been next to impossible to find the port in the blinding rain. When he asked me what kind of D.F. I was using I had to tell him that I had none, and I was a bit embarrassed when I explained how I had found the port, as I felt sure that he did not approve of my system of navigation.

2

South to Casablanca

THE following morning in beautiful weather and a nice breeze I hoisted once again the sails for France. This time there were no waving friends on the dock, as we had not met anyone ashore, so departure was easy. The breeze was nice and it was an exhilarating sail as the ship raced towards France under the large masthead Yankee-jib, the large balloon staysail and the full mainsail. The rail was just touching the water and the bow-wave reached half-way up the deck. Nothing gives me a bigger thrill than to drive a sailboat at her maximum speed and to feel the ship almost alive, forcing her way through the waves. Of course, care has to be taken not to push a boat harder than she can take, for then one risks the danger of breaking gear on board, broaching to out of control, breaking the mast or even capsizing. To ensure against these accidents most long-distance sailors will have shortened their masts, their booms and their bowsprits to such an extent that their ship will feel lifeless and very slow. To cruise in such a ship might be more comfortable and require less work to handle, but the full pleasure of sailing cannot be experienced. Lillemor, however, did not have the same point of view as I, and the great press of canvas scared her.

Outside of Ouessant, which was the most critical part of the crossing to Concarneau, and the part I hoped to be able to pass rapidly, the wind not only fell to an almost flat calm, but was accompanied by heavy fog. I will long remember that night and most of the following day, when we heard the menacing steamers' sirens without being able to see more than a few yards around us. Often they seemed to come straight for us while we blew on our tiny yacht's foghorn, which I doubted if they could hear above the noise of their bow-wave. Each time we understood that they had passed us we breathed a little easier, but as soon as one had passed it did not last too long before we started to worry about the next one. I promised I would buy the biggest and noisiest foghorn available as soon as we reached port.

Then a fresh wind sent the *Dorothea* ploughing her way at good speed again and soon to our great relief we were out of the fog. Three days after leaving Falmouth we anchored in Concarneau, a beautiful little fishing port on the Brittany coast. I had childhood friends there and I waited impatiently for the authorities to come on board, but no one seemed to take any notice of my yellow flag. Finally, hoping that the French would not be too strict in their regulations, I hoped they would not mind my going ashore to look them up instead of waiting for them. I let Lillemor stay on board just in case they should come while I was ashore looking for them. I finally located the doctor's office, the harbourmaster's office and the customs, and when I got back on board I took down the yellow flag and went with Lillemor to look up my friends.

Thanks to them, we spent a wonderful week in France. They drove us to see Brittany's beautiful countryside and they took us dining in restaurants where the French cuisine was at its best. The port itself, where we lay, was very picturesque, with many local fishing craft. I only regretted that they were all motor boats as it must have been an unforgettable sight to see them come and go under sail like they did in the old days. I was, however, glad and very impressed to see the boats of the Glenan sailing school manoeuvre not just into the port to anchor like I did, but right alongside the dock. They were all engineless like proper school boats should be, and it was for me a great joy to study every move they made. I had not had the occasion to do much studying of other yachts' technique for manoeuvring under sail since I had sailed in Norway as a teenager.

Nowadays most yachts furl their sails while they are still far out to sea, and come in invariably under power. When I sailed in Norway it was at that time considered a shame to have an engine in a sailing boat, so there when a sail was spotted heading into the port all the sailors present would rush on to the breakwater and criticise every one of his moves on board until he was safely moored inside. The discussion among the watchers would sometimes become pretty hot.

The Glenan boats were about the same size as *Dorothea*, but since they were especially made as school ships, they could accommodate an amazing number of people. For manoeuvring in a port this is a great advantage, as one man can be posted at each strategic point and several jobs can be done simultaneously. As they sailed straight for the dock in a fresh breeze all three sails went down at the same time, while eager hands gathered them up and put the gaskets on before they trailed in the water. At the same time others were putting fenders over the side, and one man jumped ashore with a heavy rope to make fast as the ship slowed down. It was a refreshing sight to see them every time get effortlessly alongside under sail, when we today see most people drive their boats the way they drive their cars.

Many have told me that a motor is necessary as a safety precaution, and that many ships have been lost because they had no engine. While this is possibly true, I think that far more have been lost because they did have an engine, for the simple reason that the man who has an engine will use it, and never learn how to handle his boat properly without it. The day the engine breaks down or refuses to start he will feel helpless and possibly wreck his ship in a situation which to a true, experienced sailing man would be mere routine. Yet that man will never admit that he lost his boat because he did not know how to handle her properly under sail. He will state flatly that he lost the boat because he was at the time engineless.

The windvane had given me a bit of trouble over the Channel and was not powerful enough in light breezes, so based on the experience I had gained so far, I made a scale drawing of a new vane and had a yard make it for me. When I got it installed a strong wind from the north-east came, so I decided that we should leave for Vigo, for it was almost September and it might have been foolish to waste a good following wind across the Bay of Biscay. The wind freshened and looked steady, so we went ashore to say good-bye to our friends, who wished us a good trip.

I hoisted the mainsail with one reef in, got the small staysail up, broke out the anchor and brought it on board, while Lillemor pulled over the tiller in order to stop the ship while I worked on the anchor. Then I pulled up the small jib, and reset the staysail the proper side. The ship gained speed and moved fast out toward the open sea. The water was calm inside the islands, but just as we left the last one the waves got very steep and confused, so Lillemor, who had not been too happy about leaving in that strong wind, begged me to turn around so she could disembark. It would have taken several hours to beat back against the strong wind and by then it would have been dark and most unpleasant to sail among the islands. Besides, I had made up my mind never to turn back, so despite her protests I adjusted the new vane for the north-west corner of Spain.

The wind was dead aft, so I lowered the jib and wanged out the staysail with the spinnaker pole on the opposite side of the mainsail. The ship was going very fast, but rolled terribly. To prevent the boom from burying itself in the water at the end of each roll, I had to lift the boom with the topping lift to avoid breaking it. The motion was so violent we did not have the courage to climb into our bunks forward, where the motion was the most violent, but preferred to lie right on the saloon floor, using a couple of spare sails as mattress.

The third day out we were both cured of our seasickness, but Lillemor was unhappy. She would pop her head up regularly through the hatch to see if the waves were getting smaller, and she would each time slam the hatch shut with a scared look and such determination as if to keep an enemy out. She swore that if we ever made land alive she would never again go to sea in anything smaller than the *Queen Mary*! I tried to reason with her, and explain that the sea was truly rough, but that the boat was under full control and that there was no danger.

No trip can be enjoyable if part of the crew is clearly unhappy, but it was still a thrill for me to see the wonderful progress the ship made every day on the chart. On the third evening I spotted land. It is always exciting to see land appear over the horizon after several days at sea. I was happy to see that my navigation had been accurate once more. Quite honestly, it never ceases to amaze me that land really comes up where it is supposed to, after the calculation of the course from the angle of the sun, the stars or the moon, and computed by a few tables. Each time, according to the calculation that land should soon appear, the same doubts arise, and I wonder if I truly can trust my old sextant and all those tables, but then suddenly there it is: a little blue shadow far away! It soon grows, until we see the contours of the mountains or of the hills; then the blue-greyish colour of the distance will gradually change into true colours. Even after a short voyage of only three days at sea it is a thrill to see the colour green again, which is the one colour we never have at sea. Then we might spot a few houses, perhaps even some people walking on shore. Sailing along the coast pleased Lillemor a lot more, and when we entered the beautiful Vigo Bay with its calm waters she had regained her confidence.

But she had not forgotten the rough crossing of the Bay and she stood by her decision not to sail any farther. I had to choose between her and the boat, she said. Any sailor will know that it is a lot more difficult to get a new boat than a new wife, so I bought a one-way ticket for her to Norway on a steamship which was due in a week. It was not as big as the *Queen Mary*, but after its photograph had been studied by Lillemor, she accepted it as sufficiently safe, despite its obvious inferiority to the *Queen*. While waiting for the ship to arrive I changed the wire halyards for ropes, so I would no longer cut my hands on them. I also felt a lot safer with ropes, for it is easy to see when a rope is getting old and you can replace it easily and cheaply. I had had bitter experiences on the *Windflower* with wire cables breaking with no warning. I had sailed so far with no life-lines, as I considered them ugly, but on several occasions I had felt a bit unsafe on the foredeck, so I installed the regular stanchions all around the ship.

The days passed rapidly in the quiet little town where Cadillacs ride side by side with ox-wagons and where we saw mixtures of old and new everywhere. Soon the day came when Lillemor stood on the steamship and leaned against the rail waving good-bye. 'Well, there goes another wife,' I thought. The ship soon faded in the distance and I felt a bit sad alone in my boat, for I knew that this time I would never see her again. Yet one might think that a man would get used to seeing a wife sail away when it is the third one. Although, to be quite honest, it was the first time I personally had had a wife sail away on a steamer. My first one waved good-bye through an aeroplane window in Burbank, California, and my second through the large, slightly dirty window of an express train in Los Angeles.

And so here I was leaving Vigo all by myself on 13th September. I sculled slowly out of the tiny harbour in beautiful sunshine, expecting the wind soon to freshen. The wind did come, but it also brought a thick fog which I had not expected. Visibility was so poor that even my own head-sails had the milky look typical of fog. I carried no log on the *Dorothea*, so for measuring the distance covered I just estimated the speed and kept track of the time elapsing, and then by transferring on to the chart the compass course I could tell reasonably closely where I was. I could not lay my course straight out of the bay, as the wind was dead against me, so I had to beat back and forth in zigzags. After a few tacks I knew that the errors of my dead-reckoning navigation would accumulate and soon I felt very unsure of my exact position.

Once when I heard a sound which probably was an automobile engine racing up a hill, straight ahead of me, I went about immediately, and marked off my position on the chart as quite close to the shore. A little later I cranked more and more frantically on my foghorn while I heard another boat's horn approaching closer and closer, until I also heard his motor and finally even his bow-wave. I kept on sounding my two short blasts to show that I was a sailboat on the port tack. I had thus the right of way of all ships except for another sailing boat if this one was on the star-board tack.

It is, of course, foolish to insist upon a right of way if it looks like the other boat has not heard your signal and a collision may occur, but on the other hand if I changed course and the other had heard my signals, a change of course might confuse him and he would no longer know what action to take. Finally, just as I was losing my nerve completely and was going to come about after all, I heard voices shouting words in Spanish which sounded like swear words, and almost immediately I heard the sound of an engine getting reversed, and then I saw through the fog, quite near, a small motor ship which disappeared again quickly as we slid apart. I realised once more that even if a yachtsman's foghorn sounds impressive in the store it is not very useful at sea when it cannot be heard above the noise of the engine or the bow-wave of the ships we might meet.

An hour or so later the fog lifted enough ahead of me so that I could see the beautiful islands which mark off the entrance to Vigo Bay. I was able to get into a quiet bay before the fog again closed in around me. I was greatly relieved to have arrived safely at anchor, despite all the fog, and promised myself not to leave again until the weather was completely clear, even if it meant waiting a whole month in that lonely bay, but by next morning the sky was clear, so I left just after breakfast for the beautiful little fishing village of Bayona, which was not too far away.

I had hardly furled the sails in the romantic little harbour when I was hailed by a rowboat manned by half a dozen lovely young ladies. Even a doctor could not have ordered a better medicine for me to get over my wife's departure, so I gallantly invited them on board. They were thrilled and rushed down below into the saloon. They asked a thousand questions of which I could only answer a few, as my Spanish was about as limited as their English and French. Our conversation was therefore not the most brilliant, but it is always pleasant for a man to be in beautiful women's company, so I was disappointed when less than half an hour after their arrival a high-pitched voice from the outside brought a sudden halt to our talk. The girls looked as though they had been caught in forbidden territory and ran up the companionway after a very hurried good-bye. As I came on deck myself the last of the girls was already jumping into their boat, while a very determined matron supervised the situation from a second boat. I had heard that Spanish women had very little personal freedom, but I was shocked to see how strict it really was.

I walked around the lovely and picturesque streets of the small town, enjoying the peace and romance of a new place. In the evening I looked up the 'divers of Vigo Bay', whom I had heard so much about. I soon found them in the house that they rented and they told me the fantastic story of their treasure hunting. They were looking for an old galleon loaded with gold from the Spanish Main which had sunk suddenly in broad daylight right in sight of the whole fleet, just outside the entrance to Vigo Bay, in fifty fathoms of water.

John Potter, jun., the head man of the divers, had read through the Admiralty's record and the original logbooks of the ship which had witnessed the tragedy. It had always been a mystery what had caused the sinking of the ship until John, after searching the area for weeks, found to his amazement, in a place marked off as fifty fathoms on the Admiralty charts, a lonely underwater peak which reached within a few fathoms of the surface. Even the local people refused to believe that there could be an underwater rock at that place, because they said that even in the roughest weather they had never seen the sea break there as it would undoubtedly have done had there been shallow water. Nevertheless the hydrographic office in England sent out a ship especially for surveying the area. All charts now have the rock marked off in the right place. The reason the sea never broke on it was probably that the peak was extremely narrow and acted on the water almost like a knife. The rock was also sufficiently deep so that only a ship with a very deep draught would hit it. But even so, it is quite frightening to think how many ships during the years must have sailed very near death without knowing.

Once the rock had been found they thought it would be easy to locate the wreck, because they felt sure that the hidden rock was the cause of the inexplicable sinking, and thus also proved the truth in the old record. Since the ship sank quickly and they knew the direction from which she came, it sounded easy to dive in the proper direction from the rock and then the wreck would have to be found. Yet they had searched for four years without finding it. They had found several wrecks around the rock, but not the one they were looking for. The greatest difficulties were the great depth, the stormy weather and the time involved since the caravel sank.

The south-west wind never stopped blowing during the week I stayed there. The port was well protected, but the wind was so strong that I was glad of the oversize anchor and the heavy chain the *Dorothea* was equipped with. Her $\frac{3}{8}$-in. diameter stud-linked chain and her 56 lb. plough anchor had made Scotty laugh, for he thought them unnecessarily heavy on my small ship inside the calm harbour of Birdham Pool, but here it did not seem an ounce too heavy. In fact, I even went through a lot of trouble one night to get out a second anchor with a heavy nylon line in order to relieve the tension on my main chain, which seemed to be stretched out dangerously tight. The force of the wind and of the sea has to be experienced to be believed.

At the end of the week the dark low clouds disappeared and the wind died down. On Monday, 21st September, I woke up in beautiful sunshine. I hoisted the sails after a hurried breakfast, and set the course south, away from the approaching northern winter.

The coast of Portugal, which can be so stormy, was in its best mood and I had a perfect voyage. Sun, fair winds and full sails the whole way to Casablanca. Not once did I have to take in a reef or do any kind of repair on a parted rope or torn sail; on the contrary, I amused myself in experimenting with the large wardrobe of sails which I had on board to see which was the most efficient. *Dorothea* had the old-fashioned cutter rig with a long boom and the jibstay fastened at the same spot as the inner staysail stay. She had no standing backstay and ordinarily a single set of runners to the root of the headstays was sufficient, but when I used the large masthead yankee jib an additional runner to the masthead was necessary. It was an efficient rig where speed was concerned, but not a very easy one to handle. While experimenting with all the sails I made sketches and calculations for improving the rig when I next reached port.

The 27th was my thirty-fifth birthday and I could hardly have wished for a better way to celebrate it. I sat on deck, admiring my ship gliding easily over the waves, gently heeled over by the breeze. I watched for hours the seagulls fly close to my boat. I sat on deck just admiring the scenery and the windvane took care of the steering for me. True, it did not steer as straight as an attentive helmsman, but the course was close enough, so I preferred small inaccuracies in steering than being chained all day to the helm. As it was, I could go on sitting on the deck or on the cabin roof or even sit on the bowsprit and admire the bow slicing the water mile after mile. I could also go down below and cook my meals while the *Dorothea* kept blindly on her course or just lie on my bunk reading one of the many books I had with me. At night I hung under the boomcroutch a paraffin light which would shine a white light all round the horizon. Presuming that the steamers were keeping a good watch and that they would give me the right of way which was due a sailboat, I slept eight hours a night while *Dorothea* kept on going by herself. I had a small compass of the inverted type which I had mounted right over my bunk, so if I woke up during the night I would shine the flashlight on it and see if the course was right. If the wind had changed and therefore also the course of the ship, I had to go on deck, readjust the pilot and the sails before returning to my warm bunk, but if the compass stayed on the same bearing I just turned over and went back to sleep.

Every morning I measured the angle of the sun, and at noon when I measured again I could transfer the calculation of the morning to obtain the exact noon position. I marked it as a cross around which I drew a small circle. Then I could measure directly on the chart the distance between the two last marks and thus determine how many miles had been covered in the last twenty-four hours. That always seemed an important matter, not so much for the idea of arriving quickly at the next port, but rather for the sport of it, as nothing is more satisfying than having a sailing ship which can really take advantage of the wind.

Cooking my meals was not too great a problem, as I had an excellent all-round recipe. It had been given to me by a recently divorced friend. When he had seen me eating in restaurants every single day after the departure of my wife number two, he changed my way of life with the following words:

'Women always try to make us believe that cooking is a difficult art, so we will think that a wife is a necessity, while in reality nothing is easier. Just remember these two basic rules: everything can be either boiled or fried. If you choose to boil it, just throw it in boiling water until it feels soft when pricked with a fork. If you choose to fry it, then lay it in a hot greased frying pan until whatever you fry looks right. That's all there is to it.'

I doubt that a master cook will agree, but it opened up the way to hot meals for me. Of course, I soon discovered a few weaknesses in the rule,

for example trying to determine when a boiled egg was of the right con-
sistency, as I could obviously not stick a fork through the shell, but this
was easily solved by having nothing but fried eggs.

The eighth day after my departure I saw a steamship a few miles ahead
of me, and I thought it would be fun to go reasonably close to her and
wave to the men on board. When I did get close I saw that she must have
been doing some kind of oceanographic work with the cables they were
lowering over the side. She flew the Blue Ensign and I saw her name in
large letters—*Discovery III*. An officer on the bridge shouted to me as I
sailed by: 'Is there anything you need which we could help you with?'

On a matter of principle, I answered instinctively: 'No, I'm all right.
Thank you so much.'

Then remembering that I had never checked my watches properly and
on their accuracy depended my navigation, I added: 'But could you please
give me my longitude?'

An instant later came the answer: 'Latitude 35° north, longitude
8°30 west.'

I wrote down the position right on the cabin top before I would forget
it, thanked him again, and when *Dorothea* had sailed away a safe distance
I went down to my charts and compared the steamer's information with
my own calculations. The latitude was only 3 miles off, but I was a bit
disappointed to see that my longitude was 20 miles off. The latitude is not
affected by an accurate time, so the 3 miles' error in the latitude was either
due to an inaccuracy in the sextant or in my calculations, or possibly inaccurate sighting through the sextant, as it is rather difficult to hold it
absolutely steady from the deck of a small ship bouncing over the waves.
But I was not concerned about a 3 miles' error which I consider close
enough, for after all I can easily see even a beach more than 3 miles, so
such a small error would not prevent me from making port.

However, the 20 miles' error worried me seriously, for it was enough to
miss many a landfall. The longitude is directly dependent on the exact
time which we call Greenwich Mean Time and therefore the most probable
reason of the error would be that my watches did not keep proper time.
What was worse was that it was an error which would keep on accumulat-
ing. An error of 4 seconds in time is equivalent to approximately 1 nautical
mile in distance, so an error of 20 miles would be an error of about 1 minute
20 seconds in time. Yet I had two chronometers and one wristwatch and
had expected much less error than that. Had I had a radio, I could have
checked the exact time from the B.B.C., or several other stations, but I had
had so much trouble and expense with my radio on the *Windflower*, which
continually broke down in the damp climate of the tropics, that I was
hoping I could manage without one this time.

As it was, I corrected the course for Casablanca, presuming that the steamer's position was correct, and disregarded my own calculations. I also wrote down the 1 minute 20 seconds error in the watches, so I would get the following observations without that error. I promised myself that I would get both chronometers checked and adjusted as soon as I got in port.

The following day around noon I saw land, and a few hours later I sent some thankful thoughts to the navigator of *Discovery III* when the entrance of the port of Casablanca opened up right in front of me.

The port of Casablanca is huge, and it was a long sail in the crowded harbour before I reached the yacht club, where I let the sails fall on deck so the ship would slow down, and as it slid alongside a moored yacht I threw a line to it and made fast to her.

The authorities came almost immediately to check my papers and gave me permission to take down my yellow flag. The only trouble was that the whole harbour was surrounded by a high fence with the entrances guarded by soldiers, and my pass was only valid for one day at a time. I therefore had to go to the police station every single day in order to get my pass stamped. A rather annoying process, but otherwise life in Casa was very pleasant and for me fascinating, as it was the first time I had touched Africa or seen an Arab country. I was amazed to see scooters racing through the streets driven by veiled women who to me looked as if they had been cut out of a two-thousand-year-old story book. I could hardly believe my own eyes when I saw men kneel down right on the sidewalks, regularly bend down until their forehead would touch the ground, then stand up for a short moment before repeating the process while mumbling prayers, completely unaffected by the passers-by or the cars.

Every day I went bicycling through the town, and liked especially the old town, the Casbah, where I felt as if I were looking into a different world, if not another age. I paid little attention to all the warnings of not going there alone, which one day nearly cost me my bicycle. I was inside one of those tiny stores and waiting to be served. I had left the bike against the wall outside, but I still could see a part of the rear wheel past the door. Suddenly I saw the wheel slide out of my sight. I rushed outside, but the bike was already twenty yards away, held by a small man who ran alongside it. I am not much of a fighter, but since I was obviously much bigger than the thief and few people can run as fast as I can, I felt sure that I soon would have my bike back, but much to my surprise I soon realised that instead of gaining on the thief he got farther and farther away, for while he seemed to have a free passage in front of him, I had continually people crossing the street right in front of me, forcing me to slow down. When he had gained sufficiently on me he tried to jump up on the seat so he could simply pedal away, but he must have misjudged the height of the seat adjusted to my long legs, for he fell flat, right in the middle of the street.

Despite all the Arabs who got in my way, I soon got to my bike, and he had just the time to get to his feet and run away. A man with more fighting spirit would probably have run after him and given him a lesson, but I was more interested in recovering my bicycle. I rode back to the store to finish my shopping, but this time, and every time thereafter I took the bike with me into the store and kept at least one hand on it.

Back at the yacht club they told me that I had been very wise not to try to chastise my thief, for assuming I had caught up with him, I would have had not one man against me, but probably a dozen or so of his friends also. Assuming again that I had survived the battle, I could have been sure that the bike would not have been waiting for me in the middle of the street where the thief had had to abandon it, but would have disappeared for good.

I had been much disappointed to learn that the Hiscocks had left just a couple of days before my arrival but while I lay in the very berth *Wanderer III* had occupied two other yachts arrived which I was never to forget.

The first one was the *Raider*, a salty-looking British gaff-ketch which made fast alongside me. The owner, Colin Gallon, and his young American crew Harriet were to become my good friends and almost every evening we shared our meals together, sometimes in the club's restaurant but more often either in their boat or in mine. Our ships were of exactly the same overall length and much of the same type except for the different rig and for the new diesel engine which Colin had had installed just before leaving England. We were both headed for Tahiti so we expected to meet again in many ports along the way and when the day of departure arrived we rendezvoused in Las Palmas where we both wanted to fit out for the Atlantic crossing.

The other boat was the *Volharding*, a Dutch boat, also headed across the Atlantic. The owner invited me on board one day for tea and none of us could know then that the following year his boat would temporarily become my property.

3

Storms Across the Atlantic

ARLY in the morning, on the day following *Raider's* departure, *Vol-harding* left port after having called the airport's weather-report station and asked what weather could be expected on the way to Las Palmas for the next few days. The officer in charge assured him he could not leave at a more favourable time, as he should get sunny skies and moderate north-east wind the whole way. So I decided to leave also—despite the heavy north-west swell and the black menacing clouds. As soon as I got some fresh food aboard and checked my chronometers I headed for the open sea a few hours after the *Volharding*.

As soon as I had rounded the outer buoy marking the entrance to the harbour I had a very uncomfortable sea caused by the wind and the swell coming from two different directions. However, the wind was fair and *Dorothea* made good speed under full mainsail out on the one side and the winged-out staysail on the other side, while the jib was sheeted hard amidship in an effort to dampen the motion which increased rapidly. During the night the wind increased steadily, so I had to pull down a reef in the mainsail, while I started to feel a bit seasick. I trusted the wind would soon moderate, so it would conform with the official weather report, but next morning the sky looked even more menacing, with low, black clouds racing close to the surface at a disconcerting speed, while the wind freshened so much that I took in a second reef in the main, and had to take in the jib completely, as it was shaking the whole rig so badly that I was afraid that something would break.

And something did break, but it was not what I had expected: the top hinge of the windvane sheared off! The vane took a sickening bend, being only held by the lower hinge, and I expected the whole thing to break off completely and disappear over the side at any moment. I hurriedly found two sticks of wood and some galvanised wire and then, hanging over the wildly rocking stern in order to reach the broken hinge, I lashed the vane tightly and the hinge between the two sticks. The operation was greatly complicated by the fact that at this stage I was very seasick. As soon as the pilot had been repaired I went down below again, on the way glancing at the glass, which was still falling. I laid down on the floor, wedging myself between some spare sails, as I was afraid of being thrown out of my bunk if I had tried to lie there.

Seasickness has the strange reputation of being reserved for landlubbers and then primarily to women and sissies. It is therefore more or less a shame to have ever been seasick. The very few people who are immune to that most miserable sickness feel entitled to make fun of their less fortunate mates, for some inexplicable reason. During the war scientific tests were carried out in order to learn more about the illness, and it was found that out of one hundred persons only two were absolutely immune, while on the other end of the scale only two were incurable and would apparently stay seasick until they reached port or until they died.

Perhaps the most usual rule was that the first three days in a rough sea after a long stay ashore would make a man sick, after which time the symptoms would disappear. Each time a sailor would again leave port the cycle would start all over again, except that over the years, little by little, a man would in the end become almost completely immune, or at least a lot less susceptible to it. It might seem surprising to many that the tests revealed that women were slightly more resistant than men and had a higher percentage of immunity. Also surprising was the fact that a seasoned seaman who never got sick on his own vessel might get deathly sick if he was transferred to another ship with a different motion.

In the afternoon the wind was really screaming, so, as much as I hated getting up and doing any work, I had to admit that I was carrying far too much canvas and had to reduce further. This time I took in the third and last reef in the mainsail, and as to the staysail I had to take it in completely. This apparently simple operation completely exhausted me in my weakened condition, because the seas were so huge and so confused that they bounced the vessel to such a degree that it was very difficult to avoid being slung overboard. I had to use most of my strength just to stay on deck, so to reef or take in sails alone on board under such conditions seemed a monstrous job, especially when I had to stop regularly and just hang on when I felt the stomach cramps starting again, making me vomit.

I thought I should force myself to cook a hot meal no matter how sick I felt, for if I could eat just a little bit, even if I should vomit immediately thereafter, I still would feel better. In any case, if I stopped eating altogether I certainly would not get my strength back, and there was no telling how long the storm might last. I decided just to boil some potatoes in a deep cooker, which I placed securely on the stove while I lay down again. A few minutes later I heard a crash among all the other noises of a ship in a gale and knew instinctively that the cooker had been flung out of the stove.

I got up immediately in order to recover it before the spilled potatoes made too much of a mess, but as I did not see it on the floor after all I wondered what had happened, when it came down in the same instant from the chart table, which was on the starboard side and several inches higher than the stove! On the following roll it had then come down on the floor. The wicked and violent motion a small boat will get in a storm cannot be imagined by those who have not experienced it themselves. I gave up cooking and was thankful that I had not been scalded by boiling water. I tried instead to eat some biscuits while listening to the whistling of the wind and the crash of the breaking waves which came constantly over the deck.

All the ports, ventilators and hatches had been closed since the day before, except the main hatch, which I had kept open about two or three inches so I could get some fresh air and so it would also facilitate my getting on deck every time I had to 'lean over the side'. The wind increased to what I estimated to be full gale strength with hurricane force in the squalls, which would be Force 11 or 12 on the Beaufort scale. I should have taken down the little bit of mainsail I still had up and either trailed one of my sea anchors or at least some warps in order to ease the ship and dampen a bit on the violence of the seas which were constantly breaking on board over the large square stern. I knew I should, but all that work seemed just too much, and I kept on telling myself that the weather report had promised good weather, so surely it could not be all that bad and it would soon calm down.

However, the glass kept on falling to such a degree that I half-way thought that the violent motion had upset the mechanism. I tried every excuse for not getting that sail down, even telling myself that if it really blew hurricane force then the sail would blow itself to ribbons and thus relieve the ship and do the job for me. But the sail was heavy flax and it did stay in one piece. Then all of a sudden the world seemed to have come to an end for me: a terrible crash and the light through the ports changed to a half light, while water poured down the slightly open main hatch as if it had come out of a high-pressure hose. My first thought was that I had been hit by a steamer, but then I understood that I was just buried under a huge wave. I still remember how, lying on the floor, I asked myself while watching helplessly the water which kept on coming down on me: 'My gosh! Isn't it ever going to stop pouring down?'

It did stop after what seemed like an eternity and full daylight came back through the ports, but by that time I was practically swimming in the bottom of the boat, for the water was about a foot above the floorboards and was washing back and forth with the motion of the ship. I stumbled on deck, to be met by a frightful sight. The seas were mountainous and the wind so strong that I had difficulty in breathing when facing it.

Obviously I had two jobs which needed immediate attention: get the rest of the sail down and empty the ship of all the water in her. The most logical would probably have been to start with the sail, so as to protect me against a second burial which on the now heavier boat could have been disastrous, but I doubted whether I would be able to lower the sail in such a gale without rounding up into the wind. The ship would then be temporarily broadside to the sea, a most dangerous position in such a sea, especially when I had so much water in her. Rather than losing time experimenting with the rig, I went to work on the bilge pump while thinking about what to do with the sail. The pump was fortunately a big one which really poured out the water, but it was extremely tiring to work, as it was the old-fashioned type with an up-and-down pulling handle which I could not hang on to for fear of bending the handle in the heavy motion. I had to hang on to the ship for dear life with one hand while pumping with the other. I pumped continuously, only stopping once in a while to vomit, or rather just to have the cramps associated with vomiting, as practically nothing could come up any more. When, after what seemed an eternity, the pump sucked air, I was so exhausted that I had to lie down and rest for a while before tackling the sail.

Down in the cabin the mess was not as bad as I had expected, although everything seemed wringing wet. The heavy teak flooring, which is very difficult to get up, was lying in disorder wedged almost on edge against the mast, while the sail bags were lying underneath, right in the bilge. I pushed one of the heavy floorboards back into place and lay down, so tired and sick that I did not even want to think about the sail which I still had to take down. This time I completely closed the hatch. I had got enough fresh air while pumping to last me a long time. I watched the upside-down compass under the deck and was thankful that the ship kept a dead straight course with no tendency to broach to. What was more, by staying dead straight ahead of the huge waves the course happened also to be straight for Las Palmas. I made a rough guess on the speed and thus on the distance covered since leaving Casa, and feeling that I could not possibly hit any land until next day at the earliest, I fell asleep in the middle of the storm while the *Dorothea* continued its wild ride.

Sleep is a wonderful medicine. When I woke up several hours later I felt a lot better and ate a few biscuits with butter on. The glass was climbing and the wind moderated to about Force 10. The seas were so huge that I did not like even to watch them. I felt that I would now be able to get the sail down, but since she had run all right since the burial I found no reason to reduce sail now that the wind was moderating, so I just let her run at her mad pace.

At noon I forced myself to cook a hot meal of potatoes and salt meat while I sat next to the stove and held a hand on the pot so it would not again get slung across the galley. After I had eaten, I felt good and all seasickness had vanished, and when I saw that the barometer kept on climbing I was really happy again and felt that I was master of my ship after all. I blessed the fact that I had taken out the deep cockpit in England and flush-decked it instead. I hated to think how long it would have taken the ship to get up to the surface again with the deep cockpit she had before. Indeed, I rather doubted if she would have come up at all.

The wind in the evening had moderated to about Force 7 or 8, so I took up the small staysail of heavy flax and winged it out on the opposite side of the triple-reefed mainsail. During the night I shook out one of the reefs and next morning I woke up to a beautiful sunshine and a wind of about Force 4. I soon had all the sails up in a sea which was still high, but flattening gradually.

For the first time since leaving Casa I was able to take a sunsight. It showed me that I soon should see land and that my course during the storm could not have been better. I took out all my things to dry in the rigging and on deck, my books, my clothes, my charts, the bedding and the mattresses. In the beautiful weather and good breeze things dried out quickly, except two of the mattresses, which had been completely soaked. I knew from previous experience that it is almost impossible ever to get back in proper shape a mattress which has been in sea water, so I preferred to let them go over the side right away. I cleaned out of the bilges the half-cooked potatoes which I had not had the courage to pull out in the storm. I laid the floorboards down properly again and cleaned up the ship so nicely that even I could see no trace of her ever having been in disorder.

Before noon I saw the characteristic three cones of the mountains around Las Palmas appear above the horizon, and in the afternoon I sailed into port just as the wind was dying completely. Four dinghies rowed out from the inner harbour to meet me and took photos, while one of them was filming.

I anchored in front of the yacht club among several other yachts, which I presumed were also headed for 'the other side', as Las Palmas has become the traditional jumping-off place for crossing the Atlantic in the late fall. There was no trace of the *Volharding*, but I was not surprised, as there was no reason to believe that he would have kept the same reckless speed as me through the storm. The chances were that he had been hove-to during the storm and I could therefore not expect him for another two or three days, depending on how long they had considered it necessary to heave-to.

Next to where I now was anchored I saw the name *Noctiluc* on a tiny 24-foot yacht of beautiful proportions flying the French flag. While I was in Casablanca I had heard a lot about the young couple on board and

I was anxious to meet them. I called over to them and invited them to come on board for a cup of tea. They brought me the daily paper, where I read that the storm had caused many lost fishing boats and also caused damage to several steamships, while on shore many houses had had their roofs blown off.

Pierre Hamel said that it must have been an unusually bad year, for they also had had a storm just a few weeks earlier south of Spain on the way to Casa. They had been hove-to, which is the accepted safest position for a small boat in a gale, and both had been lying in the same bunk with everything closed up when they felt the ship capsize until the mast got in the water. They were thrown out of their bunk above the leeboard and landed on the galley table on the opposite side, Pierre on top of his wife. An instant later the ship straightened up the same way that she had been knocked down and with such a vicious and quick motion that, as unbelievable as it sounds, they had been thrown back into the bunk. Janine said that she had had black and blue marks all over her body on the one side after hitting the galley, with the weight of her husband making it much worse. Pierre said that the only damage to the ship was to the lower part of the mast-rail, which had been torn off by the sail when this got dipped in the sea.

The days passed pleasantly in the wonderful climate of the Canaries. Life ashore was cheap and everything under the sun was available. In a small store I found an old octant which was probably made at the beginning of the nineteenth century. It seemed in good condition, so besides the curiosity of having a navigational instrument about 150 years old, it could also be used as an emergency sextant in case my present one should fall overboard or be damaged. After a bit of haggling I got it for three dollars, which I thought was very reasonable. And I had not been mistaken, for the same evening when I showed it to a Jewish yachtsman he offered me six dollars for it. That convinced me, of course, that it must have been worth at least twelve and consequently I firmly declined his offer.

In the days that followed several yachts left, among which was the *Jellicle*, the tiny 24-foot folkboat, a Swedish light-displacement design, but built in England. The owner was a British retired army major, only thirty-six years old, red hair and one front tooth missing. He was a singlehander like me and believed also in simplicity, for his boat was even more Spartan than mine. His ship is the only other cruising boat I have seen which, like the *Dorothea*, had neither motor nor electricity (not counting the school boats of the Glenan). Despite her tiny size, the ship looked extremely seaworthy and showed a very experienced owner.

Five days after my arrival I saw a sail glide slowly into port. The hull was blue. It was *Volharding*! Excited, I rowed over and saw three unshaven

men who looked several years older than they had done when they
left ten days ago from Casa. It is strange how much tiredness will show on
a face. Their first question was how long I had been here. They laughed
when I told them I had arrived five days ago. They thought that I was
joking. When they realised that I had really sailed in exactly half the time
they had taken, they shook their heads and said that I must have driven
the ship like a madman. They told me how they had lost their two sea
anchors despite all the chaffing gears, and had after their loss laid a-hull
without a stitch of canvas up. The seas washing over their ship penetrated
sufficiently through the hatches to soak their engine, and when the gale had
passed they had been unable to start the motor in the calm which soon
followed the storm. They had had a slow passage, but a much safer one
than if they had kept on running like I had.

But the days passed without the *Raider* showing up and I became
worried, but finally thought that the storm might have blown them past
the Canaries and that they therefore had decided to continue directly to
the West Indies. So after having waited a long time I finally hoisted sails
on the 9th November and heeled over to the breeze headed for the
Caribbean, 2,800 miles away. But I was not to find the *Raider* there or
anywhere else. She had disappeared without a trace. Extensive searches
on both sides of the Atlantic by the Coast Guard and even the Navy failed
to even get the slightest clue as to what had happened to her. We can
only guess. To the authorities who later contacted me on the request of
Harriet's father to hear my opinion as I had been their last friend to see
them, I simply said that in a real storm at sea no small ship is wholly safe
regardless how strong the ship and how good the crew. Accidents will
happen occasionally and that is the chance every sailor takes when leaving
port.

The trade-wind passage from the Canaries to the West Indies is considered an easy passage for a sailing ship, yet it is a bit scaring to think
about the tremendous distance which has to be covered through a very
deserted area of the ocean before the other side can be reached. Many
'experienced' week-end yachtsmen claim that it is much more difficult to
sail among the tricky English waters than it is to do a transatlantic crossing.
From a mechanical, day-by-day point of view they might be right, but if
we consider the accumulated possibilities of wear, breakage, accidents,
storms and sickness, there is indeed a great advantage in never being too
far from a port with repair shops, doctors and friends.

The moral effort to leave for an ocean crossing is amply illustrated by
the many would-be transatlantic sailors who have put up their ships for
sale in Las Palmas during the last few years. Yet they had been able to sail

out of their own home waters in England or France, and now all they had to do was to sit back and enjoy the trade-wind passage. What had made them fail except the fear of the great distance itself? A fear which is not as unreasonable as it might seem to some. When, for example, the statistics show a 2 per cent gale frequency in the lower Atlantic it might at first sound that the chance to get in a gale is almost nil, which indeed it would be for the coastwise sailor, who rarely leaves without listening to the radio report, and even then has the possibility of escaping into a port before the weather really gets bad, should the wind become stronger than foreseen. But for a crossing which will last anywhere from about twenty-two days to sixty or more, depending on chance and the ability of the ship and her skipper, conditions change completely. A 2 per cent gale really means two days of gale in every 100, or one day of gale in every fifty. In other words, if the passage takes fifty days we are almost sure to get into a gale if we believe in statistics and the law of averages. And a gale is a gale no matter where it is.

This being my second crossing, I tried to make the ship as strong as possible and carried a fair amount of tools, extra wires, ropes, and even assorted pieces of wood for carpentry work. But what I really feared was getting seasick again after my stay in port of eighteen days, which had probably been enough for me to lose my sea legs. Knowing how important it is to keep regular meals and how painful it is to do any cooking while on the verge of being sick, I had prepared a large pot of 'lapskaus' before leaving. It is a traditional Norwegian dish made of meat and potatoes cut in small cubes and cooked all together until it becomes a thick stew.

Already the first night in a very choppy sea and strong, squally wind brought back my old sickness. I wondered if I ever would get over that miserable feeling, and had I known then that it was to be the last time for many years I would have felt much happier. Next day I was already a lot better, and the following day all seasickness had vanished, but instead I had got a bad cold and a terrible headache. On the 18th I got much worse and my throat became terribly inflamed. I had never experienced anything like that before and wondered what I could do to help. It felt like a sore growth in the middle of my throat which prevented me from swallowing any food. I was afraid that it could even choke me by preventing me breathing if it got any worse. I had no thermometer on board, but I had been sick often enough to be able to tell that I was running a high temperature. The smallest job seemed an insurmountable chore and I even wondered if I would ever make shore alive and in time to get into a hospital before it was too late. In fact, even without my help *Dorothea* would probably have arrived in the West Indies all by herself, being pushed by the trades, although she could not be expected to do a record passage under such conditions. And it was no great consolation to me, as I cared little what happened to the ship or where she went if I died. I read through my medical books, but all I learned there was that with symptoms which I had I should 'seek immediate medical attention'. What to do in the meantime they did not say.

Two days later I discovered that even if I could not swallow ordinary food I could at least get down hot soups; and that discovery brought back hopes that I could make the crossing alive, for I was in no doubt that the only way the growth could be removed was with the help of surgery. The wind often got very light, but I was too weak to shake the sails out, so whether the wind was strong or weak *Dorothea* stayed reefed down for many days. Even one night when I was awakened by an unusual motion of the ship I discovered from the upside-down compass I have over my bunk that the ship had turned around 180 degrees and was going straight into the seas, but I had no hope that it would last till we got back to the Canaries, as I felt sure that it was only a squall.

Ordinarily I would have rushed on deck to turn the ship back on course, as I hate to see wasted wind, especially if it actually makes me turn back, but now I was too tired and too weak to care much. I just let the ship go in the wrong direction, thinking that anyway the wind would soon change back into the regular trades and would then automatically turn *Dorothea* back for me.

But next morning when I woke the ship was still going the wrong way, and not until late afternoon did the foul wind stop, only to be replaced by a calm. A huge swell was coming from the north, telling of some disturbance and storms up there which were probably the cause of the upset trades. I heard the sails slamming, but thanks to the well-secured wangs and also the very small area of the reefed sail the slamming was not bad enough to necessitate doing anything about it.

Next morning the ship was again going towards the West Indies and had thus picked up the right course all by herself when the wind had come back, while I slept.

That day I started to feel a little better and had much less fever. I was able to get down a thin stew, as I was getting famished from only having had soups for several days past. When I got enough ambition to take a sight and calculate my position I discovered that *Dorothea* had covered 1,145 miles and realised that I had been two weeks at sea already. It was not too impressive a speed, but then *Dorothea* had been mostly on her own.

On the 25th, as night fell, I was exactly at the half-way mark, according to my calculations, and I celebrated with an extra good stew, as I was also much better, although I was very weak and had frequent bouts of fever; but I knew that the sickness was losing and that it was only a matter of time before I would be as fit as ever. But in that assumption I was not quite right, for even today, almost four years later, I still get a little something in the back of my throat which bothers me and makes me want constantly to clear it, but even the doctors don't seem to understand what it is.

On 29th November, the twentieth day at sea, I crossed the two-thirds line after three days of rain, very strong winds and high seas, when I had to reef down the sail again which I had finally unreefed just before the bad weather came. When I could sight the sun I calculated that my average speed during those three days had been 127 miles a day. *Dorothea* was running with a bone in her mouth!

On Monday morning I discovered to my horror that the backstay had broken. The mast was bending forward almost like a fishing pole, or so it seemed to me. Full of panic at the thought that it could break at any moment, I jumped to the mast and let fly the large jib's halyard so as to relieve the mast of the pressure bending it forward in the strong quartering wind. I decided to do the rest of the trip without the jib, for it was now only 840 miles to Antigua, and I felt much too weak to do any climbing up the mast, even though I was much better. I preferred sailing a little slower.

I still had no radio with which to check my chronometers, and by Friday I was a bit in doubt about my exact position, as the two chronometers disagreed by as much as 25 minutes by now. However, my wristwatch agreed within 2 minutes and 55 seconds with one of the chronometers, so I disregarded the other one, even though it was the most expensive one. If I had chosen the right time I should be about another 360 miles from Antigua, but if the other chronometer was right I should hit land any minute. In fact, I should already have by-passed the island.

Being so unsure of my position, I did not dare to sleep more than a couple of hours at a time in the daylight and hardly at all during the night, when visibility was very poor and I could only count on seeing the unlighted shore half an hour before hitting the beach. Should I run aground during my sleep, on the weather coast with the whole Atlantic beating on the shore, I could be certain that the boat would become a total wreck in a matter of minutes, and it would not even be certain that I would be able to jump ashore without getting killed in the breakers among possible rocks.

On Monday the 7th I wrote: 'Hardly slept at all last night as land cannot be far now, and I do not want to run on to an unlighted shore. Many more of the new white birds. Should see land before nightfall.'

And then: '12.10 local time: LAND Ahoy! just as I had worked out my noon sight and went forward telling myself that I should see land, there it was!'

Those are always exciting moments, but land was almost thirty miles farther than the figures of the chronometer indicated and the most surprising thing is that had I chosen the time just from my wristwatch I would have had the smallest error, which goes to show that it is not always the most expensive which is necessarily the best. My latitude was correct within a couple of miles, which was to me a great satisfaction, as I had navigated with the old octant I had bought, and that proved that I had been right in my belief that it was just as accurate as a more modern instrument.

Visibility was so good and I was still so far from land when I spotted it, that night fell before I made port. As I did not want to attempt entering an unlit port in the dark, I hove to for the night, but next morning when I did get close I took several compass bearings on land in order to get the location of the entrance to English Harbour, where Lord Nelson hid his fleet, for I knew it was very difficult to discern from sea. Many boats had sailed right past the entrance without seeing it. As I steered toward the cliff where the entrance should be according to my bearings I recognised the land from my last visit, and suddenly, when I was very close, the gap opened up and I steered straight into the narrow pass, in squally winds coming down from the hills, and was in quiet waters for the first time in many weeks.

What a thrill to be back in the lovely West Indies and to feel the hot tropical air bring me all the familiar smells of land again. The green vegetation and the brown earth. Several yachts were there. I chose a convenient berth, let the sail fall on deck as the anchor was running out, got the dinghy in the water, rowed a line ashore and pulled the ship into the very dock where Lord Nelson had also made his own ships fast. It was 11.30, so I had made the crossing in a couple of hours less than twenty-nine days, and two days faster than last time in the much larger *Windflower*.

4

West Indian Interlude

JELLICLE was in port and was the first to greet me welcome. He had arrived a few days ahead of me and had taken thirty-six days across, and was much surprised to hear that I had done the trip in twenty-nine, as he openly admitted that he had been sure when seeing *Dorothea*'s wide stern in Las Palmas that he would have done a much faster trip than I could ever hope to do, as he considered his boat with her fine lines to be much faster. Had he known how poorly I had sailed my ship the first half of the voyage, he would have been even more surprised. It shows that it is very difficult to judge a boat's speed from what one can see of her above the water, for, after all, what really counts is the shape of the boat which is under the waterline.

Jellicle was the only other long-distance sailor in the harbour but several large charter boats of Commander Nicholson's fleet were there. English Harbour is the headquarters of the charter fleet which carries tourists from Antigua down to Grenada and back, stopping at most of the islands on the way. The Commander greeted me with a hefty handshake and invited me to his comfortable home, which was the restored house of Lord Nelson's paymaster. After telling him of my adventures since I was last there, I invited him on board the *Dorothea* and asked him if he would include me in his charter fleet, as he had done with *Windflower* during my previous stay. The Commander did not seem too enthusiastic, and said that even if the ship was extremely well fitted out she was much too small for charter work; besides, I really should have a ship-to-shore radio, so he could stay in contact with the customers in case an important message arrived for them. I explained that it was not practical for me to have such a radio, as I had no motor to charge batteries. Then I knew there was no hope for me!

'What! No motor! Are you mad? How do you expect to charter without a motor?' he bellowed.

I did not insist, as I felt that he was right. The best boat for chartering would be a two-masted boat with very short masts where only small sails can be hung, so no reefing is ever necessary, and then count on the powerful quiet diesel engine for getting into ports on schedule. It is much less work for the crew, which for this reason need very little training in handling the ship. Nicholson did not need to worry about boats getting out of schedule. The charterer feels more confident that they will not miss their return plane, and since very few of them are experienced sailors they think the small sails are the way it should be, so everybody is happy. But to my mind it is just a make-believe, an imitation—even cheating. In any case it is not the real thing.

As I certainly was not willing to spoil the fun I had had with *Dorothea* by installing a motor, I gave up the idea of chartering and thought that should everything else fail I could have a pleasant time by enjoying life as long as possible in the islands, and when running short of money I could sail to the States, work there for six months or a year at a time, saving every cent I could, then sail back to the tropics for another year or so.

English Harbour has become the traditional meeting-place for long-distance yachts for celebrating Christmas away from home. By the 24th there were half a dozen yachts in the ports, among which were several I knew from Las Palmas and during the holidays musical groups came and serenaded us from the dock where the yachts were moored. Negroes have a fantastic sense of music and rhythm, and I was especially impressed by an orchestra of young boys about 10 or 12 years old. When I jumped ashore to put a few coppers in their 'tin bank' I saw to my surprise that not one of them had a real instrument: the 'saxophone' was a piece of rusty car exhaust pipe, the 'clarinet' was a straight iron pipe also all rusty, the 'drum' was just a wooden box a bit broken, the 'Hawaiian guitar' was achieved by a boy who pinched his nose, and so on. As strange as it may seem, the music which came out of this makeshift orchestra was quite good and without any false notes. The money they seemed to collect was modest, but considering the amount of capital invested I feel sure that their books were never in the red.

I had planned to sail directly to Martinique, which is one of my favourite islands, immediately after the Christmas celebrations, but disturbing news came over the radio that a revolution was in progress and an excited mob had upturned cars, broken store windows and even caused several deaths. As I saw no point in looking for trouble, I decided to sail to St. Thomas instead, while the revolution had time to cool off, then when it had calmed down I would sail to Martinique.

I left on the 28th at 10.30 after twenty days in the idyllic port, and arrived at Charlotte Amalie at two o'clock on the morning of the 30th. As I had been warned that there was a charge of fifty dollars for entering an American port at night, I anchored outside the harbour, despite the heavy sea, and was able to catch up a bit of sleep after having made sure that my

anchor was holding properly. At eight o'clock I made the official entrance
with the yellow flag and all. Here again I was to see that everything
American is the greatest in the world: the red tape was to last more than
two hours, while in the British and French islands it rarely took more than
five minutes.

The harbour was crowded with yachts of all sizes, many of them doing
charter work by the day. They take up to six passengers, which is the limit
set by the American Coast Guard for boats which have not passed the
special safety test for regular passenger traffic. No yachts ever pass that
test, as one of the many requirements are a certain number of watertight
bulkheads, which is not possible on a yacht without ruining the inside
accommodation, especially for use in the tropics. Apparently the Coast
Guard consider that it does not matter as much if just six passengers
should drown, but this relaxation in the regulations permits many yachtsmen to make much welcome money, and it also enables many tourists to
make enjoyable trips at sea in lovely yachts. The boats generally leave at
nine in the morning and return before nightfall. The agent here thought
that I would have no difficulties in chartering, as the wind was so regular
that the customer would not even notice that I had no motor; but he said
that considering the size of my boat I should not take more than four
passengers at a time. Since each passenger was charged fifteen dollars, this
would mean that I could make sixty dollars a day, less of course the agent's
fee and the cost of sandwiches and drink for the guests, but I would
certainly clear at least thirty-five dollars a day. It seemed that it would be
a good way of life, as a few months of chartering would theoretically be
enough for the rest of the year, as life in the tropics need not be too
expensive.

Among the many boats in the port was another singlehander, Colin
Leslie Fox in the gaff cutter *Vaiger* of almost identical size to the *Dorothea*.
I was very interested in the boat, as I had been offered her at a very
interesting price while in England last. Early one morning I saw Colin
hoist his sails, and as I came out of the hatch he shouted over to me: 'I'm
sailing over to Christenstadt, the most beautiful harbour in the world.
Come on, get those sails up, and let's sail in company!'

His enthusiasm made me forget all about chartering at the thought of
that exciting sail in the fresh trade wind, closehauled for the thirty-mile
passage to St. Croix Island, so I jumped to the halyards and followed not
far behind the *Vaiger* out of the harbour. *Dorothea* was a bit faster than
Colin's boat, at least when closehauled, so I soon changed my number one
jib for the storm jib and we were then going exactly the same speed. While
changing the jibs on the bowsprit *Dorothea* plunged through a sea which
completely soaked me from top to toe, but in that wonderful climate,

where I was sailing wearing only a tiny bikini, I soon was dried by the wind with no discomfort at all.

In the late afternoon we sailed into the extraordinarily beautiful harbour of Christenstadt, right past an hotel whose guests were waving their glasses at us and to whom our boats must have been a striking sight under full sail at high speed, my blue sails closely following *Vaiger*'s red ones, within yards of the terrace. We luffed up to a stop, let the headsails down, let go the anchor, and when we were sure it held, dropped the main and furled all the sail. Then with the main halyard we got our dinghies over in the water and were ready to explore another town. The water was as clear as crystal and we could easily see the bottom with its rocks and weeds. It seemed so clean that we were tempted to drink it. Ashore the small streets and houses have remained Danish in character, despite the fact that the island was purchased long ago by the States. I felt as though I had found a little paradise, except everything in the island was extremely expensive and the natives were insolent and unfriendly, contrary to the islands farther east, where living was cheap and the natives pleasant and friendly.

I missed Martinique so much that I gave up chartering in the American Virgins even before starting, and hoisted sails for the Windward Islands. Colin wanted to get there also, so we sailed in company. The 'revolution' was said to be over and everything back in order, so we looked forward to going there, but Colin suggested that we should sail along the whole chain of islands and sleep in port every night. This had the great advantage of letting us see many islands I had never seen before; but after a few days of it I became very impatient to get to Martinique quickly to see all my old friends there, so one day north of Tortola when *Vaiger* lagged far behind I could not resist the temptation to set my course straight for Martinique out through the chain of protecting reefs and hard on the wind on the port tack. Colin, of course, could not understand what had happened to me, and I do not think he has yet quite forgiven me. But I was thrilled to do some 'real' sailing again, even though the hard slamming into the choppy seas was rough on my stomach. Thanks to all the training I now had, I did not get seasick, but I did not sleep too well at night, due to the very heavy motion.

On the third day I saw to my horror that the port spreader had broken and just supported the mast by having jammed itself on a shroud splicing. As I expected it could fall down any time, I laid the ship immediately over to the other board, thus putting all the pressure on the starboard spreader. The course was, of course, no longer Martinique, but any land where I could do some temporary repairs. That tack brought me to Guadeloupe, where I anchored in front of a tiny village called Le Baillif. I was very

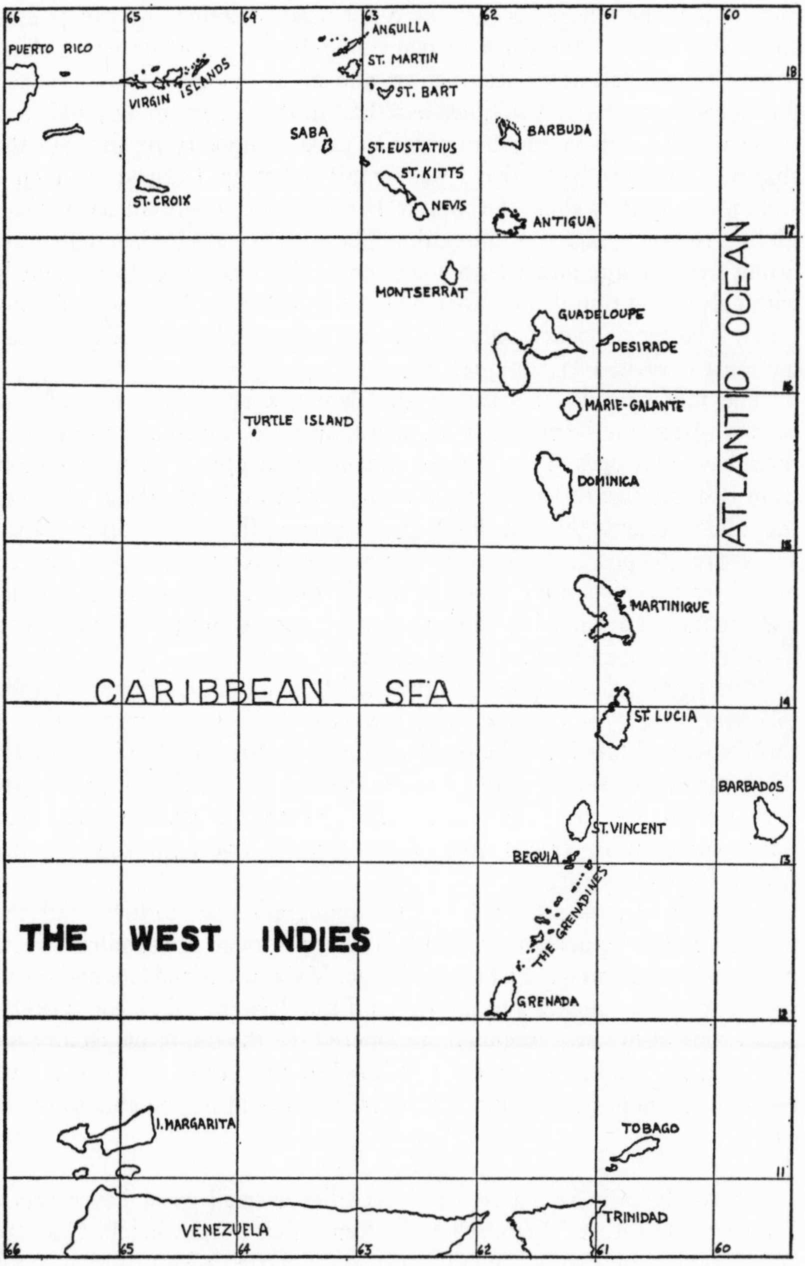

THE WEST INDIES

(Map showing:)

66 · 65 · 64 · 63 · 62 · 61 · 60

PUERTO RICO

ANGUILLA
ST. MARTIN
VIRGIN ISLANDS
ST. BART
SABA
BARBUDA
ST. EUSTATIUS
ST. KITTS
ST. CROIX
NEVIS
ANTIGUA

ATLANTIC OCEAN

MONTSERRAT
GUADELOUPE
DESIRADE
TURTLE ISLAND
MARIE-GALANTE
DOMINICA

MARTINIQUE

CARIBBEAN SEA
ST. LUCIA
BARBADOS
ST. VINCENT
BEQUIA
THE GRENADINES
GRENADA

I. MARGARITA
TOBAGO
VENEZUELA
TRINIDAD

tired, so went right to sleep, but next morning when I went ashore I was met by half the village, as they were not used to seeing any yachts ever anchoring there. I bought a nice-smelling bread, some strange-looking native fruits I had never seen before, and many oranges. These cost ten francs each, or exactly five times less than in the American Virgins!

I tried to climb the mast in order to make temporary repairs, but the ship was rolling so badly that I was unable to get up. I upped the anchor and sailed carefully along the coast to Barque Cove, where the natives had told me the anchorage was quite calm. The spreader was broken in its mast fitting from fatigue rather than a sudden strain. I fastened it temporarily with galvanized thin flexible wire which I wound round and round many times. The repair looked ugly, but it was strong and would certainly last me until I reached Martinique.

The following day I sailed to the Saints, a beautiful group of tiny islands where it is surprising to see that the natives are white and many of them have blue eyes. They are descendants from a few French emigrants from Brittany and do not seem to have mixed with black blood, although they all live exactly the same life as the negroes in the neighbouring islands and are just as poor. The local 'gendarme' checked my papers and showed me where the 'restaurant' was. It proved to be a private home where the main room was arranged as 'dining-room'. I was the only guest and I much liked the simple and friendly atmosphere.

Next day I sailed to Roseau in the British island of Dominique, and the following day, 27th January 1960, I arrived at Fort de France. What a thrill to be back! As I sailed up to the anchorage after nightfall I recognised the silhouette of several boats I knew well from my last visit. From my deck I could see the *Volharding*, and I learned that she had been sold immediately on her arrival from Las Palmas for a very low figure to my friend, Pierre Leveque.

Next day I was signalled by the immigration authorities, and the formalities were quickly completed. Walking through the familiar streets made me feel as though I had come home. My many friends invited me to their homes for lunches and dinners and the days passed all too quickly. Ricky, one of my best friends there, offered me the use of his factory for repairing my broken spreader. I redesigned the fitting so when it was repaired it would be stronger than ever, and would not be able to break again.

Across the bay from Fort de France lies a small guest house called l'Auberge de l'Anse Mitan, where I often sailed to take lunch. One day two American tourists at the table next to me started a conversation about my boat anchored just outside the restaurant, not far from the beach.

After a while they confided that they liked the West Indies a lot, but were disappointed that they were unable to find girl friends. I said laughingly that they would probably have much better luck in the neighbouring English islands, where they would be able to talk the language. I added that there were, for example, many free girls in St. Lucia, just about thirty-five miles away.

'Why not take us there? We'll charter your yacht ãnd you show us where the girls are,' they proposed.

I accepted gladly and when they paid me the charter fee I did not think it necessary to tell them that I was headed there anyway to pick up some mail I expected.

They enjoyed the wonderful sailing trip, and once in Castries, the capital of the island, I showed them 'where the girls were' and left them on their own. Next morning they came back with gleaming eyes and declared that they intended to settle down here, and as far as they were concerned 'all American women could go to hell'. So I gathered the night had been successful.

I proposed to have lunch at Pidgeon Island, just a few miles' sail along the coast in the direction back toward Martinique, and where we arrived after a refreshing sail. The island is owned by an old English lady who used to be a famous artist long ago. Mrs. Snowball lives all alone on the island, only surrounded by her staff of native servants, and runs a small bar and restaurant set up almost on the beach under a thatched hut. The place has not much to offer in the way of food, but the island is so charming that we could afford to be indulgent about the menu. I was to come often to the place, as I enjoyed chatting with the old girl and looking at the tiny surf which came within yards of the house. The charterers were also taken by its charm, but as night approached they got restless and wanted to return to Castries for some more girls. I pointed out to them that if they wanted girls we need not go that far, as there was a small village on the mainland right across from where we were. So we borrowed one of the natives' dug-outs which were lying on the beach and paddled over.

We had only walked through the streets for ten minutes or so when a girl smiled at one of my charterers, and asked if she could walk with him in the moonlight. A few minutes later another girl hung on to the arm of the other American, but time went by and no girl walked up to me, so I started to get an inferiority complex. However, finally a very nice-looking girl of only about 16 or 17 came up to me. So we all walked happily along, talking and laughing, but when one of us suggested that we should head for a lonely beach, my girl declared with a frankness which never failed to impress me that she did not like making love in the sand.

'Let your friends go to the beach,' she said; 'you come to my house.'

'Do you have your own house?' I asked, rather surprised that such a young girl should already have her own house, even if it was only a shack.

'Yes,' she answered, 'I have got a house with my mother.'

'Your mother is not home?'

'Yes, she's home, but I have my own room,' she assured me.

Knowing what kind of walls are used in the native houses, I exclaimed: 'Are you mad? Even if she does not see me come in, she will hear that I am there and will kick me out.'

The girl looked at me as if I had deeply insulted her. With a hot voice, fierce eyes and a dignified air, she replied: 'My mother would not say anything and she would leave us alone: my mother has *manners!*'

How different standards of morals and good manners are in the different parts of the world! And who is to say which ones are the best? But despite her assurances I preferred to go on the beach.

'In that case, I want to go back to the village to get my towel, because the sand is damp and I will catch cold otherwise. You wait here and I'll be back.'

The two other girls agreed with that wise decision and they all left, leaving us alone in the road.

'That's the last we see of those girls,' one of my charterers declared. 'Let's get back to Castries before it is too late.'

'Let's wait fifteen minutes,' I suggested; 'they might be back.'

Hardly had ten minutes elapsed before we heard footsteps and there were our girls running towards us all out of breath, waving their towels over their heads and laughing as if coming for a big play.

A couple of hours later we all walked back towards the village to get to our canoe. As we passed the huge church I asked my girl if she ever went to church.

'Of course I do,' she answered.

'Do you also confess yourself?'

'Yes, every good Catholic has to,' she confirmed.

'What does the priest say when you tell him that you make love?'

'He says that I should not make love when I am not married.'

'So you promise not to do it any more?'

'Of course not! I am not a liar. I just tell him that I have to.'

'What does the priest say to that?'

'He asks me why I have to. He is not a very smart man. He does not understand much, so I have to explain to him that it is in the nature of my body.'

What the priest replied to that simple and honest answer I do not know, for we had arrived at our dug-out, so the conversation was dropped and soon we pushed the heavy boat back in the water, aided by the girls, and paddled away while the girls stood at the water's edge waving after us for a long time.

' 'Just try to imagine an American girl helping us push that boat! She cannot even close her own door when we pick her up in a Cadillac!'

Back in Martinique they told me that they were returning to San Francisco just to sell all they possessed. Then they would come back and settle in the West Indies. But like so many dreams it will probably never come true.

The two Americans had hardly disembarked in Martinique when a middle-aged couple asked me if they could charter my boat for a trip to Grenada, stopping at every one of the islands on the way. Thus started for me a series of trips up and down the chain of islands which brought a nice replenishment to my bank account. I was glad after all not to have an agent, as not only did I save the agent's fee, but I was much more free and could take or decline the charterer according to my likes or dislikes. Contrary to what Commander Nicholson had said, my lack of engine did not at all prevent me from finding customers. On the contrary, it even seemed to awaken the spirit of adventure dormant in even the well-settled man, for on several occasions my ship was chosen in preference to more comfortable yachts equipped with large engines, electricity and radio telephones.

I chose St. Lucia as my headquarters, where I banked and where I received my mail. I liked the convenient stores and the friendly population. I like the two movies where the people often got so excited that there was a permanent sign over the screen which would flash in large letters 'Keep Quiet Please' every time the audience shouted, overpowering the loudspeaker.

One day I was struck by a girl with almond-shaped eyes and rolling hips. I followed her to the post office and stood behind her in the long line of Poste Restante. She had small golden earrings in her pierced ears. I pulled teasingly at one of them. She turned her head toward me and gave me a smile which encouraged me to ask her to come and visit my boat, as I would take pleasure in showing it to her. But she was not interested in boats and claimed that she knew what I really had in mind, but that I was out of luck, as she was not in the mood. But when she got to the window and a letter was given her, she asked me suddenly: 'Please read my letter for me.'

She told me her name was Bjula, that only recently had she come to town and learned English. Her mother was a voodoo sorcerer and they had until a couple of years ago lived in the interior of the island, where they had only talked their native 'patois' and, of course, had never been to school.

After having read the letter for her, she asked me if I would also write the answer for her. I gladly offered to do it, but I pointed out that I did not carry a pen and writing-paper in my pocket, so we would have to write it on my boat. She looked suspiciously at me and declared:

'Yes, I know. In the boat you don't write letters. You push me in bed. I don't want that!'

I duly promised to write the letters, so she hesitantly got into the dinghy, petticoat, high heels and all.

As soon as the letter was written and before I had had the time to propose anything, she calmly said:

'I know you want to sleep with me now. You can. But first, I want to stick a hole in your left ear, and put in my gold ring, the one you pulled in the post office.'

'What kind of foolishness are you talking about?' I asked laughingly.

'That is no foolishness. That is serious business. Then we make love.'

'Anyway, we don't have any instruments here to pierce any ears,' I said, reassured, remembering the doctor's office in Hollywood with all the shiny sterilised instruments which had been necessary to pierce my wife's ears. But I did not yet realise how much can be done by simple methods. In any case, Bjula was not easy to discourage:

'Yes, you have,' she said. 'I saw you yesterday sewing your sails on deck. Show me your needles.'

Ignoring her request, I pushed her gently on to the bed, but she screamed so horribly that I thought her cries would be heard in the police station, and I already visualised the judge saying:

'For raping an eighteen-year-old girl, I condemn you to fifteen years in jail, Amen.'

So I released her quickly. She straightened her clothes and then asked calmly for the needles again. She then picked the largest, one I had never used, as it was far too big for my sails. It was also quite rusty and dirty.

'Now get me a big uncooked potato,' she ordered.

'But this is ridiculous,' I said, 'besides the needle is much too big and should be sterilised first.'

'Get me the potato or row me ashore.'

I gave her the potato. She held it behind my ear and then quick as lightning she stuck the needle right through the ear and into the potato. Then she undid her ring and pushed it into my ear. She grabbed my pliers and squeezed the tiny lock.

'Now you cannot open it. It is in for good,' she declared, satisfied.

'You could at least have scraped off the rust and boiled the needle, so I would not risk an infection,' I reproached her.

'Don't be silly! You will not get sick. But you must spit on your fingers and rub the spit on the ring and turn the ring into the sore. That will keep the blood clean.'

I felt sure that my doctor would not approve of that method, but I had noticed that animals would often lick their wounds, and since I had no medicine on board I thought I had not much to lose by trying her method, but said to her: 'You do it for me.'

'You are silly! It is your blood. It must also be your spit. Now do as I tell you.'

She looked at me critically while I duly turned the ring full of saliva around in the sore ear.

'Good,' she declared, 'you do that many times every day. In eight days no more sore.'

She then took off her other ring, rubbed it lightly against my lips and then put it on the gold chain she had around her neck, which was all she kept on her as she let her dress fall to the ground.

'Come,' she said as she jumped into bed, while I secretly thought how fortunate it was that preliminaries are not always that painful.

Next morning as I rowed her ashore she said in a voice which became deeper and strange:

'You have had many girls in your boat. In the morning you row them ashore and at night you look for a new one. But now it is different. You will never get another black girl in these islands, because my blood has got into yours with my ring. But I will stay with you. I will come back tonight.'

Whether it was due to the magic she had learned from her mother, or rather because the other girls were afraid of her and did not want to hunt on her property, or whether I was happy with her and did not search any farther, I do not know, but the fact remained that her words came true and I never slept with another black girl in the whole of the West Indies.

When I had a charter I left her, but each time the charter was over I always sailed back to St. Lucia. News travels fast in small islands: it was seldom more than about a half an hour after my anchor was down before I saw her small silhouette walking down to the dock, where I fetched her in the dinghy. She would often stay also in the daytime and then we would go together to the market hand in hand, much to the disapproval of many, as even if most men in the Colonies have native girl friends, there seems to be an unwritten law which requires that all black girl friends should be out of the house before daybreak. I cared little for such laws, as I had neither a boss nor neighbours to please. At the market she would buy goods for the two of us for less money than I could have bought for myself. Here at last

I had found some justification in the saying that two can live as cheaply as one! She could neither read nor write but she certainly could figure out the complicated English money system which in my eyes was further complicated by the fact that it had recently been changed to W.I. dollars, while most of the natives continued to count and to charge the price of the old penny and pence system. She could buy a dozen different fruits and vegetables, add up in her head the total sum from all the penny prices and then pay in dollars. And she sure was not afraid to argue if the change was short! Then back in the boat she would cook strange native dishes which otherwise I would never have known and which were a welcome change from my bachelor diet.

It amused me to have discussions with her, as through her I was looking into a different world. She was without a doubt very intelligent, but her logic and her background was so different from mine that we often had difficulties in understanding each other, yet at other times I was startled by her simple logic, which was not distorted by our modern civilisation. In medicine, however, we had quite different views. I knew, for example, that one of their basic rules for good health was that hot and cold do not mix. Thus if we are hot and perspiring we should not expose ourselves to a cold draught, for if we do we would have great chances of catching a cold or getting rheumatism. We agreed so far, but she carried this rule much further. Bjula told me, for example, that one of her girl friends had just caught gonorrhoea, but it was all her own fault.

'Hot and cold don't mix. A warm man and a warm woman are good. A warm man and a cold woman are bad. Then both get gonorrhoea.'

She only shook her shoulders when I told her how it really works.

'You white men are often very stupid,' was all she had to say, and dropped the subject.

I decided to try to teach her to read and tell the time, but she was not interested in books or newspapers.

'I never see you read any papers. The important news I hear anyway.'

So I gave it up. And after all why is it considered so important to be able to read and write? But even the clock seemed to bore her, and soon she lost complete interest in it and declared that if I thought it too much trouble to answer her when she asked for the time, then I could not love her very much. So I gave it up, too. I did not seem to be able to teach her much, but she taught me many things. One day while in a confidential mood she told me that she had had a tiny, cute baby, but that it died a sad and unnecessary death while just a few months old, a story which I cannot describe in this book, but my first reaction was:

'Why did you not sue? You would have been certain to have won a court case.'

She gave me a look I will never forget. Her eyes were still full of tears, but her contempt for my suggesting such a thing almost scared me.

'Would that have given me back my child? I do not want to profit by my baby's death.'

I suddenly realised the bad taste in our way of thinking in such matters. Most people in our civilised world are not able to distinguish between what they are legally entitled to and what they are morally entitled to. How much cleaner were the thoughts this uneducated girl had!

She always insisted on sitting in the shade of the awning and did not like seeing me expose myself so much to the rays of the sun.

'To think you would have a nice white skin if you were a little more careful! Now you are almost as dark as I am,' she complained.

It has always surprised me that the negroes so much dislike the colour of their skin, for in my opinion their skin is the nicest thing they have. A dark beautiful skin, smooth, firm and free of all the small imperfections most whites generally have. When I saw a fresh arrival of tourists coming straight from the north they always reminded me of people just coming out of hospital after a long sickness.

One day when I took her sailing she did not have the protection of the awning and at night she complained of sunburn. I was so surprised, as I had always believed that a negro could not be burnt by the sun, but Bjula got very annoyed when I expressed surprise.

'Of course we get sunburnt also. No different to white people. We have got red blood, too. Why do you think I never go out in the sun? Because I want to stay as light as possible. Otherwise I get very black and you would be ashamed of me. Tell me, did they not teach you anything at school?'

I apologised for my ignorance and saw indeed next morning that she was a bit darker all over except where she had had her bikini, which had left its shape on her skin in a lighter colour.

She always looked at me with disapproval when I brushed my teeth vigorously every morning.

'You are going to wear them down,' she would warn me with great concern. She herself had never brushed her teeth in her life yet I have rarely seen anyone with whiter and healthier-looking teeth. She had never been to a dentist and never had a toothache.

On one of my trips to Martinique the new owner of *Volharding*, Pierre Leveque, told me that he wanted to sell his boat, but could not find a buyer in Fort de France. He wondered if I would have the time to sail his boat to the American Virgins, where the chances of finding a buyer would be much greater. As he was working with the French Line, he had no time to do it himself. We agreed that I could sell the boat for anything I pleased as long as he got the amount he expected. For simplifying the paper work for me in the American Virgins he transferred all the papers of the ship in my name, so I became the legal owner instead of just his agent. I kidded him, saying that I now could keep the whole amount of the sale for myself, but Pierre just shook his head and said simply: 'I know you would not do that.'

And he was right, for I think that even a hardened criminal would not have the conscience to cheat a friend who trusted him.

On 17th May, the Norwegian national day, I set sail with a crew of two: one English girl who wanted to get as far west as possible for a minimum of money and a Frenchwoman who had a week's vacation. It took us all of five days to get to St. Croix in a very light trade wind over a flat sea. When the girls had left the ship, the one for New York and the other back to work in Fort de France, I went to work with the paintbrush, as it is the shiny paint which sells a ship more than anything else, and I believe that the first impression is the most important one, so not until I had painted the whole ship did I set sail for St. Thomas, where I was lucky and got a reasonably good price for her within a few days.

When I had the money in my pocket I suddenly thought what fun it would be to make a surprise visit to my parents in San Francisco. I rushed back to the bank and sent the money to Pierre, then I purchased a plane ticket to Miami. From there I had a four-day bus ride across the country to San Francisco. This is a much better way of travelling than to take a plane, as not only is it much cheaper but one sees a lot which one would miss in a plane. The Greyhound buses are very comfortable and very fast. They travel by day and night, but one can leave the bus anywhere one likes, stay up to three months in any one place which might catch one's fancy, then jump on the first bus without any extra charge and without that annoying practice of the plane companies having to order and sometimes reconfirm our reservations.

Having left for the States on a sudden inspiration, I had no luggage with me, and travelled in my rather unusual-looking West Indian clothes. They were also much too cool for life in the States, for even if it was mid-summer, and very hot in the streets, the bus was 'air conditioned' to such a low temperature that I was freezing and got a very bad cold. But this was not the main trouble my clothes gave me, as at one of the first stops when I went out to stretch my legs and tried to get warm in the sun, I was stopped by a man who showed me his identification as a secret policeman. He wanted to see my papers, but left me immediately I had shown them to him.

Next day the same thing happened early in the morning, but when at noon a third policeman started to cross-examine me suspiciously, clearly showing that he suspected my papers to be forged, I did not dare leave the

bus again, which indeed was not really necessary, as I could buy sandwiches through the window and in the back of the bus was a toilet similar
to those on the planes.

I had heard about men being taken to the police station for identification
checking and some of them had spent as much as forty-eight hours before
being released. It does not pay to show individualism in a country which
is built up on standardisation, and to them a man with unusual clothes is
looked upon with suspicion. Of course, the earring made it even worse,
but it was so small that I hoped that most people would not notice it. The
simplest way would, of course, have been to take it out, even if it had meant
breaking the lock, but I felt it would have been a sort of treason towards
my little black girl friend, so I let it be, and I saw no reason to follow completely the strict American discipline despite the many glares and even
sometimes hateful remarks I had to endure.

That ring which I have never taken out was to cause many reactions
with many people in various countries, but I found it interesting to see
how different the reactions would be from place to place and from person
to person. The Americans are those who react most against it, probably
because they are the least used to personal freedom and only respect their
own customs. Sometimes they would try to ridicule me, but more often
they would just show open hate. The polite Britisher always tried to ignore
it after a quick glance at it, while the French, who never seem to be
surprised at anything, do not seem to find anything unusual about it. The
natives of many so-called primitive places often show open curiosity about
it, as they know that white men never wear any decoration in their ears,
even if it is very common among themselves. Amongst the teenagers of
most countries there is often a bit of giggling, and I often hear uncompli-
mentary remarks about it from grown-ups, but as a general rule the people
who seem to dislike it most are the narrow-minded and uninteresting
sedentary persons, while the few people who like it are without exception,
original, intelligent, amusing and well travelled. Thus by keeping the ring
I automatically got rid of the people who interested me least.

It was a thrill to ring the door bell of my parents' home after a year and
a half of absence, but the joy of being reunited was marred by the terrible
cold I had caught in the air-conditioned bus, which kept me in bed for the
first ten days of my stay. It is amazing that the air-conditioning apparatus
should have become so popular, but I am told that it is part of progress.
That magic word, which will probably become the key to the downfall of
our civilisation.

Despite the joy of being reunited with my parents, three weeks after my
arrival in San Francisco I longed so much for my boat, the tropics and for
my little black girl that I had to get back. It was hard to say good-bye to

my parents, but I decided to come back the following year, so I would not
be away too long.

The bus took me once again through the country, but this time in my
new American clothes, and my new crewcut, no secret police stopped me.
The plane took me to San Juan, where I got a transfer to St. Thomas.
What a thrill it was to step out of the plane and breathe in the hot tropical
air again! I felt as if I had come home. There was no plane to St. Lucia
that day. So I walked down to the harbour and inquired if by any odd
chance there was any yacht headed in that direction where a crew was
needed. Most yachts in the Virgins never leave the local cruising grounds,
as the trip to the Windward Islands is considered a very hard one and most
yachtsmen there are satisfied with the multitude of beautiful anchorages
they have locally. But luck smiled on me, as there was a large and beautiful
60 ft. auxiliary ketch which not only was headed for St. Lucia, where my
boat was, but was even looking for a third crew member. The ship was to
leave two days later, but I was welcome to move right in, thus saving an
hotel bill.

I was thrilled, for not only did I save the expensive air fare, but I would
get a nice trip on a luxurious yacht and even get paid for it, too! The boat
was gleaming in varnish and shiny paint. She had new dacron sails, a large
diesel auxiliary, eight large comfortable beds, and the galley was a dream,
with stainless steel all over, a large cooking stove with oven and three
burners the same as in a house and also a large sink for dishwashing. I was
impressed by all the luxury compared to my modest *Dorothea*.

I had sailed with many different sloops, cutters, schooners, yawls, both
marconi and gaff rigged, but I had never sailed in a ketch before, except for
a few short afternoon sails, so I was looking forward to it, especially since
it has become the most popular rig of all, and must have many advantages
to have gained this popularity. But it did not take me long to realise the
inferiority of the ketch when going to windward over all other rigs, including the schooner. She was desperately slow as soon as we tried to sail
really close to the wind. I could have sailed considerably faster to windward
in my little *Dorothea* than this fancy and expensive ketch could. The
skipper finally got so impatient that he started the engine, despite the
strong wind, and we had to motor-sail most of the way in order to make
reasonably good time.

The wind was sufficiently strong to make the ship bounce quite a bit,
and we soon discovered that the wide and 'comfortable' beds were impossible to sleep in, as we got thrown about on the too-soft mattresses,
where the motion seemed to be amplified, so we all three had to sleep on
the floor, which was hard indeed, but where we knew we would not risk
any danger of being thrown out, and where the motion was more com-

fortable. In my modest *Dorothea*, which hardly ever got a second glance except from a few fishermen and experienced long-distance sailors, everything on the ship worked equally well whether in port or at sea and her ability to get to windward far exceeded this much larger yacht.

On the third day the skipper spent a lot of time in the rigging, looking for land, and sure enough in the afternoon he shouted that we had land dead ahead. A few hours later he declared that it was Dominique, which indeed I also recognised a little later, due to all its churches, which gave the island the surname of 'the Church Island'. One can hardly see half a dozen shacks without seeing a large church looming over them. I do not know how many souls have been saved by this system, but I know that in no other islands have I seen fewer smiles or had more difficulty in finding girl friends.

From Dominique we sailed along the coast, then along the channels both sides of Martinique and arrived on the night of the fourth day at Castries.

Next morning as soon as we were cleared by customs I rowed over to my own boat. I found everything the way I had left it, except for a disgusting green substance which covered everything inside. I had left all the ventilators open, but I had locked the hatches. Apparently this was not enough ventilation for the tropics, especially in the hot season, so I had a busy time washing the whole boat and airing everything. An hour after we had been cleared Bjula came over, so her information service still seemed to work. It was nice to see her again after the long separation and I showed her that I still had her ring, and asked her to look at the lock to see that I had not had it broken off for a more orthodox appearance in the States, where I told her I had been for a visit to my parents; but she did not bother to look. She just said simply:

'I know you have not taken it off. You will keep it for a long time yet.'

I stayed several weeks in the port, as there was, after all, a certain risk involved by sailing during the hurricane season, and Castries is one of the safest ports in the Caribbean, and I had a lot of work to do on the boat, painting and re-sewing a new mainsail to replace the old, which was rotten, and had been torn during my absence while it served as an awning for protecting the ship. The days passed agreeably in the little island, and I felt happy.

On 16th September 1960 the other singlehander of the port, a Dutchman who also appreciated the free life of the island, rowed over to my ship when Bjula was ashore and, rather excited, told me there were two white girls in town. We both went ashore to investigate, and soon saw them window-shopping. One was a blonde looking very English and the other a brunette. Neither of them looked the least bit interested in our attention for them, and since we both preferred the brunette we gave up trying to get to know them.

However, next morning as I walked into the post office I just happened to stay in line behind them, but none of us said a word and they left with their mail. When my turn came the mail man told me there was a package for me at the other office around the corner, so I went there immediately, only to discover that I was standing right behind the two girls again. When they turned around and saw me I had to laugh and assure them that I was really picking up a package also, and not just following them. The blonde answered that I by all means should not delay picking up the package, but her English had the easily recognisable French accent, so, surprised, I had to ask: '*Oh! Mais vous êtes Francaises, n'est-ce pas?*'

They were indeed, and the ice was broken. I invited them to have dinner with me on board and they were thrilled about the yacht, as it was the first time either of them had ever been on a sailboat. I enjoyed being able to talk with girls I could truly understand and was disappointed when they took their plane to Martinique the next day. They were both schoolteachers and only had a couple of weeks' vacation left, which they wanted to spend among their friends in Fort de France. But I kept on thinking about the brunette, and then two days after their departure I suddenly decided to sail over to Martinique to see her again. The new mainsail was not yet finished, but I had a storm trysail which with the help of large headsails should be enough to take me there. The barnacles had grown to an impressive length on the old copper, so I spent a couple of hours diving, to scrape them all off with a large wooden scraper so they would not stop the ship and make her hard to manoeuvre, then I rowed Bjula ashore; but even though I had left many times before without any trouble at all, this time she looked at me very suspiciously when I said good-bye.

'Do not take out my ring,' was all she said, as I rowed away.

Both girls had signed my guest book, so it was an easy matter for me to find the brunette's apartment. She answered the door bell and did not even look surprised to see me, but when after half an hour's polite conversation I asked her to sail with me to Tahiti, she laughed as if I was joking, yet I meant it seriously.

'Well, if you think Tahiti is too far, let's sail to the Grenadines in the ten days' vacation you have left. Then you do not even have to ask for leave of absence from school.'

To that she said 'Yes' with no hesitation, and we agreed that she should come to the boat next morning at ten o'clock.

That morning I could hardly wait for ten o'clock to arrive. However, at ten there was no one on the dock. Neither was there anyone at five past ten, nor at quarter past. At 10.30 I felt she was not coming. These things happen, but it hurts every time, and this time I was seriously disappointed, for I had felt so sure she was sincere when she said she would come. I rowed over to the *Noctiluc* to try to get some consolation there. Pierre Hamel told me that women were all the same, and Janine his wife claimed there were many other girls in the world. But at past eleven o'clock I jumped up in joy when I saw her walking briskly towards the dock, while Janine tried to push me back into the cockpit: 'Do not get so excited. Just sit down here for a little while. Pretend you have forgotten about her, and let her wait for you now,' she advised.

But I was already jumping into the dinghy and sculling as fast as I could towards shore, as I heard Janine lament: 'Oh! What fools men can be! . . .'

We sailed to the lonely and beautiful Tobago Keys in the Grenadine Islands, where we enjoyed life in general and where we snorkled and swam in the beautiful clear and warm waters and finished the new mainsail for the trip back.

Upon our return to Martinique I moved into Simonne's apartment while I put the ship on the slip for changing the copper bottom, which was worn out after about twenty years' service. Simonne suggested that I use her apartment as my mailing address instead of St. Lucia; when I agreed that it would be more convenient, she immediately wrote my name in large letters on a card which she fastened on the door next to hers, so the mailman would know where to put my letters.

But I had lived too long in the States, where everyone's life is well regulated by countless restrictions and where I had been kicked out of several apartments for having had female visitors staying after ten o'clock at night, so I was now afraid of trouble with the landlord if we openly declared that I lived with one of his tenants. Simonne looked rather surprised when I told her about my fears and reminded me that she was over 21 and could not at all see what the landlord had to do with her personal life. Rather to please me, she nevertheless went down to introduce me to the landlord and asked if it would be O.K. for me to stay as a guest in her apartment for a while. He seemed a bit surprised and just said: 'But, mademoiselle, you do as you wish in your own home.'

Simonne laughed, and I felt a bit foolish, but was happy to be back in a country where landlords did not rule people's private lives.

Then started a soft life for me which I had not had since leaving my parents' home. In the morning I was awakened by the maid's happy voice as she lifted the mosquito netting which completely surrounded our huge bed, and installed carefully the breakfast-tray in front of us, while greeting us: 'Bonjour, mademoiselle. Bonjour, monsieur.' Such an easy life should have given me twice as much strength for doing a lot of work on the boat, but on the contrary it just seemed to make me lazy, for I decided after just one look at the many copperplates and their thousands of coppernail-holes that it was too big a job to change the complete bottom and plug all those nail holes. I decided it could be done 'next time' and preferred just to patch the many holes and do the bare minimum. Even then it took me all of ten days on the slip before the boat again was in the water. I anchored the ship in the roadstead right in front of town, where I could watch her from the apartment with my binoculars.

Life was good to me and I had everything a man could dream of. Simonne worked only seventeen hours a week as a gymnastics teacher, so she had a lot of free time to be with me. We went sailing, swimming, driving with our friends, partying and just loafing. When she was working I would go on the boat and do some of the never-ending maintenance work which no yacht-owner can get away from for very long at a time, especially in the tropics, where the sun burns off the varnish and paint at an amazing speed and where everything seems to rust despite regular painting and care.

In the morning I would go through the town in proper clothes and sandals, carrying a small portable ice chest. Ordinarily such a chest would be filled with ice, drinks and food, but I always had it empty. The only reason I carried it was that I knew that it was absolutely watertight, so when I arrived at the public dock I would strip off all my clothes except a miniature bikini (after a quick look around to make sure no policeman was watching), stuff them all in the box, carefully securing the watertight lid, and then dive in the water with it, and swim to my boat anchored a few hundred feet from shore. I had, of course, a dinghy, but this I preferred to leave on the boat, as it seemed to be a popular form of amusement for somebody to untie a dinghy which was attached to the dock at night and to see the offshore trade wind carry it out to sea.

To get ashore, the reverse operation was done, and I noticed a few people were surprised to see a white, almost nude man arrive at the dock out of the water with his luggage, pull out his clothes, dress and walk into the town 'correctly' attired.

Life could have gone on like this indefinitely, but the urge to travel and to see what was on the other side of the horizon was too strong, and I finally persuaded Simonne to ask for a year's leave of absence from her job and sail with me to Tahiti, as I had suggested in the first place. When her leave was granted she sold her furniture and most of the things she would not need on the trip so all her belongings would fit into one of *Dorothea*'s lockers. In order to replenish the bank account for the long voyage I accepted a last charter which started from Barbados and took me through the whole chain of islands back to Martinique.

When we arrived at Castries, where the charter ended, I saw Bjula again and had to tell her that she would not see me any more, as I was leaving for the Pacific and would not come back. Her eyes went hard and she stared in front of her without answering.

'I will keep your ring and never take it out,' I added, I do not know why.

Then she looked at me and her voice sounded strange as if from another person when she answered: 'You are wrong. You will take it off. Not now, but later.'

She paused, and then added: 'I even know when you will take it off: you will take it off seven months before your death.'

Then she turned around as if I was a perfect stranger and left with her peculiar feline walk.

Since that time I have often nearly taken out the ring, but each time her strange voice and glassy eyes come back to me with all the magic of the voodoo in which she was raised in the interior of the island. And the ring stays in my ear, I hope, for many more years.

5

Bound for Tahiti

THE last days before a long voyage a thousand things have to be attended to and there just does not seem to be enough hours in each day for getting everything done, yet it is always during these very days that farewell parties are held by well-meaning friends. While we appreciated their kindness, we were absolutely worn out when the time of departure finally arrived.

As Simonne had never seen the islands north of Martinique, we decided to sail along the whole chain of islands all the way to the American Virgins, but the trip had a bad start, as in the very first channel we got into an extremely squally and fierce rainstorm with winds changing rapidly, so it became necessary for me to sit and steer in the rain and I caught such a chill that as night fell I was already sick with a high fever. When the wind dropped I decided to anchor as soon as possible for a rest and sailed carefully in the dark, towards the shore, sounding all the way. When I had the proper depth I let the anchor go and went to bed, but next morning rather than feeling rested I was so sick that I was unable to get up, so weak was I with a terrible fever, but it was a great comfort to have Simonne with me, as one feels helpless indeed in such conditions when alone.

For four days I lay in bed, shivering with cold one minute and feeling terribly hot and perspiring the next. Many natives came during those four days in their heavy dug-outs to investigate, as we happened to have anchored at an entirely unprotected shore where they had never seen a yacht before. As sick as I was, I still suffered by hearing their boats bumping continuously against *Dorothea*'s topsides, as I knew from bitter experience that they can do considerable damage to the smooth sides of a yacht. I told Simonne to chase them away, but she did it so carefully and with so little conviction for fear of hurting their feelings, that if they left at all they were back a few minutes later, bumping the topsides as before, while they looked and looked, for hours.

Simonne had brought a small Christmas tree so we could celebrate Christmas in style, and despite my sickness I thought I had a good Christmas and felt happy. When on the fifth day the fever left me we went

Native dugout canoe in the West Indies. The man standing up is using his weight to hold up the canoe and will lean farther out as the wind increases, in the same way modern dinghy sailors are doing. (St. Lucie, West Indies)

(Courtesy Monsieur Henri Domergue)

Native fisherman blowing through a large shell, thus producing a powerful trumpet noise which is the signal to all housewives that fish are for sale. (Martinique)

Simonne cleaning
fish at sea.
(Pacific Ocean)

The author taking a sight. (Pacific Ocean)

ashore for a short walk and were met apparently by half the village as we disembarked on the beach. They asked if 'I was all healthy again', as evidently the canoes had spread the news of my fever, and as we walked everybody walked with us. I felt so weak that every hundred yards or so I had to stop and sit down for a rest. Everybody stopped also, and waited patiently for me to get up again before continuing the walk.

It was only a few miles to Portsmouth, where the harbour was a lot safer, so not wanting to push my luck too far I felt it safer to leave this open roadstead. Simonne helped me to get in the anchor and to hoist the sails, which seemed to weigh so much more than their usual weight, but we soon arrived in the beautiful bay of Portsmouth. A few days after our arrival we were offered a beautiful stick of bananas for just fifty cents. The price was very low and the bananas were of the best quality, but the day was hot and we were not too anxious to carry them all the way down to the beach where our dinghy waited for us. Unfortunately the man was firm about it: the price was low, but we had to carry them ourselves. We had to accept his terms, as we wanted the bananas, but we were soon perspiring heavily under our heavy load.

Many natives were also walking our way, all of them carrying the same load as us, but when we came to the water's edge we were stupefied seeing them just dump the bananas in the water and walk away, apparently to fetch another load! The whole bay was full of floating bananas, many hundreds of bunches drifting out to sea in the offshore breeze. Only then did we understand that a strike or some other trouble must have prevented the expected banana boat arriving for the waiting bananas. As nothing keeps in the tropics, and since there is a limit to how many bananas a small village could consume, there was no other alternative to just throwing them away.

We felt rather foolish, for not only had we carried the bananas for the man but we had even paid him for letting us do it. No wonder that I thought I had seen some hidden smiles and giggles when we made the deal. As I got on board with my cumbersome load a banana bunch drifted by within a couple of feet of *Dorothea*, and I could not resist the temptation to gaff it and get it on board, but instead of being glad of the new fruit it just made me regret my foolish purchase even more. But at least we were able to give them to some grateful natives on an island later on where no bananas were growing.

Simonne was thrilled by the 'secret entrance' to English Harbour and loved the beautiful scenery. In order to avoid the annoying charges levied on all yachts which tie up to the dock, we preferred swinging at anchor, which gave us the advantage of more privacy. There I worked on the ship, repainting her topside and splicing her new stainless-steel shrouds, which

I had purchased in Martinique, but had not yet had the time to install. Instead of the inefficient 'baggywrinkles', I threaded a plastic hose around the wire before doing the splicing and this precaution against chafing was to prove extremely efficient.

St. Yves d'Armor, a very large French yacht converted from a tuna fishing boat, came into port a few days after us, and we became very friendly with her owner, Robert le Serrec, who was a keen photographer and gave me many valuable tips. As they also were headed for St. Thomas, we decided to sail in company so we could take photographs of each other. Robert took it for granted that his much larger ship would be the fastest, for he said that after we had taken enough pictures he would let his boat sail her normal speed and would wait for me in Nevis. He even said that he would hang a powerful white lantern in his rig so when I got in to port I could easily see where he was anchored. Not knowing his boat, I did not question his speed, but I was a bit surprised that he took it for granted that I would not arrive before dark, as that was really underestimating *Dorothea*'s speed.

We took many pictures on all points of sailing and then Robert signalled that it was enough. We both set our course for Nevis and determined to get there in ample time before dark. I hung up all the canvas I had in the fresh breeze. And so did *St. Yves d'Armor*, but it was not his boat which jumped into the leading position. *Dorothea* went, in fact, so much faster that we soon lost him below the horizon! When he arrived at anchor just before nightfall we had already been there a long time. As soon as he had anchored he came over in his dinghy and did not hide his surprise.

We visited the islands, then sailed to St. Kitts, then St. Eustatius, which is a Dutch country and where we were amused and charmed to see that there were no licencé plates on any of the cars. There were so few of them that the authorities knew each one by its looks!

On Saturday the 14th, at seven o'clock in the morning, we left together for Saba, the isolated island with no harbour where it is said that all the men are gone most of the year working outside while the women are left alone spending their time doing embroidery work by their windows. We intended to anchor close to the shore on its lee side, as we thought the island well worth visiting, especially as so few yachts ever go there because of its lack of harbour. The island being the top of an underwater volcano, all its sides are steep, so we had to get very close to shore before finding sufficiently shallow water for anchoring. The anchor seemed to hold, but the heavy swell coming around the island from its windward side made us roll considerably, so when *St. Yves* came close to us, they took one look before they declared it too dangerous an anchorage and shouted to us that they would wait for us in St. Thomas.

I had dropped the hook opposite a long stairway which seemed to be cut right into the mountainside, and which I knew led to the top of the island, where the population lived. I could see the waves beating savagely against the shore and did not think it would be possible to disembark in our dinghy without smashing it to pieces, so we decided to swim ashore with our shore clothes in a watertight rubber bag. To get ashore just in our swimsuits I knew was not possible, for even if the temperature was more than warm enough for a minimum of clothes, progress and civilisation required that even in the most remote islands we wore a shirt and shorts and shoes even if they were soaking wet with perspiration within the first few minutes.

Timing the waves carefully, we got ashore with no trouble, while *St. Yves d'Armor* disappeared towards the horizon. Some boys had spotted our yacht and came running down the stairway towards us. They confirmed that these were the stairs leading to the village at the top of the island, so we started the long fascinating climb through the picturesque winding stairway. But when we finally arrived all out of breath at the top we were disappointed to discover several taxis waiting for us! No matter how isolated a place is, tourists are finding their way to it, but we had not expected even to see taxis there, and I still wonder how they had been disembarked, even though there was some kind of a crude dock on the other side of the island where on calm days small coasters could lie-to temporarily.

In the small stores prices were ridiculously high, and much of the food cost exactly twice the price it would have cost in the U.S., where it was far from cheap. The population was mostly white, but not particularly good-looking, and it seemed to me there were just as many men around as there were women, so I think bachelors are wasting their time if they go with the idea of easy woman-chasing. They would probably do better in their home towns like London, Paris or Cannes.

It was just before nightfall when we hoisted sail for the Virgins. As soon as we were at a safe distance from the island I set the automatic pilot and we went to bed, as we were tired after the long walk. During the night I heard vaguely a strong rain squall and the rush of water past the hull as the speed increased, but I was too tired to bother to get out of bed and check. I felt sure it was just a squall and everything would soon get back to normal. Next morning at daybreak we saw a tiny spot ahead of us on the horizon. The spot grew and soon there was no doubt about it: it was the *St. Yves d'Armor*! As we sailed close past him Robert shouted over complaining about the last night's terrible weather when all hands had been on deck fighting wildly flogging canvas. When he asked how we had managed, just the two of us on board, I really enjoyed telling him that we had heard the blow, but did not like to get wet, so we had stayed in bed. I can still hear his good-natured swearing, but I think this is rather typical, and many people who say that they want large boats because they have 'got to have their comfort' do not realise that sometimes one has more comfort in a smaller boat (unless, of course, one can afford a large professional crew who do all the work).

Simonne was thrilled at the beauty of the Virgin Islands, which she thought the nicest of them all. It was the first time she had been in American territory, and she was very impressed by the big supermarkets she had heard so much about. She loved seeing the neatly cellophane-wrapped frozen meat and vegetables. And all the ready-made cakes she had heard so much about filled her with joy and she bought enough to last us for many days. Back on the boat she prepared the dinner in the minimum of time, so handy was everything, but already at the first mouthful she looked surprised. After having tasted the frozen vegetables also, she laughed and exclaimed:

'It certainly looks nice, but it has no taste whatsoever. It just tastes like water!'

As to the cakes, she really had difficulty in getting them down, with all their artificial colouring and flavouring. She did not seem to believe me when I told her that one gets used to it after a few months in the States, and that she should not feel sorry for Americans having to be satisfied with such food, for most of them firmly believe that their food is the best in the world.

Remembering how quickly I had sold the *Volharding* in St. Thomas, I thought this would be the best place to sell my dinghy, which I considered too cumbersome to have on deck for a long trip. I would rather have the decks uncluttered and just use the little folding dinghy I had below in the forecastle. I gave the dinghy a fresh coat of paint and put it up for sale for 100 dollars U.S. Two days later it was sold to the very man who had bought the *Volharding*. But I spent the money the same day by buying a hundred yards of anti-mildew sail canvas for sewing new headsails.

On 24th January at twelve o'clock we broke out the anchor and sailed towards Panama. This was a big day for us, as we felt that we now had started the voyage in earnest. So far we had really just sailed among the islands of the West Indies, which by now almost felt like our home.

The wind was astern and very fresh. It gave us a good speed, but made us roll madly. Simonne got very seasick almost immediately we had lost the protection of land, and at first I did not feel too good myself, but three days later even Simonne was feeling wonderful again, except that she had great difficulty in sleeping in the heavy motion, which caused a thousand

different noises. I had grown so accustomed to these that I considered
them as normal and unavoidable in any ship at sea and none of those noises
prevented me from sleeping.

However, Simonne had an entirely different opinion about the noises
unavoidable at sea, and she decided to eliminate all of them, so *Dorothea*
would be 'the silent sailing ship' so often described by various authors who
have never been at sea. She started to hunt the noises, sometimes even in
the middle of the night with the help of a flashlight, gradually working
closer to the offending noise until she pinpointed it. Then she had the
problem of curing it. This was sometimes done simply by re-stowing the
offending object, sometimes by jamming paper or rags around it and sometimes even by the foolproof method of simply throwing the noisy article
over the side.

Everyone knows that a double bed cannot be used at sea, as in any kind
of a sea its occupants would be thrown against each other, so I slept alone
in the saloon in the double bunk, while Simonne slept in one of the
forward bunks just under the forehatch. The hatch was of massive teak
construction and so heavy that I did not consider it necessary to lock it,
although of course it was closed.

On the night of the 28th I was awakened by a choked cry from Simonne
as if someone had tried to hold her head under the water, but almost
immediately it was followed by a happy laugh. Asking what was the matter,
she told me to come and see for myself. There were several inches of water
in her bunk and she looked as if she had just come in from a swim! A big
wave must have come on deck, lifted the hatch, rushed down on Simonne
sleeping in her bunk and then closed the hatch again! I admired Simonne's
good humour, as I think that most people awakened in this manner would
have failed to see anything funny about it. The water ran quickly out of her
bunk, but the mattress was soaked and could hardly be used any more. We
laid another mattress on the floor in the main saloon, where she slept until
we reached Panama, and she was well secured with sailbags on both sides
to prevent her from being thrown from side to side.

On the 30th in the evening the wind moderated to Force 6, so I took out
the reefs, and after having figured out the afternoon sight I announced to
Simonne that we should see the lights of Panama during the night and be
in port next day. We therefore kept watch during the night and Simonne
was very impressed when a light became visible straight ahead of the ship
at three o'clock in the morning. At noon we dropped anchor, and had thus
sailed the 1,050 miles from Charlotte Amalie to Panama in seven days flat
from anchor to anchor, which is an average speed of exactly 150 miles a
day. This was the fastest run I had ever made and one not often achieved
in a ship only 32 feet in length, but then *Dorothea* has beautiful underwater

lines and can run safely in weather which would have forced other yachts
to heave-to or reef down excessively.

I had anchored between the three marker buoys, where I knew we were
expected to await the immigration officer, and I did not have to wait long
before the efficient American organisation had me cross-examined by a
very pale-looking officer. For more than an hour I patiently answered all
his questions, as I knew from bitter experience that it does not pay to show
one's contempt for certain officials no matter how ridiculous many of their
questions might be. When he wanted to see my vaccination certificate I
was unable to find it, but showed him the ship's papers of my previous
visit, when I had been vaccinated by them, a fact of which they probably
had records in their office. But he was not impressed by my argument and
told me to take off my shirt; whereupon he vaccinated me with no further
ado, which gave me the right to get a brand-new piece of paper stating that
I had been vaccinated on this day of the 31st January 1961 and thus O.K.'d
for the next six years (if I did not lose it again).

When he asked to see my deratification certificate I had to admit that
I never had had one on this ship, as no other port in the world had asked
for one, considering that I was a yacht. He said he would send me a man
who would take care of it, and I knew that that would cost me thirteen
dollars unless the price had gone up since my last transit. Then he pro-
ceeded to measure my ship in order to establish its 'Panama Canal
tonnage', upon which the charges of my transit would be based. After
half an hour of tape measurements and then a bit of figuring the tonnage
was established, and I was much surprised to see that *Dorothea*'s Panama
tonnage was higher than *Windflower*'s tonnage had been, though in reality
the *Windflower* was exactly twice as big a ship, but as the charges for the
transit itself were very reasonable, I preferred not to mention it, in case he
objected to having his ability as measurer questioned.

The formalities over, I lost no time in hoisting the sails before night fell
and sailed over to the yacht club. It was quite tricky sailing into our berth
and I was doubly anxious not to make a false manoeuvre, as the many
yachtsmen on the shady terrace were watching us. It would, of course, have
been much easier had one of them walked down the few yards to the dock
in order to take our lines, but as I had no right to expect any help I did not
ask for any.

Two years before with Lillemor I had made many friends at this club
and had often been invited to their homes or for long car drives through
the tropical country. I looked forward to seeing them again, although I
knew, of course, that some of them would object to seeing me with a new
woman. One of them came over, and we offered him some tea in *Dorothea*,
but he soon excused himself, and for the rest of our stay we met no one

else. I had forgotten how narrow-minded the average American is and how strictly we have to obey their rules if we want to be accepted by them. To have arrived with Simonne instead of Lillemor was in their minds inexcusable, but it was only inexcusable because the red tape had not been taken care of: in other words, had I got through all the paper work and expense involved with a divorce, and then signed some additional papers called 'marriage certificate', everything would have been honourable and everybody would have accepted my new 'wife', but failing this we were undesirable.

If we made no friends, we were not lacking in spectators. They often came down on the dock and would discuss my ship while I was there as if I was completely deaf. I was much annoyed by remarks about my ropes being too thin, my wire rigging being too thick, my lack of cockpit being very dangerous, my mast being too weak and so on. One day when we were down below, but of course with all the portholes open in the heat, we heard one voice say:

'Do you know that that guy does not even have a motor in that boat and he thinks that he will get to the Galapagos!'

Whereupon they all burst out laughing as they walked away. I was furious, but I consoled myself that Simonne at least did not doubt that we could sail anywhere with *Dorothea* the way she was, which made me grateful, as I knew that many other girls would have lost confidence in me, hearing such remarks constantly from 'experienced' yachtsmen, and would probably have disembarked right there.

There were plenty of ways of spending money in Panama: walking in one of the main streets with Simonne, my pocket was picked. When I complained to the police that I had had thirty dollars stolen they asked me if I had been hurt. I admitted no harm had been done to myself.

'In that case,' they answered, 'you should consider yourself lucky: men have been knifed and killed for less money than that. We would advise you to carry as little money as possible and in any case never show more than one bill at a time.'

I overhauled most of the rigging, changing all the wires which were rusty, changing those of the ropes which looked tired, made a bar across the galley so Simonne would be held securely while she cooked, and I solved the sleeping-accommodation problem by making a removable leeboard right in the middle of the double bed in the saloon, thus changing it into two single bunks for sea use. We could then both lie in the main saloon, where the motion was least violent, and have the whole forepart of the ship for storage.

While this work was going on I had also tried to make arrangements for transiting the canal and was much discouraged by all the difficulties. First

of all, I learned that it was against the regulations for a sailing vessel to sail
through and that a tow was mandatory. They also obligingly told me that
the fee for towing me through the canal was 250 dollars, provided they
could get another customer for their return trip; otherwise they had to
charge me another 250 dollars for the return trip. As I was neither prepared
to pay 500 nor the 250, I hoped to find either another yacht or a small
native boat willing to pull me through for a moderate figure. Several
yachts transited while I was at the club, and I proposed to each one that
I would pay their canal fees and their fuel if they were willing to pull me
through. Except for one who said plain 'No', they were all willing until
they had been in the canal office to get their clearance, when they invariably
came back with some excuse like having thought it over they considered
their engine was not powerful enough, or the locks too dangerous, or my
ship too heavy. I also tried the native boats and finally from one of them I
got the real reason why nobody wanted to tow me: the canal company told
the skippers of all the boats willing to do it that they would be respon-
sible for all damages done in the locks by either vessel in case of an
accident. I was getting discouraged, and even started to consider the
possibility of sailing around Cape Horn, when finally, after five weeks'
waiting, I found a fat and happy-looking negro skipper who did not
seem to worry about possible disasters and who appreciated the money
offered.

'For fifteen dollars I'll tow you anywhere, man. But I am not permitted
to pick you up at the yacht club. You'll have to wait for me at the "Flats".
We go through tomorrow at ten o'clock.'

Unfortunately my troubles in Panama were not yet over. I sailed straight
over to the 'Flats' as ordered by the officer, and while the weather was good
during the night it blew up extremely fresh by next morning when *Nellie*,
our tug boat, came to the rendezvous spot. Instead of just taking the line I
wanted to throw to him so he could wait to windward of me till I got my
anchor up, he just steered at me at forty-five degrees angle and tried to lie
alongside despite the very choppy waters and strong winds. Fortunately I
had rigged twelve truck fenders along the side, but even then I was not
safe, as his flaring bow hit my shrouds with a sickening noise, breaking my
topmast stay. In the confusion no lines were attached and he drifted away,
but soon charged me for another try.

I did not dare argue with him, as I was afraid that he might change his
mind about towing me through. At the third try we got our lines coupled,
but, of course, having the heavy banana boat at my side made us lie at a
great angle to my anchor chain, making it impossible for me to crank it in.
Furthermore, his big ship put such a strain on my chain that I was afraid
it might even break. Realising my trouble, he let go and said he would

come alongside again when I was straight over my anchor and it would be ready to break out. Fortunately before he had had time to do any further damage the pilot came over and immediately understood the situation:

'What's the matter, boy? Are you trying to sink that poor yacht? Just throw him a line and wait a hundred feet ahead of him till he gets his anchor up.'

Greatly relieved at his appearance, the situation was immediately under control and I was soon safely towed towards the locks. Not until we were inside the smooth water of the first lock did he pull me alongside him, for greater manoeuvrability while towing me through the three locks leading to the man-made lake crossing most of the estuary separating the Atlantic from the Pacific Ocean. In the lake I was again towed behind the banana boat with a beautiful following wind, and I thought how much easier it would have been and how much safer if I had been permitted to sail through. I would have avoided the damage done to my rigging, and it would have been easy to sail from the 'Flats' to the first lock, get pulled through the three locks by manpower with lines ashore, then hoist the sails again in the lake, but man is more and more convinced that sails are a risky and dangerous means of propulsion, disregarding completely the fact that oceans have been sailed for thousands of years under canvas.

The three locks leading down to sea-level again on the other side were handled in the same way and it was a great moment for both Simonne and I when the third lock opened up: we were in the Pacific Ocean!

I had, of course, no intention of climbing to the top of *Dorothea*'s tall mast at sea to carry out the repairs, but I had recalled that just a few miles outside the town was a tiny island called Tobago where the anchorage was reasonably good and, even more important, where there were no authorities to bother us. As the top of the mast was unsupported on the one side, I sailed under extremely short canvas despite the wind here being very light, so it took us a long time to get there, but the place was so quiet and so beautiful that we were glad we had decided to stop.

I spent most of the next day repairing the rigging, but when it was done and the ship seemed well prepared for its long trip across the Pacific we went ashore to enjoy the little place and relax. In addition to the little village, there was an hotel and several luxurious homes.

On Sunday morning ferry boats powered into the bay carrying a large amount of Sunday tourists from Panama. On seeing them I immediately hoisted the sails, brought in the anchor and left in a very light northerly breeze. This was 5th March 1961.

The first few days the wind stayed very light and irregular, constantly changing in direction, but by conscientiously readjusting the sails day and night at even the slightest change we still covered more than a hundred miles a day for the first few days.

We steered out of the steamers' lane, as we had some doubt about how well they kept look-outs, and one night our fears were confirmed in a rather convincing way. We were in a position about 4 degrees north and 80 degrees west. The sky was clear except for a very light haze close to the surface. We were almost becalmed and coasted slowly towards the south.

We were both sleeping, but had taken care to hang a white light in the rigging before turning in. Simonne was awakened by a strange sound and tried to wake me to tell me that something unusual had scared her. I heard her voice in a half sleep, but was so tired that her words did not register and I just grunted some unintelligible reply. Then as in a dream I heard the noise of a waterfall! Even today, three years later, while writing these words a sudden chill sweeps over me. In a fraction of a second I was fully awake, and practically flew out of bed and through the hatch, as the sound of a waterfall at sea could only be the bow-wave of a steamer, and when one hears the wave rather than the motor she cannot be far away! The steamer was indeed coming from behind and cutting our course at a slight angle.

I instinctively threw the tiller over, but knew it was of little use, as we were hardly moving in the light breeze. The bow-wave rocked us and the ship slid past barely missing us, but I looked up at my mast, wondering if it would hit the towering wall as we bounced violently, swinging our mast back and forth, but it cleared and no damage was done, except perhaps to my nerves. My heart was pounding heavily, but Simonne looked perfectly calm. Half an hour later we were back in our comfortable bunk, sleeping as before, but hoping that steamers keep a better watch in future and respect the rules of the road, giving priority to sailing vessels.

About seven o'clock on Saturday the 11th we crossed the Equator. It was the first time for both of us, so we considered it a great day, and we celebrated it with a tinned cake which we had purchased especially in anticipation of the occasion.

The 13th, for the first time since leaving Panama we had the lovely small cumulus clouds and the warm sun instead of a constantly grey sky. In fact, the sun got so hot that we could not walk barefooted on the wood of the cockpit, but only where the decks were painted white, as this white colour reflected the sun's heat and thus stayed surprisingly cool compared with the scorching heat of any dark surface. For the tropics, a boat should be painted white all over, as it protects the ship against extremes of temperature as well as making life on board much more tolerable, but even so, one should never forget sun glasses, as the glare is rather startling!

On the 14th and especially the 15th I knew we were getting close to our landfall, but I was very annoyed that I had been unable to get my noon sight for lack of sun just at that time. Under ordinary conditions, and always outside the tropics, it is easy to determine latitude without the aid of a noon sight, but now the sun just happened to be almost exactly ninety degrees over my head, and therefore even a few minutes before and/or after noon my line of position was practically straight north-south and thus I had no indication of latitude except at noon. A very good way of calculating latitude is the use of the North Star, but, of course, below the Equator it is not visible. There are several other stars and planets I could theoretically have used, but the light night haze which seemed to be prevalent in this region prevented me from seeing the horizon with sufficient clearness to get an accurate star sight.

I was especially worried as the islands have been named 'The Enchanted Islands' by early navigators, not because the islands were so wonderful, but because of their seemingly magical habit of disappearing and re-appearing at the most unexpected times and places, due to the very strong and irregular currents which, coupled with light and often fickle winds, made them extremely difficult to find.

I was very relieved when we spotted land at six o'clock, just before dark, which gave us a positive check on our latitude—provided, of course, that we could presume that it really was the island of Espanola as I expected it to be (an island we were not permitted to land on, as by law we had to clear with the authorities at the island of San Cristobal before setting our foot anywhere in this group of islands). Soon we were completely becalmed, so in order to save the sails from the slamming, I lowered them all while waiting for a breeze to get up. The night was beautiful, the stars were bright, the dolphins were jumping around us, leaving a trail of phosphorus behind them in the water, and we thought how fortunate we were to be able to see all these wonders of nature, while our fellow workers were still sitting behind their desks wondering whether they would get enough over-time this month to be able to pay their monthly instalments on the car, the television, the new refrigerator, and maybe also a fur coat. Next day we were fascinated to see sea-dogs and hear their barking. Sea-dogs right on the Equator!

We travelled slowly in light winds, but the following night we were close to our destination and could already smell the wonderful fragrance of land coming towards us at sea. That night we did not dare go to sleep, as we were too close to land, even though progress was slow, for we had not forgotten the fact that not less than three yachts had been wrecked on the coast of the Galapagos within the last two years. At dawn we rounded the island, and at five minutes past eight we dropped anchor in Wreck Bay on the island of San Cristobal, waiting for the authorities to board us.

We had sailed from Panama in twelve days, which was a very fast

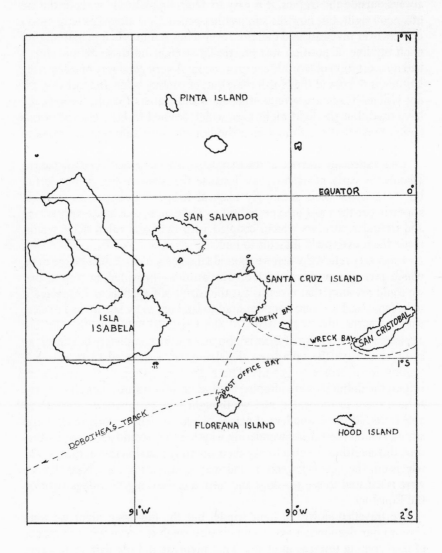

1°N

PINTA ISLAND

EQUATOR   0°

SAN SALVADOR

SANTA CRUZ ISLAND

ISLA
ISABELA

ACADEMY BAY

WRECK BAY SAN CRISTOBAL

1°S

POST OFFICE BAY

DOROTHEA'S TRACK

FLOREANA ISLAND

HOOD ISLAND

91°W   90°W   2°S

GALAPAGOS ISLANDS

passage, especially for an engineless craft, and I wished some of the wise guys of the dock at the yacht club in Panama could have seen us sail in. But it was a consolation for me to see that Simonne showed no surprise whatsoever about the fast passage, which proved to me that she had never doubted me when I had assured her that we could sail anywhere in the world with the *Dorothea*.

A delegation of four men in uniform came on board and asked for our passports and all our papers, which they kept and said we would get them back upon leaving the island, which is a thing one never likes, as one is always afraid of the papers getting lost or of the possibility of being forced to sea one night because of anchor failures, in which case one would have to return into the same harbour later on just to pick up the passports. This has never happened and probably never will, but nevertheless it is annoying to be unable to leave when one feels like it. They were, however, very nice and extremely polite, both toward me and Simonne, which was appreciated after the Americans in Panama, who had treated her almost as a whore because our passports did not have the same name. They even invited us both ashore to their canteen for a drink. There we soon got on friendly terms, so I even had the courage to ask them if it was true what I had heard about yachts often being fined when arriving in the Galapagos. The young officer with, I believe, a captain's rank and functioning as port captain answered with a smile:

'Of course, when yachtsmen break our laws we have to fine them and also when they do not respect our office hours we charge them overtime. Discipline is good for all people, even for yachtsmen.'

This might sound reasonable, but 'breaking the law' could consist of arriving without an Ecuadorian courtesy flag, in which case ten American dollars had to be paid. In Panama we had been unable to buy such a flag anywhere, but we had fortunately sewn a flag ourselves with odd pieces of old dress materials, copying the design from my geography book, as I have to admit that neither of us knew what an Ecuadorian flag looked like. I am not too ashamed to admit my ignorance, as I am sure ninety per cent of my readers would also be unable to make such a flag without a model. Anyway, the one hour it took Simonne to make the flag at sea saved us ten dollars, which has to be considered as a good hourly wage. The overtime charge is even more annoying, especially since it involves no extra work for the authorities, who still wait till office hours for doing their paperwork. What counts is the time one drops anchor. The young captain told me, still with a smile, that had I arrived six minutes earlier, that is one minute before eight o'clock, I would also have had to pay ten dollars. They had watched me with binoculars, but he said that they appreciated that for once they had met a yachtsman who had timed it right and had respected their 'office hours' and had waited to drop anchor until five minutes after eight. Therefore I had nothing to pay.

Is it really necessary to entangle in red tape even lost islands in the middle of nowhere? It seems to me life went on as well and a lot more agreeably before each little island got its 'port captain' and accompanying paperwork. What difference could it make if a few boats were free to come and go as they pleased and no one was there to 'check their papers'?

However, not everybody dislikes red tape as much as I do, and the captain for one seemed very happy about it, when he told me about the last yacht which had passed before me: it had been an American yacht, he said, and when he had been charged the ten dollars for arriving at seven o'clock in the morning he had paid immediately with no comments. However, when he had asked the port captain to make out his papers a few days later for leaving the following morning at five, he was asked for another ten-dollar bill, to which he then had replied that in that case he would wait till eight so no overtime would have to be charged. The captain had then pointed out that the papers had just been made out for five, so it was too late for him to change his mind, whereupon the American had lost his temper and called them all a bunch of thieves. When the captain got this far in his story he did not try to hide his triumph when he added to me:

'I did not lose my temper, as I was entitled to do when someone insults an officer. No, on the contrary, I just smiled at him and said that now in addition to the ten dollars overtime charge there was an additional charge of twenty-five dollars for insulting an officer of the Ecuadorian Navy, but that if he preferred not to pay he could serve the sentence in our jail instead.'

He even showed me their jail, with its three empty cells, and I can imagine that he would have been only too glad to get a customer. Needless to say, the American paid the thirty-five dollars, but I am not surprised that he did not sail to Academy Bay as he had cleared for, but instead sailed directly for the Marquesas.

Fortunately we avoided all charges or other frustrations and we saw nothing but smiles everywhere. Walking in the town we were surprised to find the Galapagos much more 'civilised' than we had anticipated from the stories we had read. The mail went twice a month and most things could be bought in the various stores, although some things were lacking, like butter and margarine, at least at the time we were there. Likewise we were unable to get any form of meat, but got both fish and lobsters at a very low price. Meat was available, but only on certain days of the month.

We left at five o'clock in the afternoon so we would not be liable for any overtime pay and cleared for Academy Bay on the island of Santa Cruz, where most of the European colony was settled. The wind was extremely light, so in order to be able to get a good night's sleep, without watches, we took down all sails and went to sleep. Next morning the wind returned and I hoisted the sails again, but discovered at dawn that we were not where I had expected and that the current must have been south-westerly rather than nor-nor-westerly as the pilot charts indicated. We progressed very slowly all day, and as night fell I realised through the last cross bearings I had been taking that a very strong current was carrying us quickly past the island, as the wind was dying completely. I recalled all the stories of boats and yachts which had been swept past the islands and never been able to return; I also recalled the 'I told you so' and was quite decided to make Academy Bay as planned.

The most logical thing to do when becalmed in a strong unfavourable current is to anchor, but according to the chart and my latest cross bearing I had 75 fathoms of water under me, and most yachtsmen consider that 15 fathoms is about the deepest waters they should ever anchor in. I had, however, on a couple of occasions anchored in as much as 35 fathoms and decided to try it now in the 75 fathoms. I took my 28 lb. fisherman anchor, shackled to it first 5 fathoms of chain, then 70 fathoms of very heavy nylon and then finally 45 fathoms of my heavy $\frac{3}{8}$ in. stud-linked chain. This did not make the prescribed three times the depth of water for the anchor line, but the proportion changes over great depth. Anyway, it was sufficient to hold the ship and I knew we were at anchor by the fact that the ship turned towards the current and got a nice little wave on either side of her bow, while the fishing line trailed straight aft, close to the surface, instead of hanging almost straight down as it had been doing while we were drifting with the three-knot current.

Next morning after a restful night we had a leisurely breakfast, and when at eleven o'clock a light but seemingly steady breeze sprang up, we decided to up the anchor and set our course toward Academy Bay again. Those who have ever anchored in the 15 fathoms already considered as very deep can surely visualise the great amount of work we had to get our anchor up to the surface. The two of us, working one on either side of the winch handle, soon stood in a pool of sweat. And this is not just figuratively speaking! The beginning was the hardest, for not only did we have to force the ship against the current with the winch, but we had the whole weight of the chain hanging straight up and down. As the chain came on board and most of the gear consisted of nylon, the effort got less, but so did our strength, so when after fifty minutes of continuous work on the winch the anchor finally was on board we were rather tired.

It was good to be sailing again, but the current was very strong and the wind not quite strong enough to give us sufficient speed to make port before the deadline of six o'clock, for it is not just in the port of entry that the overtime rule is valid, but in every one of the islands, except, of course, those which were uninhabited. It was annoying, for we did not miss it by much. In fact, it was just 6.15 when we anchored in ten fathoms at a safe distance from the harbourmaster's jurisdiction. As soon as it got dark and the authorities could not see what was going on, two motor boats came out to us, guided by our light, which always hung in our rigging whether at sea or at anchor in order to avoid being run down. It was the Baldwins of the yacht *Faith*, whom I had met in Los Angeles while on the *Windflower* and who now were at anchor inside the harbour; and in the other boat was Gus Angelmeyer, who hardly needs an introduction, as he is probably the most well-known figure of the Galapagos. We had a little party in the darkness and were thrilled that we had finally arrived at that port of the Galapagos we had heard so much about. Next morning we sailed serenely in at 8.30 and the harbourmaster came on board, checked my papers, and gave me permission to go ashore and to receive guests on board.

In this island live about a dozen European families of various nationalities and also about 150 Ecuadorian as well as two American families. When we went ashore we soon met most of the immigrants and each one had a story to tell. The three Angelmeyer brothers are the true pioneer type who came there without a cent to their name and had been able to make a happy life for themselves. In fact, they had each built their own house, using large stones to build up the walls and a beautiful local hardwood which, of course, had not cost them a cent.

Walking to the village, we saw that they had the inevitable church, but this one was of modest scale and of good taste, in contrast to most other primitive places, where a huge and obviously expensive church looms over a few shacks, always making me think that the money could have been better used for building better houses for the inhabitants.

We got home-baked bread on order at 'Gloria's', a Swedish woman who lived with an Ecuadorian and was therefore not accepted by the other Europeans, who had strangely enough brought with them most of civilised man's narrow-mindedness. She was running a 'restaurant', where we were to be regular customers. The restaurant consisted of a large table in her living-room, which was also the kitchen. She charged three sucre a meal, which was the equivalent of two shillings, the cheapest restaurant we had ever seen. The food was not too exciting and consisted mostly of rice, lentils, beans, bread, fruits and sometimes a little meat or fish. Only much later were we to realise that her food was probably about the healthiest we had on the whole voyage. In any case we enjoyed her modest restaurant, and it was a nice break for Simonne not to have to cook in the scorching heat.

We went to see the Ranbecks, a Norwegian couple who had also settled in the Galapagos forty years earlier and had never left the islands since. Mrs. Ranbeck told me that when she had been a teenage girl she had been in love with a Tangvald, even though he had never known about it, in fact had not even known her, but he had walked past her school every day in his pilot's uniform. 'He was a lieutenant and I was so much in love with him, but I was never able to get him to even notice me.'

I had to smile when I told her that if he was a pilot he could only have been my future father, as Tangvald is a name carried by only half a dozen men, and there has in any case been no other pilot by that name and in those days there were less than twenty pilots in the whole of Norway. I wrote to my father about the adventure he had missed, but he ignored my information, which indeed came much too late to do him any good.

Then we met the Gianella, a Belgian family of man, wife and two children who had arrived a year and a half earlier. They invited us to a goat-steak meal, which was deliciously prepared, and during the evening entertained us with the local gossip, which I wish could be printed here. Noting our delight about the goat steak, they suggested that we join their son the following day on his hunt, so we could, if we so wished, go hunting on our own afterwards when we had seen where they were to be found. But first we were shown all the neighbours' tame goats and begged to try to remember their looks so we would not shoot any of them, even though they sometimes went for a walk in the bush.

Early next morning Simonne, Michael, the Belgians' eldest son, and I left on our hunting expedition. We walked for hours in the scorching heat between gigantic cactus, and I bitterly regretted not having brought any water. It was only eleven o'clock when we got back with the hindquarters of the goat Michael had shot. He seemed to be used to the climate and hardly even perspired, while I, soaked with sweat, was firmly convinced that I would have died myself before sundown had I stayed in that bush without water till then. Simonne cooked no doubt as good a meal as had the Gianella, but somehow it did not taste as good to us, perhaps because of the thought of the rest of the animal lying there with a million flies on it. I oiled the gun, hung it up and we went more regularly to Gloria's for meals during the rest of our stay.

After about a month in the island we decided to push on, and having started, made our rounds of good-byes. On 18th April we sailed out of the bay, after having had to wait for forty minutes for the port captain to find our papers, which he had mislaid. It was still well within the office hours when I got the anchor up, so we were all right as far as overtime pay was concerned. By ten o'clock next morning, again well within the office hours, we let the anchor go in front of the Wittmers' house. We thought it very exciting to visit the Wittmers, whom we had read so much about. They even surprised us by giving us two letters which had been addressed 'care of the Wittmers' by friends who knew we intended to pass by their place! We were invited for tea and home-baked cakes and were even introduced to Mrs. Wittmer's sister, who had come for a few weeks' visit from London, where she had settled some forty years ago. During the tea I saw Simonne having great difficulty in hiding her desire to burst out laughing when she saw me swallow one of the thousand flies swarming around us while taking in a breath of air between two sentences, choke as it came into my wind-pipe, and cough it out, still flying, without hardly having let it interrupt my story.

When I signed their guest book I was surprised to see that on an average about a dozen yachts visited them each year. The guest book was arranged like a questionnaire and I was much amused by the answers on the question 'Finance'. A few had written: 'Adequate', but most were less fortunate and answered: 'Poor but honest', 'S.O.S.', or simply like my friends on their Norwegian Colin Archer *Rundo*: '47 dollars.' And that is not a large amount of money for going around the world! But they were fortunate and were able to make some money on the way and thus complete their voyage successfully; not everyone is as lucky, and there is more than one ship which has been sold at a ridiculously low figure at some distant port just because the crew was faced with starving through lack of money.

Mrs. Wittmer told us a lot about life in the island, and again I realised that when the white man emigrates to lost places, thinking that he is tired of civilisation, he still insists on bringing all civilisation's habits, customs, narrow-mindedness and complications with him. She told us, for example, about the endless trouble they had had to find a white dress for their daughter for her marriage and of the great difficulty of finding a priest able to perform the ceremony after having had the whole affair registered with the proper authorities! I quietly thought that they would have even more trouble when they wanted a divorce! But even admitting that they would never divorce and even admitting that it was on religious grounds that they had insisted on having the priest, I feel sure God would have been broad-minded enough to accept their union as a valid one even if they had had a simple ceremony in their home with the sincere undertaking to stay united for life.

Now that her daughter's marriage problem had been solved to her satisfaction, Mrs. Wittmer concentrated on new problems: now she wanted electric light from part of the money she was making on the book, and then they just had to get a school with a teacher for the 'Europeans' in the islands. And the teacher had to be a real one from the mainland. I cannot help thinking that if all these things mean so much it would be better to remain in one's own country rather than to go to all the trouble of looking for a virgin place only to try to make it a duplicate of the land one had just left!

The following day we sailed along the coast to Post Office Bay, in order to see the famous mail barrel which has never stopped functioning since the old sailing ships used it several hundred years ago, when outward-bound ships left their mail in the barrel for homeward-bound vessels to take it home. The barrel is not the original one, of course, and has been renewed several times during the years, so all the inscriptions on the barrel were of a fairly recent date. I added the following engraving: '*Dorothea*—Oslo—20-4-61', among all the other yachts which had been there before us.

The bay was beautiful. We heard wild asses braying in the hills, but it was forbidden to hunt them, and neither did it matter, for we would not have had the courage to butcher one even presuming that I had been able to shoot it. It was strange to think that in this very bay the old sailships had also anchored; not, of course, just for their mail, but principally for filling their water barrels and for hunting so they could replenish their stores.

From here we had our longest voyage yet to Nuku-Hiva in the Marquesas, a stretch of 3,000 miles without any land at all, and thus even longer than the voyage across the Atlantic. Today being Friday, we decided to wait till the following day, for any experienced seaman will know that it brings bad luck to sail on a Friday, and for such a long stretch I found it wisest not to take any unnecessary chances! We spent the day giving each other a short haircut, bathing in the rather cold water using a salt-water soap, resting and also, for me, doing several sun sights right at anchor, not, of course, for finding our position, which I was in no doubt about, but rather to check my sextant and my chronometer, which could easily be done by working the problem the opposite way and taking the position as a known factor instead of the unknown one. In this manner we can calculate the exact time within a few seconds and it was common practice in the old days before ships were equipped with powerful radios.

6

Fair Winds Across the Pacific

O N Saturday, 22nd April, we left at nine in the morning, to Simonne's great relief, as the enormous number of green flies constantly bothering us had started to get on her nerves. The wind was extremely light, so we inched our way out of the bay, but as soon as the distance from land had grown a little all the flies left us, as they do not seem to like the sea.

Most yachts doing this crossing take more than a month, but we were to be fortunate with the wind, which gave us a good speed almost the whole way and thus helped us to make a very fast crossing. Perhaps another reason for her speed was the fact that I let her run under full sail day and night rather than using the twin spinnakers so common among most ocean voyagers. However, most of all I should give the credit to her clever designer, the late Dr. Harrison Butler, who had designed boats not for maximum speed in calm waters, but made comfortable, seaworthy yachts of good all-round performance able to sustain high average speeds from port to port. *Dorothea* ghosts surprisingly well in even the lightest of breezes, yet in gales is able to keep going under shortened canvas while many other yachts would have found it necessary to heave-to and stop. *Dorothea* inspired such confidence that I never shortened canvas before it was absolutely necessary and never did I follow the common practice of so many cruising people of always reducing sail at sundown. Many times have we gone to sleep while the ship was racing all by herself at top speed under full sail with her lee deck awash. I knew it would be soon enough to reef when the ship really demanded it, in which case the more violent motion would wake me up. Then in the flickering light hung in the rigging I would either take a reef or two or take in the staysail or change the no. 1 jib for the no. 2 or 3, all depending on the circumstances, choosing the sail reduction which would keep the maximum speed and yet relieve the ship sufficiently.

This constant driving of the vessel is not just for getting into the next port as quickly as possible, but rather for the wonderful sensation of power and grace one gets from a sailing ship which is efficiently driven.

In the day-time I often enjoyed sitting at the very tip of the bowsprit 7 feet ahead of the ship and watching the slim bow slicing her way through the water with a slow easy motion pushed by the large sails high above the ship. At night I could sit on deck for hours just watching the stars, the moon and the clouds racing past the moon, while listening to the surge of the water and feeling the speed of the ship rushing through the night. And down below in my bunk I could fall asleep in a few minutes despite the hard and narrow bunk and despite the uncertainty of the sea. Yet in California I had had great difficulty in sleeping, despite having had a quiet house in a quiet district, an extra soft bed, king size, and no imminent dangers around me. Sleep is a strange thing, but perhaps the most important factor for good sleep is happiness.

It is a wonderful experience to cross a large ocean successfully under sail alone. It is hard to describe the sensation of happiness, of freedom and of general satisfaction given by such a voyage. It is true that the best part of such a voyage is to see the landfall, but this is not so because we will again be able to get ashore, but rather because it is the culmination of our effort and proves that the voyage was successful and the navigation accurate. Every day spent aboard during the voyage was well worth living, even including the one when the weather was less pleasant.

I would never lose the wonderful atmosphere and romance of sail which can only be experienced in a true sailing boat. And by a true sailing boat I mean one which is not spoilt by any of the modern mechanics and gadgets. I mean one which simply uses the wind as propulsion and uses it in the same way as our forefathers have done for several thousands of years and which has proved satisfactory with a minimum of headaches, a minimum of expenses and a minimum of failures. Why should modern people always feel so sure of being smarter than our forefathers? Just because we have stumbled into the combustion engine and from there into the atomic age? But that does not mean that our intelligence has grown, nor indeed does it prove that we are any happier.

Taio Hae Bay was a deep fjord completely protected from the sea and surrounded by high tropical mountains. Its beauty was almost breath-taking, especially after many days at sea, when we were no longer used to seeing any green colours at all; the rich tropical vegetation surrounding us left an unforgettable impression. But if we were both impressed by the beauty of nature, we were disappointed in the beauty of the natives. They were admittedly healthy-looking and strong, but to my taste the girls were grossly overweight, with huge thighs, huge behinds, big hands, and their feet were unbelievably large with all their toes sticking out like a fan. Their smiles were, however, pleasant and friendly, and their brown skin very smooth-looking, so I can now understand why sailors having been at sea for a long time without having seen a woman would find them gorgeous, but since this was not the case for me I did not quite find them as attractive as I had expected from all the stories I had been reading.

We purchased eggs, bread, bananas, potatoes, papayas and beautiful avocado pears, all at a very low price, which rather surprised us, as we had been told that Tahiti was extremely expensive. But we were later to learn that if the Marquesas had been cheap, Tahiti was indeed very expensive. We also purchased a native weapon, a wooden spear beautifully carved, which we fastened to the foot of the mast in the saloon, and also a small traditional Tiki which the carver finished while we waited and then polished with ordinary brown shoe polish.

In the days which followed we often went visiting Bob McKitrick, the trader. Bob had jumped ship in his young days, and had never left the island since. He was now getting a bit old and was almost blind and his old boat was laid high and dry on the beach. Neither of them would navigate any more, and I thought it rather sad that men and things had to get old and worn out with age. He was an Irishman, but after such a long life in the islands he had gained much of the mentality and the way of life of the natives, so through talking to him we got a first understanding of the natives.

He was rather sad when he told us about the problem of the native youth of today, as all the girls who were reasonably good-looking were leaving the Marquesas at the first opportunity to seek their fortune in the bars of Papeete. Many of the men left also, as they did not want to stay behind with no women, but since they could not make a living in the same way a woman can, they had to look for manual work in the town. And according to Bob most of those remaining passed their time in drinking beer whenever they could sell enough copra to buy some. It was indeed very sad to think that these few natives were all that remained from a once large and powerful race.

When the white man first came to the Marquesas many thousands lived on the island and led an easy existence with a minimum of work and a maximum of play. The country is fertile, fruits are to be had for the picking, fish are plentiful, clothes are hardly necessary, a straw hut is built in a matter of days and is very comfortable in the tropics, divorces never presented any problems, since they never married, raising children presented no problems, as they were loved by everyone and in such a community were not a liability as they are in our civilised world. A boat only cost the trouble of carving out a tree-trunk, but now that 'progress' had arrived, the natives wanted money for buying plywood boats, outboards, gasoline, clothes, beer, corned beef, radios, and we even saw one girl driving slowly up and down the road on a scooter, but I should add that the total length of the only road did not exceed 200 yards! She was the native wife of the local doctor and a very beautiful girl, so I guess he had to give in to some of her wishes.

I drew a straight line between Nuku-Hiva and Tahiti on the chart and saw that it went straight through the Tuamotus, next to an island called Manihi. The Tuamotus have caused many shipwrecks and have gained their bad reputation for several reasons. First of all they are all just a few feet above water-level, so they cannot be seen from very far. In fact, what one sees first is the top of the palm trees, in those islands where trees grow, and then one sees the beach. In the best of conditions one cannot hope to see the island more than about five or six miles away and at night, of course, this distance is much reduced. In fact, most of the native boats navigating those waters expect to hear the surf long before they can see the island, should their landfall be at night. Another danger is the strong and entirely irregular currents, and finally the strange fact that there are a great number of violent squalls in that locality.

The combination of these three things can, of course, become a serious hazard, but I consider that if the natives can navigate regularly in those waters there is no reason why I cannot do the same. Besides, I had been warned all the way from England that to get into the passes of the South Seas lagoon a motor was absolutely essential; just to prove them wrong I wanted to sail into one which was among those considered to be the worst in the world. The *Pilot* indeed warned me that in many of those atolls, among which was Manihi, the current would attain a speed of eight knots! The passes were narrow and no beacons or other aids to navigation indicated where the coral heads were. Some of these reefs were just below the surface and would break up a ship in a short time. All this sounded awful. But the natives did it—not just once, but regularly. So there had to be a way for *Dorothea* also.

A few days later at sea, after my sixth or seventh sight that day, I announced to Simonne that we would make our landfall during the night. We would have to sail between two of the Tuamotus islands and then make port in Manihi the next morning. As night fell I had been up in the rigging just in case we were closer to land than my calculations told me, but I saw nothing but the sea, as I had expected. We had our evening meal down below as usual, but afterwards I told Simonne that one of us had to stay on the foredeck all through the night, for even if there was some moon we could not be sure of spotting land more than a few minutes before hitting the beach.

She volunteered to take the first watch and to wake me as soon as she suspected that land was near, and in any case not later than two in the morning, when I would take over. For once we sailed without any lights at all so that we would not be blinded by our own light and would be able

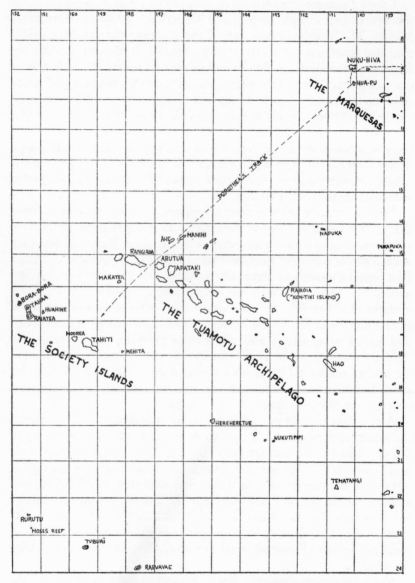

FRENCH POLYNESIA

to see farther in the dark. I woke up a couple of times, but fell asleep again as soon as I had seen the silhouette of Simonne faithfully standing on deck, one hand holding the shrouds, and trying to pierce the darkness in front of the boat. At about one in the morning she woke me gently, telling me that she thought she saw land ahead to our left. I grabbed the night glasses on my way up to deck and saw indeed land not too far on our port bow. We stayed together on deck for a while in the excitement of our landfall in these notorious waters, but after a while Simonne looked so sleepy that I urged her to go to bed.

At sunrise we were outside the pass to Manihi and wondered if it was going to be as hard as everybody had been so anxious to let us believe. I hesitated whether or not I should take in the jib, as I often did before entering a port, so it would be easier to manoeuvre, but then at the thought of the strong current I decided it was better to carry as much canvas as possible, but I did prepare the kedge anchor with its long nylon line so I could anchor at a few seconds' notice. Once more I looked at the chart and tried to remember all its proportions by heart, as in an emergency there might be no time to study it for taking a quick decision, then a couple more bearings, and then finally I put the bow resolutely toward the middle of the pass. I saw people running down to the shore. One man rushed to the flagpole and hoisted the French flag as we approached at a surprising speed. We did not travel more than about five knots through the water, yet the shore came closer as if we had been going about ten! Then I realised that the current was sucking us into the pass at a great speed. Just as this fact dawned on me Simonne's anguished voice shouted out in alarm:

'Look at the bottom! We are going to go aground!'

My heart was pounding in my chest when I looked over the side, as the bottom seemed to be just a couple of feet below the surface! According to the charts I should have a minimum of two fathoms, but they could, of course, be wrong, as most of them dated from the last century and even warned one that they did not guarantee their exactitude. I had disconnected the pilot, but I still let go the tiller for an instant while throwing the lead, which did agree with the chart, so I got my confidence back. Right inside the pass, next to a small wooden pier, I rounded up and let go the anchor immediately, as we were being swept backwards by the current until the anchor held us firmly. Then all sails went down on deck and we were in safety.

An outrigger canoe paddled violently by many natives came alongside after having paddled close to the shore up against the current, so they would gain enough to be certain of not being swept past us. After having entertained each other for several hours the current slowed down, and they declared that now would be a good time to come alongside the dock. Then, by releasing the anchor warp, the natives pulled our ship towards the dock by pulling on the rope from shore. They did so with so much enthusiasm and energy that I was glad that I had not upped the anchor as they had suggested, as how would I otherwise have slowed the ship down before smashing it against the dock when it was pulled by more than fifty eager pairs of strong hands? As it was, I was able to slow her down in time by taking a turn against the strong samson post while hoping that the anchor would not fail me.

As soon as we were made fast along the dock the invasion began: men, women, girls, boys, guitars, babies and dogs, all came on board with happy smiles. Simonne and I were pushed into a corner while not just all the sitting-places got occupied, but also the floor, the table and the kitchen sink; in fact, there were no more for the simple reason that they could not squeeze in. All our new friends opened our closets to see what was inside, lifted the lid of the toilet to see how it worked, and helped themselves to candies, cakes, fruits and anything else which caught their fancy. It was a constant rotation: as soon as one went out his place was immediately taken by another. Under such circumstances we could not even use our toilet and had to excuse ourselves when the time came, and went ashore behind some bushes to get sufficient privacy.

I have never had much trouble getting rid of undesirable characters who in so many ports are a pest for small boats, but here I felt helpless against these friendly people who sang, played guitars, laughed and looked happy, but nevertheless bothered us, as we were tired after the last night and would have much preferred some sleep and then a walk to see their island, rather than just being a source of entertainment to a large crowd of people we did not know and with whom we had great difficulty in talking, as only a few could speak French or English and then only in a very limited way. Who was it that made the following prayer: 'Dear God, I can take care of my enemies myself, but please deliver me from my friends!'

Finally they left at about ten in the evening, so we could at least get some sleep. Next morning at sun-up we were awakened by new visitors and in despair we decided to leave right away, but first had to go to the kind breakfast invitation which had been given us for eight o'clock. Sitting in a large house, we were surprised and even a bit disappointed to see it equipped with a noisy radio, a flashy gramophone and even a refrigerator! The woman of the house spoke quite good French, so she explained to us that her husband was a pearl-diver and made very good money while the six weeks' season lasted—enough money, in fact, to allow them to live well for the whole year.

We were greatly touched by the present they gave us at the end of the meal of a necklace of shells which must have taken endless patience to make out of many hundreds of small shells, each one pierced and threaded on a line. It has been carefully put on our saloon bulkhead and has occupied a place of honour ever since. They explained to us that it was not meant to be worn around a woman's neck but on top of a man's hat, resting on the brim, so it would prevent it from flying away in the wind, which was always blowing. They all laughed when Simonne had it around her neck already, as she had not at first understood their explanation. It must have seemed doubly funny to them, as I am sure none of the native girls could have got it over their heads, as they were all so much bigger than petite Simonne.

But much of their sense of logic amused us, as it was rather unusual to our minds, as, for example, when I asked them if many foreign yachts came to their island:

'Yes, many come here,' was the answer. But this gave me not much of an idea about how many did visit them, for what would seem like 'many' to some might seem like very little to others. Languages are really very unprecise. When I asked how many a year visited them I only got a great silence as my answer. So to make it easier for them and still give me a slight idea about how often they got visiting yachtsmen I asked:

'When did you last have a visiting yacht stopping in your island?'

This started a great discussion in Tahitian and then finally I got the answer after the deliberations:

'The last yacht did not stop in our island. It stopped in a neighbouring island.'

After that I gave up.

We were to get many squalls on our way to Tahiti, which made the voyage more worrying, as we were afraid of the poor visibility during these violent rainstorms, but we did see the next two atolls in good time as we sailed between them, the fine shiny lines of their beaches showing clearly in the moonlight while we could even guess the outline of the coconut trees above the beach.

Next day, Saturday, 27th May, the heavy rain squalls became even more frequent, but in the afternoon the sun was back. It did not, however, make us too happy, as the wind died at the same time, thus letting the heat become almost intolerable. I had to take down the sails, as they were beating themselves horribly in the choppy sea. We then tried to cool off a bit by swimming around our becalmed vessel, but even though we could not even get a fish on our line we always had the feeling of great monsters swimming next to us in the great ocean and did not wish to stay too long away from the relative safety of our dry deck.

That day we ate the last of our salt meat from the Galapagos which had served us well almost every day of the trip, but it was without regret that

we had the last bite, for even if we did not find it quite as unpleasant as
tinned food, we ate it with no great love. We looked forward to getting to
Papeete and getting fresh food again. After nightfall the wind came back
and we again got a good speed, but next morning there were calms interrupted by violent rain squalls. It was tiring, but we did progress, and in the
afternoon we saw the high mountains of Tahiti far in the distance. In the
evening I had to take down the sails again, as a heavy swell from the south
shook the sails horribly whenever the wind died down. At three o'clock in
the morning I was awakened by a light breeze from the north-west, which
is the exact opposite of what we expected in the south-east trade-wind belt!
But any wind is better than no wind at all, so I hoisted all sails and set the
course back towards Tahiti. At five o'clock I got so hungry that I could not
resist the temptation of waking up Simonne and asking for breakfast. She
woke up with a smile as usual, lit the lights as it was still night, and made
breakfast with no complaints, although I know a few women who would
have told their men under such circumstances to go to a very specific hot
place or else wait till the clock has had the time to get a bit farther around
the dial.

At ten o'clock Tahiti reappeared through a light haze, but this time
quite close. We both declared that it looked just like Martinique and had
plenty of time to admire it, as we travelled very slowly. Just as we rounded
Pointe Venus, the extremity of the island, the wind died and we soon
realised that we would not be able to make port before dark. As we laid
there completely becalmed we were astonished to see a ship in the distance
looking as though it belonged to Captain Cook about 200 years ago. As it
came closer we were even more surprised, for this could not possibly be a
native craft, as it was too close in every detail to the old warships. We
guessed it had to be some kind of movie for which the ship had been built.
She came toward us at about eight knots and we could soon hear the noise
of her engines and breathe in the fumes of her diesel. It reassured us that
we were not dreaming, because as she passed we saw large projectors and
movie rigs at various places in the ship. Just behind her came a large
native-type motor vessel which stopped next to us and offered us a tow.
Even though it was tempting to get to port that night, I hated so much
letting myself be pulled by the nose that I, without hesitation, declined
their kind offer.

Occasional breaths of wind during the night made us progress slowly,
so by three o'clock in the morning we were outside the entrance pass to
the port of Papeete. Just as I set the course for the pass a rain squall hit us,
so I immediately changed the course, as I did not care to get through the
pass in the fury of a squall with its poor visibility. By the time it was over
it was almost seven, and we finally entered the gates of Paradise.

7

Tahiti and Her Sisters

THE pass was much larger than I had expected from the tales I had been told and gave me ample room for tacking back and forth in it, for we had the wind dead against us. I became, however, rather apprehensive when I saw that the large steamer full of tourists which apparently also had been waiting for daylight entered the pass at a great speed before I had time to clear it. I had to sail rather close to the one side of the pass in order to give them enough room. Sailing vessels do have the right of way over steam, but of course we cannot really insist on that right in a narrow pass where it must be extremely difficult to manoeuvre such large ships.

As soon as we got inside the lagoon all the rolling and pitching stopped and we sailed in a perfectly flat sea. We steered for the yacht anchorage which we could see clearly, as there were already about a dozen yachts there. I had a detailed chart of the harbour, the clouds had gone, and the light breeze gave us a nice easy speed. With the binoculars I had already picked out a spot for mooring the ship, so I made my anchor ready and had all set when with about 300 feet to go the pilot boat came alongside with a heavy bump, shaking my boat so that I felt it all the way into my bones, and a man jumped aboard ordering me to take down the sails, as they were going to tow us to our mooring place.

Greatly annoyed I muttered that I did not need his services now that I had entered the port and just had a few yards left and that I especially did not need a tow in such a nice breeze, but when he insisted that they could take no chances I obeyed and let all sails fall on deck. But when the heavy steel boat got under my bowsprit while wanting to pass me a tow-line, thus threatening to break the spar should the slightest wave make me pitch up and down, I lost all control of myself and insulted them in no uncertain terms, and with such a loud voice that people on shore no doubt heard every word I said.

The little tugboat reacted by immediately giving a quick short blast of power ahead, thus getting out of reach of my bowsprit, as soon as they saw that I had their line, but much to my surprise no one insulted me back, like most other people would have done whether they had been in their rights or not. The pilot, holding my tiller, never for an instant raised his voice and apologised for the bumping, but mentioned quietly that the bump had been very light and felt sure that no damage had been done. I looked over the side and could indeed only just see a tiny scratch on the paint, which hardly mattered, and when he added that I must have had a very hard trip and was probably tired from lack of sleep I calmed down completely, for he did not say it insolently but sounded genuinely friendly.

We were soon securely moored at the dock and the pilot was most kind in helping me fill out the complicated paperwork in Tahiti. He was, in fact, so nice and pleasant that I later went over especially to his office in order to present him my apologies for the rude words I had used, which he accepted with a friendly laugh and put me completely at ease. These excuses I addressed to the man as such and not to the uniform, for I always consider that a pilot is a great nuisance for a yachtsman, but this man had not made the law and all he did was to do his job in the best way he knew.

The police came on board just a few minutes and left with our passports, telling us to come the next day to the station to fix up the paperwork. As soon as the authorities had left we got many visitors on board. One man gave us some new baked bread, which we both bit into immediately, as it tasted to us better than any cake we had ever had. The man who has never been many weeks without a bite of bread cannot imagine how wonderful this simple food seems when one gets it again. That must have been known by our friend, and we were indeed pleased to see that it was almost a custom to greet a newly arrived yacht with a fresh loaf of bread. It was in any case a present which for its outlay in money could hardly give more pleasure to men who have been without bread for a long time. Tahiti is really in the middle of a large ocean and even the fastest yacht will have been many days at sea in order to get there.

Another present from another yachtsman which thrilled us was a huge pamplemouse which was the juiciest and the sweetest we had ever tasted. The pamplemouse-givers introduced themselves as Mr. and Mrs. Kittredge from Arizona. They had sailed here from San Diego in their 38-foot ketch *Svea*, which had been built in Denmark and shipped over to the States on a freighter. They invited us over to look at their boat, which impressed us greatly, as it was extremely well kept and so cosy that we felt right at home in it, a feeling we very seldom got in boats other than *Dorothea*. We were to become good friends and spend much time together.

Most of the yachts along the waterfront of Papeete were American, coming from Hawaii or California, but there were also a couple of English yachts and one from New Zealand, and even one from France. Since long before the war the population of Papeete has been used to seeing yachts arriving all through the year, so a new arrival does not get much attention, except for the few minutes it takes to carry out the manoeuvre into the dock, or rather into the town's main street, to which the yachts, in fact, are moored with two lines to hold their stern close to shore while the yacht's anchor holds the bow pointed towards the sea. Thus with a plank between the yacht and the shore one can step ashore without using the dinghy, as there is no tide there and the boat will always remain at a convenient height in relation to the shore. In fact, to be quite exact, there is a small tide of about one foot, and the strange thing about it is that high waters are always, all the year round, at noon and midnight! The tide pays no attention whatsoever to either the moon, the sun or the winds! I had heard about it before my arrival, but never quite believed it, but during the months I was to stay here I had ample time to notice that it was indeed a fact.

From the deck of the boat we could see all the traffic passing by in the street. I was very impressed by some native girls speeding past on scooters, with their long hair trailing straight behind them for a couple of feet from the windspeed. Some of them were indeed neither too fat nor without charm, but I was to hear later that most of the best-looking girls were half Chinese and half Polynesian, a most pleasant combination. However, it looked as though there were many more white men in town than there were attractive native girls, and I was later to hear about many complaints from the single men that they had more difficulty in finding a girl in Tahiti than they had in their own home town.

Contrary to what one might think, Papeete, the capital of French Polynesia, is a very small town. Probably due to its fame, we were surprised just to see a small town not much different from what we could expect to see in almost any tropical island which had gained enough importance to be on the map, yet we immediately were taken by the strange charm which has probably helped make Papeete as famous as it is. Just walking through its streets was a thrill. There was a small Chinese restaurant, there a small shop selling dresses and pareos, there on the corner a girl and a man laughing together—maybe over some joke, but maybe just being happy to be alive.

In one of the Chinese restaurants which served all kinds of food we both ordered a rare fillet mignon steak, french fried potatoes, a large green salad, and as dessert a lot of fresh fruit. We had been warned never to give any tips to anyone in Tahiti, as tips are an unknown custom, and since I hate that custom anyway I was not going to be the one to introduce it into the island. In fact, when some tourists still leave a tip the waitress has to give it to the house, and I was to hear about one waitress getting fired just from that very restaurant because she had kept a very large tip left by an

American who was trying to date her. Her boss had considered that she had been stealing from the house and therefore did not want to keep her in his service!

A few days after our arrival I went to the hospital in order to have a complete check-up, as I honestly had started to worry that I might have tuberculosis, as I had an almost constant fever which at night gave me often terrible fits of perspiration, despite the nights in Papeete being rather chilly. Fortunately the tests revealed that there was nothing wrong with me, so the fever must have been caused by just general poor health rather than any particular sickness. But if the tests did not explain my fever, the visit to the hospital had not been in vain, as it introduced us to the head doctor, who was to become a good friend of ours.

Making one good friend in a new place is so often like starting a snowball rolling: we soon had many friends in Tahiti, which made our stay not only much more pleasant but also much more interesting, as we had a good chance of understanding life in the island much more than if we had just been ordinary tourists to whom the private homes are closed.

So many people have talked about the wonderful climate of Tahiti that we were a bit disappointed about its terrible heat in the middle of the day, followed by a rather chilly night. The climate did not seem to do us much good, judging from all the troubles we had. I constantly had to stay in bed for one reason or another. One violent cold with high fever had me in bed for several days, then the 'flu with terrible stomach pains, then constant perspiration fits—not just in the day-time when it was hot but often also in the chilly nights. Simonne was not much more fortunate, and in addition had much female trouble which had been unknown to her before she got to the tropics. The climate did not seem to be all that healthy for the natives, as many of them had tuberculosis.

One night at about four in the morning we were awakened by a commotion on the neighbouring yacht. She was a 32-foot yacht from New Zealand; the two men on board had each found their woman with whom they now shared the boat. As we looked out of our porthole we saw the one girl just lying down on the deck vomiting. We could not see in the dark that it was blood she was vomiting, so we did not at first understand the cries of despair of the other girl as she came on deck and leaned over her friend. One of the men shouted to a native passing on a bicycle to get the ambulance. Less than five minutes elapsed before the ambulance arrived and the doctor rushed to the girl. He leaned over her, but almost immediately rose and announced her as dead. A few buckets of salt water thrown on the girl washed away the blood, while the other girl cried almost like a dog will cry when her newly born have been killed, a most terrifying cry when it comes from a human.

Papeete's waterfront with all its yachts, as seen from
the *Bounty*'s rigging.

The author in a small stream at Pointe Venus.
(Tahiti)

The author watching *Dorothea* by the Pointe Venus. (Tahiti)

A mother playing with her child in a one-stringed swing. (Tahaa in the Society Islands)

When her boy friend came back from the burial I had trouble in recognising him. His face was swollen from continuous and unashamed crying, and he looked almost ten years older. The following day the dead girl's friend who had cried like a dog in pain was playing a guitar on another yacht, but this man looked for the rest of his stay as if he would never be able to forget his sweetheart and just stayed sadly on his boat and did not look for another love to replace the one he had lost.

That the dead girl's girl friend had mourned less than twenty-four hours was not due to lack of heart, nor did it tend to show that her crying had been insincere; it just showed once more the typical character of the natives, who live just in the present, and neither in the past nor the future. This peculiarity of the Polynesian race was demonstrated also in its daily customs: early in the morning when we went to the store for shopping we would see the Tahitian women purchasing a spoonful of ground coffee, just the length of bread necessary for breakfast, a couple of spoonfuls of butter, and anything else she desired or could afford, but the quantity would be figured just for that breakfast! But what surprised us a bit was to see that they even purchased the hot water for making their coffee! The Tahitian is too lazy to heat up the water at his home and the Chinese storekeeper, always eager to make an extra penny, continuously had boiling water which he sold to his customers! They would hurry back to their houses near by and then fix the coffee before the water had had time to cool off.

The old-time three-master which we had seen the first day at sea was indeed a movie ship, as we had guessed, and was still going out every day finishing the film *Mutiny on the Bounty*. As I thought it would be fun to see such a ship from the inside, I applied for a job as an extra. In the office they told me that I would be paid seven dollars a day plus the noon meal, but the condition was that I shaved off my beard, which I had grown to a frightful size since I had left Panama. I gladly promised to shave it off, so much more as it had become rather grey, despite the fact that I was not yet 37, and grey is a colour I hate.

I stayed several weeks on the ship, going out every morning and coming back at night. This time was a mixture of great excitement and of disappointment, as most things are in life. I was especially disappointed that the *Bounty* was equipped with huge diesel engines and most of all that these were never stopped, even when we supposedly were under sail. Furthermore, only those sails which could be seen by the cameras were ever hoisted. Sometimes the ship would be pushed by the engine faster than the light wind, with the result that the sails were aback while the bow-wave stood impressively high.

But if I felt cheated from the sensation of being on an old three-master at sea under a press of canvas, I did have fun climbing in the rigging for setting and furling the sails. Working up in the rigging was, in fact, rather easy, and as long as we did not get careless presented very little danger. Of course, should a man lose his grip and fall down he would have little hope of survival. Neither is it recommended for a man who easily gets dizzy. It is rather far down from up there. The uppermost yard will slide down to the yard below it, and no one therefore has ever to climb all the way up, but after one of the other extras had teased me that I would not be able to get all the way to the top and touch the very cap of the mainmast, I immediately felt obliged to do so.

On the way up I remembered to climb on the outside of all the platforms instead of passing through the manhole which I knew the sailors called the 'landlubberhole', and I soon reached the top where the ratlines go. In order to get all the way to the peak I had to climb the very pole, which there was not stayed. This was not very difficult and certainly a lot easier than when I had had to do it a couple of times on the *Windflower*, so I quickly reached the cap, and even got so high that I leaned over it on my stomach. Once there I wanted to turn over and sit on the cap, which was about eight inches in diameter—even the thought of then standing up flashed through my head—but I must admit that I did not dare take the chance. In any case I had won the bet and it would be silly to take a chance of falling down, which furthermore might spoil my chances to collect!

I had various roles in the film, mostly just standing in the background in my sailor's dress or climbing in the rigging (still in the background), but one day I had my big chance: I was to be a movie star and my partner would be no less than Marlon Brando, the main star himself. Marlon Brando was the hero although he had mutinied and I was one still faithful to Captain Bligh and wanted to follow him. Unfortunately for me there was no more room in the small ship's boat and I had to stay with the mutineers despite my wishes. All this was explained to me and I had to learn my 'lines' right away.

On the fourth try we finally got everything right. We had had a few difficulties, but I was nevertheless exuberant: not everyone gets a well-known star as a partner at his movie début! I was a bit disappointed to see that my wages were still only seven dollars a day, while everyone knew that Brando was getting several thousands in the same length of time, but then the world is not always fair. I wrote to my parents to tell them to be sure not to miss the movie when it appeared, and was much disappointed when they wrote me after the première that they had not seen me. Only two years later did I finally see the film myself and was much excited when my scene approached: would I be on or no? And there I was, right in front of Brando! But while the camera dwelled a long time on Brando, I stayed only seconds on the screen and could easily understand that my parents had missed me altogether! And no wonder that my name did not figure on the bill-board next to Brando. . . .

The last day I had been on the *Bounty* I got rather a bad friction burn on the top of my foot from sliding down the rigging. Often in the tropics these burns heal very slowly, often getting infected despite careful cleaning. While I nursed my wound the yachts in the Los Angeles to Tahiti race arrived one after the other. Some of the crews were rather drunk even before the gangplank was in place and as soon as the immigration had cleared them they all rushed directly to Quinn's bar. The Quinn's is famous all over the world for its many girls, and for its common toilet for men and women. In fact, the women in order to get to the single common toilet have to walk past the row of men standing toward the wall using the urinator. Especially American women come out of the toilet with a rather hard to describe look on their faces. But they all have to walk in and take a look, to see for themselves if it really is true what they have been told back in the States.

The 14th July is France's national holiday. I doubt whether many Tahitians know what the day stands for, but it is certain that they could not have celebrated it with more enthusiasm. In fact, they celebrate it so thoroughly that they do not even say 'the 14th of July', but simply 'the July'. This is also much more suitable, since they seem to need the whole month in order to celebrate it properly. During that month one can see traditional dancing, done in beautiful palm and bark dresses, by girls, women and men from all of the Society Islands who have come to the capital in an effort to win the prize for the best dances and the best costumes. Simonne, who is a dancer herself, was greatly impressed by the virtuosity of the girls in shaking their hips in a frantically rapid motion, but even though I am not a born dancer I was even more interested and could hardly take my eyes off the girls' hips.

Ever since we had decided to sail to Tahiti, and until we got there, we had had only one thing in our minds: get there. But now that we had arrived we knew that we also had reached a cross-roads in our lives: where were we to go from here? Simonne did not get the job there which she had counted on, and as for me, being a foreigner I could only stay a maximum of six months in the year. In most countries a foreigner can stay for ever, as long as he arrives on his own yacht, and no papers are even required apart from the ship's paper. Only a few countries have different laws. The States, the Galapagos and Tahiti were the three countries that I had found so far where a foreigner was considered just as much a tourist whether he came on a yacht or if he arrived by any other means.

Another drawback for foreigners is that no work is permitted (except for a very few exceptions), the same as it is in most other places. Even chartering is strictly forbidden. One can, of course, say that one is taking some friends around for a ride, but this would hardly work for very long, considering that every time we got the anchor up or down we had to get the authorities' permission. Since rumours travel fast in a place like Tahiti, it would not be long before the authorities knew that the 'friends' were paying guests. Life in Tahiti is very expensive, so we both knew that without income we would soon have to leave and find another paradise, if there were such a place. We had enough money left for about a year's cruise, and we wondered whether we should sail back to Martinique, to France, to the Orient, to Australia or to the States.

I had not seen my parents for a year, so it was decided that I should sail to San Francisco and stay there for the winter, while Simonne returned to Martinique. We both could work and thus have comfortable savings when we met again nine months later to continue our cruising. I would wait for Simonne in San Francisco and then decide where to set the course. A ship was leaving direct from Papeete to Martinique on the 26th August, which would bring Simonne to Fort de France in time for the beginning of the next school year. That left us another month together, and while we both liked the dances we had become tired of all the drinking and all the noise which went on during the 'fête', so we took the opportunity of making a cruise to the other islands of the Society.

On Friday, 21st July, we broke out the anchor in a fresh breeze among the yachts and rather close to a large steamer, but all went well under full control. Despite the fresh breeze at the anchorage, when we could have done with a lot less, the wind died almost completely when we were in the middle of the pass, which is notorious for its strong cross-current. I stood ready for anchoring before we got so close to the reef that anchoring would even be impossible, but the wind came back in a few puffs sufficiently to get us out. Once outside we had a very fresh trade which made Simonne rather seasick. I proposed to reduce sail, as she would probably feel a bit better if I eased the motion of the ship, but as usual she insisted that we kept our full speed. The night was rough, but then already at sunrise we saw our first destination: the beautiful island of Huahine.

We sailed along its coast, which except for its coral reef strongly reminded us of the West Indies; and at one o'clock in the afternoon we sailed easily through the pass in a fresh beam wind and anchored by a nice beach, not far from a little village. No 'authority' seemed to come out for checking our papers, so after having had lunch we went to bed in order to catch up on the sleep which had been a bit disturbed during the night. Later in the afternoon we went ashore and were thrilled to find an island which seemed almost untouched by the tourists. The natives were smiling at us, but stayed very reserved. The landscape was just out of this world, the houses were for the most part built of palms and blended nicely with the landscape; we saw a few girls washing without any bras on, although they did cover themselves lazily when they saw us.

Some of the houses were built on pilotis which we thought looked so nice, but there it is no doubt done so the floors stay dry even in the worst of rains. The kitchens were all separated from the main hut, thus keeping the kitchen smells and smoke away from the living and sleeping quarters. Among some of the huts we noticed a few tombs over which was raised a small palm roof so the tomb would stay in the shade. The village was tiny, but there was a 'restaurant' there which delighted Simonne. It was run by a Chinese, of course, and was combined with a store where everything could be bought: corned beef, tinned fruits, dresses, tools, beer, diving-goggles, etc. etc. We ordered 'chow mein', which proved to be a lot better made than the one we generally got in Papeete, yet cost us a bit less.

Back in the boat as night fell we were bewitched by the calm of the lagoon among the lush vegetation of the island. This island we really liked. We could have stayed there many days and been perfectly happy, but we wanted to see the other islands of the group, so on Tuesday we upped anchor and set the cap on Raiatea, where we arrived at noon. We used the pass at Uturoa, which presented no difficulties, as we could get in without tacking, although we were closehauled. We anchored close to the village and rowed ashore to visit this new island. For once Simonne and I disagreed about a place, for she disliked both the village and the island as a whole, while I thought that the village had a Wild West atmosphere which I did not find unpleasant.

We were surprised about the large amount of 'natives' who looked completely white, even having blue eyes. They were in strong contrast to the 'fonctionnaires', who lived in concrete houses and kept all their habits of the 'metropole', had cars, maids and refrigerators. These whites lived in the same type of houses as the regular natives and seemed to share their customs and their way of life. I never found an explanation for this, but I presume that they must have been descendants of earlier immigrants who had 'gone native'.

We were very interested to see the 'crowning stone' which was used in the days when the Pacific was unknown to the white man, for selecting a new king when the old one had died. Or rather, to be exact, to eliminate unworthy candidates. This stone was the height of a very tall man and was in the middle of sacred territory where no one was ever allowed to trespass. Any violators were immediately punished by death. No one today knows exactly what the conditions were to become a successful candidate as a new king, but we do know that the final test for the candidate was to stand in front of the 'crowning stone'. If he was taller than the stone he was then elected king, but if he happened to be shorter he was immediately put to death. This system of election seems rather strange to us today, but after all might not be much worse than ours, for while today's politicians need first of all a slick tongue, the old Polynesian kings needed in addition to their height a certain amount of personal courage, for they could never really be sure of being sufficiently tall, since the stone was on sacred ground.

Raiatea is historically the most interesting of all the Society Islands, because once it had been the capital of the group before the coming of the white man. It was from here that regular voyages had been made to the Hawaiian Islands more than two thousand miles to the north, across the doldrums, long before the white man even dreamed about making voyages across the open sea and long before we knew anything about celestial navigation, or indeed had even invented the compass. Many theories have been made about how they were able to find their way to tiny islands after so many miles at sea, but most historians admit that it is to us today a complete mystery how those voyages could repeatedly be done successfully.

Next day we sailed in the lagoon over to Tahaa, the neighbouring island which could almost be called the twin sister of Raiatea, as they both were encircled by the same coral reef. Sailing inside that reef was most exciting, as the islands are too low to stop the wind, but the reef is efficient enough to stop all the waves. Thus one gets ideal sailing conditions: a good, fresh breeze yet a flat sea.

We had heard so much about Bora-Bora that we were impatient to get there and thus by-passed Tahaa without stopping. We just sailed along its shore until we got to its north-west pass, which we used for getting out into the open sea again for our passage to Bora-Bora. The breakers on either side of this pass were most frightening, and perhaps especially so because they overlapped each other and as seen from a ninety degrees angle we would swear there could not possibly be a pass there at all. But when we approached the pass or rather where the pass is supposed to be, according to the chart, we saw that the overlapping reef was farther forward and that by going out at an angle between the two rows of breakers there is a safe passage. Here again we were closehauled through the pass, but could make it without tacking, so we did get out without any difficulty.

The sail over to Bora-Bora was a short one, as the wind was fresh and the distance modest. Soon we sailed along its reef, which extends a fair distance to sea, and admired the beauty of it all; the colours close to the reef, the palm trees ashore, and perhaps most of all the island's spectacular peaks, which looked even more impressive than on the famous prospectus.

When we approached the pass we got a little apprehensive, for here we did have to beat our way into it against a wind which came straight at us. The pass was rather narrow, although we had ample room to tack, but we had not gained much speed on the new tack before it was again time to come about and thus lose all speed again. The great danger was not to get up enough speed on the new tack for the ship to respond to her rudder, for should the ship refuse to come about we would not get a second chance, and would then fall back on the reef, where the huge breakers would break up the ship in a matter of seconds.

In this pass I had ample time to notice how awkward *Dorothea* was to handle with her twin runners and two headsails; this made four ropes on either side to loosen and four others to tighten on each tack! I had no standing backstay, so the main runner had to be tight if I wanted the headstay to be straight. In fact, with no runners tight at all I even took a chance of seeing the mast fall over the side. Often for ease of handling getting into a port I would take down the jib and disregard the second pair of backstays, thus only having two ropes on either side. Due to the short time we had in this narrow pass, we entered like that, or rather we tried to enter like that. We soon realised that we were just tacking back and forth at the same spot without getting in. The explanation was simple: the current was going out at just the same speed as we were gaining into the wind. In most passes the current reversed direction every few hours, but not in all of them and not always. If the wind was very fresh, as it had been during the last few days, the seas washed over the reefs at the windward side of the island and would then always rush out through the passes, which were generally more or less on the lee side. Unfortunately, this did not always prevent them from having large breakers on the lee side, as large swell often came from any direction.

As it was, we needed more power to get in against the current, so I had no choice but to hoist hurriedly the jib between two tacks. I got it up on the one tack, turned, and then winched it tight on the next tack. The increase in speed was enough to make us gain on the current, so after another half a dozen tacks we were inside the lagoon and out of the current which accelerated in the pass. The best anchorage for the wind prevailing at the time was just outside the hotel at the other end of the lagoon, so we had a beautiful sail across the calm water before arriving there. We sailed into the anchorage at great speed among the several yachts already lying there. The sails fell on deck, the anchor went over the side and we were peacefully at anchor once more.

Next to us were *Svea*, then the large and beautiful *Wanderer* dating from 1893 and being an example that beauty will always remain beautiful through the ages, providing it has originated from usefulness and true beauty, and not just out of some ridiculous fashion popular at the moment. There was also the *Farida*, which was, except for her paint, a most beautiful 38-foot Colin Archer type, built in Norway two years before. The American owner had singlehanded her from the south of Norway to England, taking nine days for the trip, during which time he said he had a total of two hours' sleep. I can well understand why he then shipped his boat on a steamer for the remaining distance to California. Now, with the help of several crew on board, he had sailed the ship from Los Angeles to Tahiti and from there to Bora-Bora. His wife had joined him by air at Tahiti and seemed to like island-hopping, but did not care for any ocean crossing. In fact, very few women do, and Simonne is one of the exceptions.

We were all moored outside the hotel, which was built in 'native style' and indeed very skilfully done. We were invited to have dinner at the hotel and we thoroughly enjoyed the décor, which was most attractive, but we were a bit disappointed about the food, which certainly did not measure up to its high prices. After dinner, walking back to the beach under the palm trees bathed in full moonlight, we were in a landscape of dreams. Rowing back to our ship we had the impression the dinghy was floating on air, so clear was the water: we could see every detail in the bottom as the rays of the moon penetrated the clear water all the way down. The beauty of Bora-Bora cannot be denied, and I could well understand that this had been Alain Gerbault's favourite island. He died during the war in Java and no one knows what happened to his handsome vessel, but after the war some of his admirers were able to have his body brought back to his favourite island, where he was buried next to the beach, close to where he usually anchored his yacht. We visited his grave and to me it was a solemn moment, for he had been one of my childhood heroes, and even though I had decided in my early teens to sail around the world like he had, I had also been painfully aware of the fact that there would be a thousand reasons for me never to be able to do it. Yet here I was. Not yet around the world, in fact not even half-way, but still I had reached the islands I had dreamed about.

The place was every bit as nice as it had been at the time Gerbault had been here, but the natives were no longer the same. The men kept at a cool distance, and the girls now knew the value of money. Several thousand American soldiers had been stationed on the island during the war, so it stands to reason that the natives would have changed. Now the island had even become a tourist centre, and there is no doubt that we would have liked it a lot more had we arrived a couple of generations before, but nevertheless we still enjoyed our stay immensely.

We stayed a few more days at Bora-Bora before leaving, but while there I cut a new large jib which I intended to keep on sewing on my passage to

Tahiti. I marked all the corresponding seams with numbers so I would not go wrong when assembling the sail in the little saloon at sea.

After having sailed out of the pass just five days after our arrival, we set course for Tahaa again on the way to Tahiti. This time we had both the wind and the current behind us, so we got out at great speed with no trouble, but when a few hours later we were outside the pass for getting into the lagoon encircling Raiatea and Tahaa we knew that we would have some hard work to get in again. The breakers on either side of the pass were rather frightening and much larger than I had ever seen before, possibly due to the recent gale, which had been building up rather a heavy sea, of which a huge swell still remained. This was the pass on the north-east side of Raiatea and not the pass we had taken out from Tahaa last time, for we wanted to do some shopping in Raiatea before arriving in Tahaa, where we had been told nothing could be purchased.

But everything went well. At each tack the faithful little ship came around with no hesitation and each time showed us that we had gained a few feet, except on two of the tacks when I had been a bit slow to trim the sheets and was much annoyed at myself for having lost several yards. When we came past the narrowest spot of the pass the current must have had less force, for we then gained a lot more at each tack and then finally got out of the pass and its current altogether, while we sailed at a good speed inside the protected and beautiful lagoon.

When we arrived at Tahaa we went to see Monique, a Frenchwoman whom some people we had met in Bora-Bora had told us of. A little later we stood outside her house introducing ourselves. She was surprised to get visitors; her English was not the best, so she seemed truly delighted to be able to speak French this time. She told us her story in a few words, for she must well have guessed that we wondered about how fate had sent her from a French 'bourgeois' family to this rather lost place. She had simply been on a vacation from France at the hotel in Bora-Bora. There she had met the native orchestra leader. That was just about the whole story. As simple as that. The orchestra leader was called Sikki, he fell as much for Monique as she had for him, so he left his 'wife' and they both changed islands altogether and had lived in Tahaa now for several years, after having been legally married in Raiatea. They had a baby and expected another one, this time a boy, said Sikki. They had a small vanilla plantation which seemed to bring them enough money to live on. Their village was very small and consisted of less than a dozen huts. All the inhabitants were related to each other, and were, in fact, one big family.

We were introduced to most of the inhabitants and were much interested to see the inside of their huts. Most of them were built on stakes about four feet above the ground, so all dampness from the ground was eliminated.

This must have been especially appreciated during heavy rains. The roofs were made out of plaited palm leaves, which surprisingly enough never leaked as long as they were fairly new. They explained to us that it took one man about two weeks to make one of these houses and just a few francs for nails and for the floorboards. All the rest they just picked from nature, like the palm leaves which also served as the sides of the house, but they added that neither the nails nor the floorboards were strictly necessary: if a man had no money at all he could just make an attractive house using thin flexible branches as lashings instead of nails, and he could make the floor by first lashing sticks of wood side and side and covering this rather uneven floor with mats made out of plaited palm leaves. The result was just as good, but required a lot more work to do it properly, so when they had the money they preferred to pay for the nails and the floorboards. The average life expectancy of such a house was only three or four years and it could, in fact, even fly away the first year if a hurricane struck the island, but then all they had lost would have been two weeks' work and a few francs. They could then sell a few coconuts to the 'Chinaman' and for the money get the needed nails and boards and two weeks later they would have a new house again.

We stayed almost a week in the village and during that time got invited to dinner in several of the huts. We shall never forget those days, which gave us an idea of life in the South Seas before all the tourists arrived. We went out with them in their dug-out pirogues for fishing in the lagoon, we picked coconuts with them and watched them make coconut milk, which was not simply the inside juice of the nut as we had thought. That juice they call coconut water and is refreshing but has nothing to do with milk and is as clear as water. The 'milk' was made from the meat of the nut by rasping it on a specially made bench, then they squeezed the juices out of this mashed nut and a whitish substance came out which looked like milk and even reminded me slightly of milk, although this had, of course, an entirely different origin. What is very surprising and might even interest nutrition specialists is the fact that babies are often raised on that milk.

Their food was indeed delicious and had been prepared in the 'Tahitian oven', which consisted of heating up a hole in the ground with a wood fire which had been burning for many hours. When the fire is almost dead most of the ashes are taken out, the food is laid in the hole after having been carefully covered with leaves, the hole is covered above the food with numerous layers of plaited mats and then all one has to do is to wait the proper amount of time, when the food is dug out and served. I doubt if there is a better way of cooking food and this way was certainly the method of cooking by prehistoric man. If modern cooking methods have made the job easier for the woman, it certainly has done nothing to improve the flavour. This meal in a modest hut made us once more realise that money is not only unnecessary for happiness, but also for comfort: the food could not have tasted better, yet had cost nothing in money, the hut was extremely comfortable and we were feeling happy among friends who had plenty of time.

When we left almost a week later several of our new friends cried openly when we bid them farewell, and we were ourselves rather sad, for we felt that we left a part of ourselves behind us. We had not just made some new friends, but we had gained a new philosophy of life. There are still many places on earth which are rather primitive, but in most of those places the natives speak another language altogether, and it must be hard for a white man to get on sufficiently equal terms to be able to understand them fully. Here we found that rare combination of intelligent people speaking our own language, who were friendly and hospitable towards us, yet lived almost as they did several thousands of years ago.

They stood on the water's edge and waved farewell to us while the ship heeled over in the breeze, gained speed and slipped away. We got out through the eastern pass of Tahaa with no difficulty, as we had a beam wind, and we had thus tried all four of the passes encircling the twin islands. We plunged immediately into a very short and steep headsea as we tried to lay course for Moorea. We had the wind dead against us, but it was no use waiting for more favourable winds, as these were the natural trade winds and everybody had to expect to get headwinds when sailing back to Tahiti. The bowsprit lifted high in the sky over one wave before plunging straight through the next one, letting the sea wash over the ship from end to end, but despite the rather rough motion we were making good speed through the water. As night fell the wind became very light, while the choppy seas stayed rather steep, so our speed then dropped to almost nothing, and thus under unfavourable conditions it took us two whole days to get to Moorea, where we anchored under the famous spectacular peaks after having sailed through the pass in a single tack.

We had read a lot about the beauty of Moorea and we were not disappointed. I do not think it would be possible for anyone to be disappointed about the beauty of any one of these islands: they are all as if cut out of a story book.

We were not alone in the deep fjord which was our anchorage, as another cutter lay also at anchor there. She was the *Phoebe* from South Africa, a cutter of heavy traditional construction a few feet larger than *Dorothea*. I had laid next to her in St. Lucia while she had still been with her previous owners, a nice elderly couple. They had sailed through Panama and had come as far as Tahiti, where the husband had become seriously sick and had been flown back to their home in South Africa, while the ship, abandoned in Tahiti, had been put up for sale. One of my friends, Bill Lohr, who had arrived in Panama in his small ketch *Serai II*, heard about the ship being for sale and remembered her well from her passage through Panama, when they had laid there next to each other, and purchased the yacht through the mail. Then he had hurriedly sold the *Serai* and flown to Tahiti to pick up his new ship. And here we were, anchored next to each other.

I saw Bill later in Papeete; he had planned to sail to Panama, but had been demasted in a squall. I have always been extremely interested in studying other peoples' mishaps, as it helps me to understand what to guard against so the same accidents do not happen to me. Looking carefully over his rigging, I was surprised to see that not one of the shrouds was broken, nor indeed had any of the spreaders failed; so the mast must have split from compression strain, which in a modern Bermudian rig is considerable. We could clearly see the glue joint in the hollow mast being open a long way, so that must have started the splitting. It is claimed that the modern glues are so good that the wood will even be torn before the glue fails. Maybe it is true. Nevertheless, I have seen many glue failures in the tropics.

Many will think that such an accident was unusually bad luck, but even yachtsmen generally do not know that there is a fantastic number of yacht accidents of one sort or another. The reason most people greatly underestimate the dangers of the sea is no doubt because we hear a lot about the successful voyages, while no one is inclined to talk much about their failures. The daily newspaper will put in a few lines when a yacht meets disaster, but news is fast forgotten, while the books and yachting magazines will last, will be reread and talked about. Many will claim that there is no safer place than the sea for a good boat, but then how can one be sure one's boat is the 'good' one?

Let's take a look at the yachts I saw while I was in Tahiti. A large percentage of them met with disaster within the space of one year. Let's call *Phoebe* case number 1, and then go on with the next along the quay which met with hard luck.

Case number two, *Si Ye Pambili*, was a British-made yacht which had been purchased by five ex-policemen from Rhodesia. Their ship was a total wreck on the shores of Rurutu. Their chain had broken while they were ashore and even though they saw it happening from land they had not the time to save the vessel; by the time they got back on board she struck the first time and they were unable to get her off before the heavy swell pounding her up and down on the reef had broken her up. A safe precaution would have been to drop two anchors over the side instead of just one.

Case number three, *Marinero*, was laying a little farther away. She was a

38-foot ketch, American, owned by Floyd Petersen, who sailed with his wife and a crew. They were finishing the repairs after the damage they had received in the hurricane which hit Raiatea while they had been lying there six months earlier. When the accident happened Floyd had been away from his boat, as he had had to fly to Tahiti in order to get his wife in to the hospital, but the crew, Fred, had been on board, taking care of the vessel until the owners' return. Fred lived on the vessel with a native girl friend, which contrary to popular belief is greatly disliked by many, especially the missionaries. The hurricane had struck so suddenly in the middle of the night that Fred had been unable to get the ship away from the dock, despite the ship's powerful motor, as the terrific wind held the ship tight against it. Fred got help from a whole gang of natives who hunted for old automobile tyres, and then by timing the surge of the vessel were able to slip them between the ship and the dock.

This would have saved the situation, but one of the missionaries came down to the dock. When he saw that the natives were busy helping a foreigner who had led one of his followers to live in sin, he shouted up above the shrieks of the wind that he forbade them all to have anything to do with 'that ship of the devil' and commanded them all to go immediately to church and pray for forgiveness. After a moment's hesitation they left the ship and walked towards the church. Next morning when the storm was over the dock had chowed not just through the planking but also into the deck all the way to the cabin coachroof. Fred, left alone with the girl, had been unable to find new tyres in time as they had worn down. Then it had not taken long before the first plank was holed, and from then on they had been busy bailing through the rest of the night to prevent the ship sinking. All the holes were above the waterline, but in the terrific winds and short seas the water was washing all over the ship. It was, in fact, a miracle that the ship stayed afloat, but it did and they were even able to repair her so she again looked like new.

Case number four, *Sea Star*, which we first saw at Nuku-Hiva, got into a choppy sea not far from Raiatea, and in one heavy lurch threw the owner's wife so hard across the cabin that she broke her shoulder and had to be taken to hospital.

Case number five, *Sea Wind*, a 38-foot American ketch with a clipper-bow and gleaming paint moored next to me, started suddenly to make a lot of water, much to the owner's surprise, as the ship had never leaked a drop until then. Upon investigation he traced the leak to a tiny hole in the planking just by the waterline. Wondering what it could be, he wanted to scrape off the paint with his knife, but as soon as he put some pressure on the knife it went straight through the planking, which crumbled away, leaving a hole where water then rushed through. He hurriedly stowed some heavy gear, spare anchor, spare chains, jerricans and such, over to the undamaged side of the boat so the list would raise the leak out of the water. Further investigation showed that the plank had been completely undermined by tropical teredo worms. In a few days the yacht was repaired and as good as new again, but I wonder what would have happened had he not discovered the damage before putting to sea on his way to Australia?

Case number six, two Tahitians went out in their modern outboard for fishing offshore. The boat capsized when a fair distance from land, filled, and sank due to the weight of the two outboards. Ordinarily men in such a situation would be doomed unless the accident had been witnessed by another ship which would have rescued them. But these men were not ordinary men: they were Tahitian and Tahitian pearl divers to boot. To them the sea is almost a natural element. Realising immediately the situation, one of the men hung on to the sinking boat as it went down, while he unscrewed the motors. First the one, then the other, and pushed them clear of the sinking boat. By the time he had the second motor cast off the boat was so deep below the surface that he knew that he would be unable to swim to the surface, but he also knew that without the weight of the motors the boat had to float up to the surface, as it had no ballast and was built all out of wood, so he just hung on to the craft and was thus brought up to the surface. There with the help of the other man they bailed her out and he crawled on board. Unfortunately they had neither sails, oars, food nor water on board, so all they could do was to hope either to drift ashore or be picked up by a passing ship before it was too late. The wind and the current were not in their favour and they drifted out to sea, missing Moorea, but a search was started when they did not return at night and they were found the following day in good shape.

Case number seven, a 28-foot-long motor yacht owned by a Frenchman who had been on the famous raft expedition of Erick Bishop from Tahiti to South America, laid for a while fender to fender with me in Papeete. Six months after I had left the island she went aground in the pass of Moorea, and became a total wreck.

These are just a few of those boats which met disaster shortly after they had been my neighbours during a few months' stay in that port. There were at least five more. In most other ports I could also bring many similar accounts, but I do not want to tire my readers with continuous lists of hard luck. Nor have I mentioned accidents to persuade anyone that the sea is so dangerous that no one should go to sea, but rather to show that it is ridiculous to be lulled into a false sense of security. We should admit that the sea is dangerous, but that it is still very possible to travel on it with a minimum of risk if we study what is dangerous and prepare ourselves and our ship accordingly.

The remaining time we had together before Simonne's ship took her back to Martinique went all too fast. Before we fully realised it the day of separation had come. Simonne had great difficulty in holding back her tears, and I could hardly remember having felt so sad before. On our way towards the ship with all her luggage we very nearly stopped by the steamship office to try to get the ticket refunded, in which case we would sail together towards Europe in *Dorothea*, for after all I still had money enough to get that far. But we decided to follow our reason rather than our hearts and that was, of course, a great mistake. The ship soon moved away from the dock, taking Simonne with her, while I waved until I could no longer see her in the distance. I felt utterly lonesome when I walked back alone to the empty boat.

8

Alone to Honolulu

DUE to the direction of the prevailing winds in the Pacific between Tahiti and San Francisco my route would take me so close to the Hawaiian Islands that it seemed logical to make a stop there for a rest and for buying fresh food; I therefore cleared port for Honolulu.

In the lee of the Tuamotus, I had very squally weather with sudden increases of wind strength, often accompanied by heavy rain and poor visibility, but these waters have such a bad reputation that I almost thought it normal. However, I was disappointed when after leaving the parallel of those islands the wind stayed stubbornly in the north-east and blew extremely fresh, kicking up a nasty sea and forcing me to lay close-hauled and to plough into the waves when I should have had a south-east wind to give me an easy ride. Not only did I have a very hard sail, but I was unable to make the easting I should have done in this latitude, for according to the *Sailing Directions* it would be almost impossible for me to lay the Hawaiian Islands should I get into the north-east trades north of the Equator, unless I had already done sufficient easting. As it was, I was even lucky to reach the Equator on the same longitude as Papeete without even falling farther to leeward.

Just north of the Equator I lost the trades and came into the doldrums. This region was dreaded by the old square riggers for a good reason: it is extremely difficult and tiring for a sailing ship to get through it. Most people who have never been through it will imagine this as a belt of no winds and a perfectly flat sea, but this is far from the case. It is just calm in the respect that the trade winds do not blow there, but otherwise there are winds there. The trouble is that it comes in spurts and from all directions, and varying in force from a light zephyr to a full gale, the change sometimes happening in a matter of seconds. Then after a burst of wind it could be absolutely calm for several hours, but never long enough for the sea to calm down. Since the wind changed so often, each time kicking up waves from a different direction, the sea was extremely confused and looked almost as if it was boiling with its waves shooting straight up into the sky.

For a sailing boat every breath of air has to be utilised if one wants to get through the region in a reasonable amount of time. The great difficulty was that when the wind died I had to take down all sails, for in the very rough sea the motion was so violent that the sails were flogging the whole rigging too severely if I left them up. The problem was to get the sails up fast enough when a squall arrived, so I would make good use of the wind before it again died down, but I had to guess ahead of time the approximate force of the wind so I would not hoist too much sail, as that could have grave consequences, yet if I was too careful I was wasting time, for sometimes the squall would be all over by the time I had my sails up.

I generally could see the squalls coming and by the ripples on top of the old waves I could estimate the wind's direction so all sails could be trimmed ahead of time, and thus I drew maximum miles out of every squall. At night conditions were a bit more difficult, as I had to do the estimation solely by the sound of the coming squalls. Very often this was accompanied by torrential rain, which did not make it too tempting to get out of the comfortable bunk, but I still wanted to get through as fast as possible, although I had chosen this miserable belt for catching up the easting I had been unable to achieve in the trades south of the Equator. Here it was no harder to do easting than any other course, as the wind blew from any odd corner of the compass, but it did mean that I had to stay even longer than necessary in that miserable region.

Here I could no longer sleep all through the night as I could when in a steady trade wind, but had to tend to the sailing twenty-four hours a day and slept in short periods of ten to twenty minutes each time.

The wind could attain a very high velocity, and I especially remember one time when I had left a small storm jib up sheeted hard amidship in an effort to dampen the violent motion while I waited for wind with all the other sails lashed on deck: I was having my evening meal and it was night when I heard the rain squall coming, or rather what I presumed to be a rain squall, but somehow the sound was not quite familiar and I was not too anxious to interrupt my dinner, so for once I decided to forget about this squall and let it go to waste. A moment later the 'rain squall' hit me like a steam hammer and laid my ship over more than forty-five degrees. It was not the rain I had heard, for this was a 'white squall' without rain. What I had heard was the sound of the sea being whipped up by the wind as it swept towards me. The strength of the wind was unimaginable and must have been full hurricane force. My ship is extremely stiff and it is almost impossible to believe that any wind could heel her over so far just under bare poles and that tiny jib. The squall lasted only five minutes at this strength, during which time she raced along at full speed out of control, while I had ample time to wonder what would have happened had I hoisted the mainsail as I usually did. Even with the double reefs I permanently kept in at night in this region it would have either torn the sails to ribbons or broken her mast, or simply capsized the ship.

After that experience I became more careful and never hoisted any part of the mainsail at night until I had felt the strength of the squall. This was a lot safer, but also more work, for it is very difficult to hoist a Bermudian mainsail when it is full of wind, and I also lost valuable miles while doing it. In this manner I sailed an average of fifty miles a day through the doldrums. This is not a very great speed compared with what the *Dorothea* generally was good for, but it was a far cry from 'being becalmed for weeks' which had been the warnings I had received from so many.

I finally crossed the latitude where I was supposed to get the north-east trades with its easy sail, small cumulus and no more rain squalls. I had done ample easting and should now get an easy ride, but the days and the miles passed and the weather improved very little and I saw nothing of the trades. When I reached the twelfth parallel and should have been in the middle of the trades, I heard on the Honolulu Radio that they had unusually clammy weather with 100 per cent humidity, terrific heat and that the usual trade wind had died down completely, much to the distress of the inhabitants, who count on that wind for making the climate of Hawaii agreeable. This was to me really bad news, for it meant that the whole trade-wind belt was upset and that I could not count on getting the trades for several days yet. What annoyed me even more was that I had done all that easting in the doldrums for nothing, but here I was also getting winds from all kinds of direction and could as well have sailed in a straight line.

On the twenty-seventh day out I spotted land. It was the big island of the southernmost of the Hawaiian chain. I sailed for another two days before getting to Oahu, the island where Honolulu is situated, and I felt fate was teasing me, for just as I sailed into the channel south of the island the sky cleared, the small cumulus appeared and the trade wind blew! Sailing in the lee of land I was thrilled to see the catamarans sailing through the surf all full of tourists, as I had seen on so many prospectuses; I saw the huge luxury hotels and cars speeding along the road. It was strange to see a big 'civilised' town after all this time in the tropics.

I was a bit in doubt about where I should sail, for I well remembered how much trouble I ran into last time in California when I had not anchored at the place reserved for that purpose. I hailed a sailing yacht as I crossed her path and shouted through my loud hailer asking if he knew where I could anchor for immigration.

'Just sail over there,' he said, while vaguely pointing in the distance: 'Sail through the pass and anchor in front of the yacht club. They will call immigration for you.'

I soon found the pass, which was very narrow, but I was just able to get through on the one tack as closehauled as it was possible. Huge breakers were rolling in on either side of it, and surfboarders were sliding in on the waves at high speed not far from the pass. In fact, I almost went aground when watching two girls surfing just yards away from me! It was strange to feel the motion of the ship suddenly calming down to the firmness of the ground after all these days in unusually rough motion.

The immigration was soon there and consisted of four officers. They took one look at my long bowsprit, which was the only way to embark at the place I had been given, and told me that they would prefer me to come ashore so we could fix up the paperwork at the club instead of on board. They could not have been more pleasant and, in fact, even offered me a Coca-Cola. After they had left, the yacht club invited me to be a temporary member for two weeks, during which time I could use all their facilities without any charge.

The yacht harbour was extremely pleasant and well organised. Each yacht laid to a small pier on to which it was very easy to embark and disembark. On each of the small docks there was a freshwater tap and a plug for electricity. For those who so desired a telephone could also be installed right inside the boat. All we had to remember was to unplug when leaving for a cruise. At regular intervals on land were installed public toilets, as it was against the law to use the yacht's heads.

Walking along the docks I recognised many yachts. There was the *Farida*, still painted red. She had had fair winds on her passage from Tahiti. Then there was the *Viejero*, a Tahitian ketch which had left Tahiti about a month before me and which also had had a good trip, and a little farther was the *Manu Rere*, a rather romantic-looking gaff schooner of 36 feet overall.

The route to San Francisco would take me through cold waters and I would have to expect to lay closehauled most of the way. Leaking decks are under such conditions a terrible nuisance so I decided to repair *Dorothea's* deck once and for all by removing the old deck completely and laying a brand new one before attempting the crossing. It took me about three months to complete the job working alone and just using the ship's handtools; by that time I was getting very tired of a big city's hustle and bustle and decided to sail to tiny Lahaina on a neighbouring island for doing the painting of the new decks as it had the reputation of never having any rain, which would be a great relief after Honolulu's daily afternoon rainsqualls.

I arrived the next day in a strong wind. On this occasion I saw once more how stiff *Dorothea* was as I sailed under no. 2 jib, full staysail and just one reef in the main, and still had the deck out of the water, while a

Tahiti ketch travelled with the deck in the water under just staysail and mizzen. The pass into the tiny port of Lahaina was extremely narrow, and it would have been impossible to tack in the channel, but the wind was favourable, so I sailed straight in under just the staysail with the idea of letting it go down on deck as soon as I passed the breakwater and let the ship just glide slowly in until the right moment for anchoring.

Unfortunately, I soon realised, while about half-way in the channel with sharp coral reef on either side of me, that a strong cross current was pushing *Dorothea* on the breakers. I had no room for turning and going back out again. Neither did I have room to anchor before getting on the reef, as by the time I would have enough scope out to make the anchor hold the ship would be on the reef. I only had one possibility of saving the vessel, and that was to get more power in order to overcome the current. I jumped to the main halyard and never before have I got up the mainsail in such a short time! The ship heeled over under the press of canvas and easily overcame the cross current, but I had an anxious moment as I turned the breakwater and shot at high speed into that tiny harbour where there was absolutely no room to turn the ship for manoeuvring or for slowing down by shooting into the wind. Fortunately my vessel is so rigged that I can always get down the canvas on any point of sailing, even in a strong wind, so I got the sails down in a hurry and stopped the way on the ship with the anchor.

A friendly-looking man with a snow-white beard rowed over to me and surprised me by saying:

'Welcome to Lahaina, Peter. Give me a stern line and I'll row it ashore for you.'

As I had never seen the man before, I was a bit surprised that he knew my name:

'Thank you so much, but you surprise me by knowing my name.'

'Well, yachtsmen hear about each other, and I could hardly be wrong considering that not too many yachtsmen wear a gold ring in their left ear!'

His boat was a very nice and husky ketch about 50 feet overall, and he was fitting out for a round trip to the South Sea Islands with his wife, grown-up children and a crew.

As soon as I was made fast at the dock with the bow out towards the anchor the Tahiti ketch came in under power and was soon moored next to me. George, the owner, who in Honolulu had given me so much valuable advice, explained to me that they had had a terrible storm after leaving the 'Big Island' and had had to turn back to port, where they had waited for better weather. They had then sailed here to Lahaina for a trial sail before leaving for the south, to check and see if everything was in order and had not been damaged.

Lahaina was indeed a beautiful little place and a great relief after all the noise, strain and hurried life of the big city of Honolulu. Had I come directly to this charming place I would probably have left for San Francisco as planned, and had a wonderful souvenir of the Hawaiian Islands, but as it was I had been reminded too much of the unpleasant atmosphere of my life in California and I had lost all desire to sail to San Francisco.

About two weeks after my arrival at Lahaina the wind surprised us all by blowing from the north-west, which is very unusual. My white-bearded friend said laughingly that it would be the perfect wind to start for Tahiti. George said that he still had some work to do. So did the white-bearded one. But the very word 'Tahiti' had made me dream. What a wonderful moment it would be to sail into the quiet and beautiful lagoon again! We only live once, don't we? I still had a lot of work to do, the ship was still not painted everywhere, I still had many splices to do on the rigging in addition to those thousands of small jobs which seem to delay a ship's departure for ever, but then if I had considered the ship seaworthy enough to sail from Honolulu to Lahaina, why could I not sail to Tahiti and finish all the work there? I made up my mind on the spot and exclaimed:

'You are right. It would be a wonderful wind for sailing towards Tahiti! I think I'll forget about San Francisco. I'll sail to Tahiti instead.'

They all laughed and thought I was joking, but looked like they did not quite know what to believe when they saw me rush over to the grocery store. An hour later I was back at the dock, having been driven by the stores truck for carrying all the food to the ship. I then hurriedly added a a few bulldog clamps where I had not yet had the time to do any splicing, lashed the dinghy, stowed my tools and paintpots and took off that very day for Tahiti!

The beautiful wind which had prompted me to leave died even before I cleared the island and I lay most of the night close to shore, completely becalmed. Early morning saw an easterly wind which gradually increased in force. The third day out it was so strong that I was under close-reefed main and reefed staysail with no jib and still had the deck in the water and travelling too great a speed. The bowsprit was plunging through the waves and solid water was washing clear over the ship all the way back to the main hatch, which had to stay closed. I should no doubt have hove-to, but I hate such a waste of time and prefer to keep on going. As I got farther south the wind moderated gradually, but it was not until the tenth day that I could take out the reefs and feel reasonably comfortable. On the other hand, the wind had stayed absolutely steady in direction, so I had had to do no work at all and had been able to lie in my bunk, sleep, read or just daydream. As I crossed the line demarcating on the chart the limit of the doldrums I was prepared again to get the typical and miserable weather that region is noted for, but the days passed with the most beautiful flat sea, sunny sky and light easterly breeze which under all light-weather canvas day and night gave me an average of a little over a hundred miles a day.

Soon, and much to my surprise, I crossed the line marking the southerly limit of the doldrums and had thus made it across that notorious sea under ideal conditions and without even a single squall! In the lee of the Tuamotus, however, I got one sudden squall which made my large yankee jib disintegrate into ribbons. It was old and rather ripe, so I was not too surprised, but as my new yankee was not quite finished my daily average dropped about twenty miles a day with my no. 1 jib. This was another demonstration of how important it is to carry sufficient sail area, yet even with just my no. 1 I was still carrying more sails than most cruising boats today. In fact, many cruising boats rigged with 'snug, all inboard rigs' and trailing large propellers would probably have considered the winds I had as too light for sailing and would prefer to power, and would never have experienced the wonderful feeling a ship will give under large sails able to take advantage of light breezes which leave a flat sea.

I stayed as closehauled as I could for the whole voyage from Hawaii and, as unbelievable as it sounds, I thus arrived on Moorea, the neighbouring island of Tahiti, only missing my destination by about ten miles in a distance of 2,400 miles! Only there did I tack the ship for the first time for the remaining distance. Two thousand four hundred miles closehauled on one tack.

The wind was fresh as I approached the entrance pass to Papeete and entered it at a great speed; I hoisted the sails and followed the tug which most patiently waited for me tacking back and forth. I dropped the anchor at the indicated spot and then the tug took my stern line ashore. As soon as I had my gangplank ashore the authorities came on board and the immigration officer laughed when he saw my passport and remarked that I had calculated my absence pretty close, since I had been away exactly six months and two days, which was just two days more than the minimum absence permitted before I could apply for a new visa.

Within a couple of hours of my return to Papeete most of my friends had already come to the dock to welcome me back. Most were surprised to see me, as they knew that I was headed for San Francisco, but they also easily understood when I explained that I had changed my mind. I was thrilled to be back and felt almost as if I had been reborn after the long dull months in Honolulu. For three months I was to have a life of party-going, dating and excursions to the neighbouring islands. Tahiti has always had the reputation of being a bachelor's paradise. Some men who have come a long way to take advantage of such a situation have been bitterly disappointed, but it is, however, still a fact that a girl never sleeps alone in Tahiti. In fact, a girl would prefer to spend the night with a lover she did not particularly like rather than be alone. This might sound surprising to many, but to them it is just as much a dishonour to sleep alone as it is a dishonour for a girl in our civilisation to be in a ballroom without being invited to dance.

How is it, then, that some men have difficulty in finding the sex they expected to be so abundant in Tahiti? The reason is simple: the reputation of Tahiti brings men from all over the world to the island, with the result that there are far more men in the island than women, so even if each woman is free with her favours, most of them prefer to have only one lover at a time and therefore the surplus of men will necessarily sleep alone. As in most other countries, the girls prefer to have a lover on a long-term basis, so the tourist who has only a couple of weeks' vacation is at a distinct disadvantage. On the other hand, few of the girls will worry about next year, and most will consider that the possibility of the relationship lasting a couple of months or more will be satisfactory.

Any bachelor who wants to dance all night at Quinns' and is able to keep on buying beers for his dance partner at a frightful speed can feel entitled to take her home when the dancing is over. With the Tahitian girls we don't have to go courting for weeks, as we so often must in our world, for in Tahiti it will be either 'yes' or 'no' the very first night. If it is 'no' it will be firm and not just because she thinks it sounds more respectable to let a man wait.

On one occasion, however, I was much amused to see the Tahitians interpretation of our code of morals. I had been invited to a party at the Administrator's house and there met a girl who offered to drive me home in her 'Deux Chevaux' (which is the popular name for the two-horse Citroen cars). She was a rather attractive girl of almost white skin. She told me that she was a quarter Tahitian and three-quarters white, as both her father and her mother were each half white and half Tahitian. I am sure that my mathematics teacher in school would have claimed that under such circumstances she was just as half Tahitian as her parents, but I did not question her reasoning. I invited her to visit my boat and after much hesitation she accepted, provided I would get out of the car first and signal to her when the street was deserted, as she wanted no one to see that she would 'do the boats'.

After about half an hour's conversation I thought it would be rather impolite not to at least kiss a girl who sits alone with me in my boat at two o'clock in the middle of the night, but when I took her in my arms she very firmly pushed me away and declared very seriously that she knew perfectly well what a 'Popaa'[1] thought about a girl who gave herself away on the first night they met and she did not want me to think that she was such a girl, but said that if I wanted her she would come back the following night. I did not insist and soon followed her back to the car, feeling that she had promised to come back the following night just so I would let her go more easily, but she rather surprised me when I said good night to her ashore and she looked me deep in my eyes and said almost tenderly:

'If you think it will be hard to wait until tomorrow night, I can come back early in the morning, as I don't start work in the office until eight o'clock.'

It sounded like a joke, but something in her face made me resist the temptation to laugh, and I just assured her that she would be welcome any time. I had hardly fallen asleep when I was awakened by a kiss. I looked at the clock. It was a quarter to six and the sun was barely up. She was back, and assured that she would now be considered a respectable girl by anyone's standards, for this was a new day!

Once while airing my hate for motors of any kind in yachts one man told me that motors are sometimes good to have and a boat without an engine will get into many situations where she will be wrecked while an engine would have taken her easily to safety. As I consider that a properly run pure sailing ship is at least as safe as most auxiliaries, I challenged him to give me just one example if he could. Much to my surprise he answered with a smile:

'I can easily give you an example, as the wreck of a yacht still lies on the reef by the southern pass of Huahine. She was thrown on the reef in the narrow passage for lack of an engine.'

I was very intrigued about what had happened exactly, for while I, of course, admit that in the hands of a novice a pure sailing boat would have many chances to get into trouble, I felt that by the time a yacht has sailed as far as the South Seas her crew must know exactly what the ship will do and what she cannot do.

The best way to find out would no doubt be to sail over there myself and ask the local residents who might have witnessed the accident. My 'quarter-Tahitian' girl friend had often told me that she would so much like to try a sail in *Dorothea*, so I thought it a good occasion to invite her for the ride. She was overjoyed at the idea and asked for a week's advance on her vacation and told me that her fiancé would not come back from Noumea for another fortnight, so everything would work out for the best. We did have a fast and enjoyable trip in the fresh trades all the way to Huahine, and I was surprised to see that she did not show the slightest

[1] 'Popaa' in Tahitian means a white man or woman.

sign of seasickness, which is rather rare among people who have never had
any experience with the sea before.

Shooting through the southern pass at great speed in a beam wind I was
surprised to see no trace of the wreck which supposedly was there. We
anchored and then went straight to the local 'gendarme' office in search of
information. The gendarme proved to be the only white man on the island
and seemed only too happy to chat with us. He offered us Coca-Cola (which
seems to be sold even in the most remote places) and bade us sit down in
the saloon of his airy house. When I asked about the wreck and explained
the reasons I had for being interested, he pulled out the file on the accident
and explained that the swell had not taken long to break up the wreck.

The first thing I noticed looking over the photographs taken immediately after the accident, when the ship was high on the reef, was the fact
that the sails seemed to be nicely furled with the sailcovers on! Why should
anyone worry about putting on sailcovers when a ship is lying at a forty-five
degrees angle, pounding itself to death on a sharp coral reef? As I read the
report the explanation became obvious: no one had put them on. Rather,
no one had had the time to take them off and hoist the sails *when the engine
stalled right in the middle of the pass with a strong beam wind*. Thus it was a
most misleading half-truth to say that she was wrecked for lack of an
engine! She had in reality been wrecked because her skipper had trusted
the engine too much and the engine had failed at a critical moment.

My girl crew was anxious to visit some relatives in Raiatea, so since I
liked that island we set the course towards it before returning to Tahiti.
After two days in Raiatea we set sail again in a very fresh trade wind, but
this time we had it dead against us and the trip was rather rough, well
reefed down and the seas washing clear across the ship from forward aft,
much to the fright of my friend. Thirty-six hours later we were outside the
pass of Papeete with the wind still blowing hard. It was the middle of the
night and pitch dark with no moon. I don't like to enter ports in the dark,
but I felt that I knew the port well enough now to risk it rather than to
spend many hours hove-to outside in the rough sea.

I told my crew to stand forward on the bowsprit inside the pulpit and
shout to me when she could either see or hear the breakers on either side
of the pass, while I steered straight in on the two alignment lights. I was as
closehauled as the ship would go, but I could just lay the course as long as
the wind did not turn. It was so dark that I could not even see the girl. In
a sudden panic that she must have fallen overboard in the rough sea I
flashed my torch on the foredeck and there saw her half sitting, half lying
on the foredeck, holding on to the samson-post with both arms, while her
dress, soaked by the flying spray, was glued to her body. I saw her face
turned forward, no doubt trying to pierce the darkness, while she shivered

in the wet dress. I wondered for a moment if I asked too much of girl crews, but then a South Sea pass is worthy of all the look-outs we can afford, especially on a dark night. The ship was heeled over sharply, plunging through the seas, and then all of a sudden the motion quietened down, but I could still feel that the ship was travelling at great speed through the water.

I realised that we were inside the lagoon: we had entered the pass without either of us seeing or hearing the breakers just yards away! I was thankful for the two lights' accuracy and that everything had gone well.

At seven o'clock next morning, after just a few hours' sleep, we were awakened by the pilot launch telling us which berth to take, and soon the girl left ship with her suitcase after what she declared to have been the adventure of her life. Less than an hour later the girl was back with her suitcase, tears running down: she explained that her parents had refused to see her in their home and that they did not consider her their daughter any more now that she had brought shame on them by running off with a foreigner, and a yachtsman at that! They had said that they would only reconsider her their daughter if she came home with a marriage licence! In the meantime the girl had nowhere to go, so she moved on board. I thought about parents' stupidity, for surely that would be the last thing they had wanted, yet apparently they no longer lost face, since 'it was no longer their daughter'. The fiancé came a week later and did not look too happy about the situation, but when he still wanted to marry the girl I was so grateful that I even offered to be best man at the wedding, an offer he very firmly declined.

While many of the other yachtsmen were working on their engines I had been busy sewing new sails for my ship. Sails purchased at a sail-maker's are very expensive, but if we are able to sew them ourselves they will only cost the price of the canvas, which is just a fraction of the sail-maker's price and, most of all, the result will be much more satisfying, as a hand-sewn sail will considerably outlast a machine-sewn one. Just as I had finished my new large jib a neighbouring yachtsman who had watched me work asked if I could do some work for him on his sails and would in that case pay me two and a half dollars an hour. I gladly accepted the offer and made thus several hundred dollars in the weeks which followed, sitting under his awning and just restitching the machine seams of his sails, while watching the girls pass by.

One day my friend Mark, who had the only boat in Tahiti doing charter work, came over to my ship with a panic-look on his face and told me that he was in trouble and that I had to help him out. Both he and his wife had accepted a charter for the same two weeks and they were now double booked.

'Well, can't you send a letter to one of them telling them of the mistake and hope that they will want to come later?' I asked.

'The trouble is that they have both already left the States and are on their way. Just imagine their fury when they get here and see that they can't both have the ship! Please, Peter, you have got to help me out and take one couple for a fortnight's cruise. Otherwise I will have no end of trouble with my agents as well as with this customer.'

I did not know how to get out of the situation, for I did not want to refuse Mark that service, but really two weeks seemed a lot of work for rendering a service to a friend, and it could not have been less convenient, for I expected Simonne to join me the following week and had looked forward to being there on the dock to greet her and kiss her welcome on her return to Tahiti. I tried to explain all this to him, but it did not convince him at all.

'I will meet her for you,' he offered, but when he saw the expression on my face he quickly added, 'With my wife, of course. We will lodge her in our house until the first plane goes to Bora-Bora, where she can meet you. I'll pay her ticket, so it won't reduce the thousand-dollar fee you get for the charter.'

My eyes popped open at these last words: a thousand dollars!

'You must be kidding! I couldn't possibly get a thousand dollars for a fortnight's sail with my thirty-two-foot boat!'

'Who do you take me for? Do you think that I'll keep the money while you do the work? A thousand dollars is, of course, too much for a boat your size, but they have already sent the money and it will look funny if we tell them now that it costs less. Of course, this fee includes everything to amuse your customers for two weeks, and not just the food which they are free to ask for in the best hotels, but even taxi rides, speedboat rides, and everything they might dream of.'

Since a licence is required in Tahiti for doing charter work, it had not occurred to me that I was going to get any money for the job, but still I did not see how I could let him be stuck with the double booking, and when he made such a generous offer I was in no doubt any more. It was arranged that I would avoid the charter restriction by clearing the port definitely before leaving and list the two charterers as my personal friends going as crew. For additional safety we decided that I was to leave the Society Islands for good as soon as the charterer disembarked in Bora-Bora. Rumours travel fast in Tahiti, and I was not quite sure that the port captain really believed me or whether he just knew the whole truth and was nice enough to close his eyes and just wished me a good trip.

I was so worried that something should go wrong with Mark and his wife meeting Simonne, as should no one meet her she would have thought that I had stood her up, and I dreaded to think of her disappointment and of the risk it could entail, for, after all, I was not the only man on Tahiti.

I therefore wrote as many as six different letters (carbon copies to save work) explaining the reason for my not being at the dock on her arrival and asking her also to join me by the first plane either in Bora-Bora or in Raiatea, depending on the plane schedules, at the time of the ship's arrival; these letters I gave to six different friends, asking them to give the message to Simonne for me. I omitted, of course, to tell each one that I had asked five other friends to do the same service, as I then ran the risk that each one would think that the others would take care of it and Simonne might not get a single one.

This precaution proved to be wise, for Mark had not been able to stay in Papeete any more than I, as his charterers had wanted to leave immediately, and his wife had completely forgotten about Simonne until the day after the ship's arrival, and out of the six letters she only got four. Now, four letters are, of course, ample, but suppose that I had just written the two which were never handed her? Of course, it could have been a most embarrassing situation when Simonne was met by several friends each with an identical letter and the same verbal message, but I knew that Simonne had an easy laugh and the ability always to put everyone at ease. Nevertheless, even now, two years later, when I write these lines, she has not yet quite forgiven me the disappointment I had caused her by not being on the dock on her arrival. She thought that any amount of money would have been a poor excuse, for money means little to her.

The charterers proved to be a young couple, sporty and very pleasant. They had never been on a boat my size before in the open sea, but were thrilled about everything. The first port was Moorea, where we went to a 'native roast pig dinner' arranged by the hotel and the following day a taxi ride was arranged for driving around the island.

From there the trip went to the Leeward Islands. First to Huahine, where we hired a speedboat for driving around the islands inside the lagoon in very shallow water, beautifully clear. At the village on the opposite side of the island from *Dorothea*'s anchorage we stopped to take a look at the unusual huts all constructed on tall wooden piles over the water. We were informed that they liked it better over the water, because it was much cooler than on shore. I also noticed that the plumbing was simplified: a convenient hole in one corner of the house was all that was needed. In addition to the houses over the water, there were also quite a few on shore, but close to the water's edge.

From Huahine the trip went on to Raiatea and Tahaa, where after a few days Simonne landed at the airstrip of Raiatea. What a thrill to be together again! We promised each other never to part any more, for no one knows what can happen during these long separations and so much could prevent us ever meeting again.

A few days later in Bora-Bora the charterer left the ship, the two weeks having ended, and we were alone on board again. We decided to leave westward immediately, as we were at the end of the good season and sailing in the unfavourable time of the year is never as pleasant. So a little later *Dorothea* sailed out of the pass for what we considered the second half of the world.

9

The Second Half of the World

'PARTIR, c'est mourir un peu . . .' say the French, yet we felt like we were being born afresh as we sailed out into the ocean towards new and distant horizons. It could not be because we were glad to sail *away* from anything, for a more pleasant place than the French islands would be hard to find, but it must rather have been for the exciting feeling of sailing towards new adventures.

Perhaps we had been too anxious to get going, for we soon discovered that we had forgotten to take bread, potatoes, butter, fresh fruit and fresh vegetables with us. To make matters worse, we were soon to discover that it had been a mistake to tell the Chinese storekeeper that he had to make sure that the twelve dozen eggs we ordered from him had to be absolutely fresh because we were leaving on a long voyage to Europe. He had then apparently considered that it was an excellent opportunity to get rid of his old eggs, for out of the first ten eggs we opened at random three were completely rotten and filled the whole boat with a sickening smell, while most of the others were so doubtful that we did not eat a single one, but threw the whole lot of 144 eggs over the side, damning the Chinese store-keeper while doing it.

The rotten smell soon disappeared, but nevertheless it had not helped Simonne's seasickness, which had returned after her long stay ashore. We had rather a heavy sea and strong winds mostly from the beam, but also often from forward of the beam, which was disappointing, as we were right in the trade belt and should have been able to count on having good strong following winds. The day's run was to vary between our poorest run of 70 miles to our best run of 166, but on an average we were to cover a little more than 100 miles a day before our landfall twenty-four days later.

Leaving Tahiti I had cleared for Noumea, but on the way we changed our minds and decided to visit the New Hebrides instead. There were really no special reasons for us to change our plans, except that we were free to do what we pleased and we thought that the New Hebrides sounded more exciting and much more virgin than the commercial Noumea. The days on board passed quickly as usual. Simonne spent a lot of time figuring new ways to prepare our fast-disappearing tins, while I shared my time between sewing the old sail I had purchased in Papeete for six dollars, reading magazines and books, figuring my position, dreaming up improvements in *Dorothea*'s rigging and retrimming the sails and the pilot whenever the wind changed. We chatted together and made plans for the future consisting mostly in how to keep on sailing till we were 90 years old.

On 2nd August I threw overboard the 20-foot-long squareyard which I had expected to be so useful according to the many books I had read on the subject and which had described the great advantages of having a square-sail for trade-wind work. But now, after having tried it from Papeete, I had only found it cumbersome and awkward. I much preferred to run under the mainsail well boomed out on the one side and balanced off on the other side by a flat spinnaker sheeted to a very long spinnaker pole on one side and to the foot of the mast on its other corner. So, being tired of the space the pole occupied on the deck when the wind was not free enough for it to be used, I preferred to get rid of it altogether, despite all the work it had taken me to make it. It floated high on the water, being hollow, and we both stood on deck watching it disappear below the horizon, wondering where it would finally be washed up and to what use it would be put by the people finding it.

At noon, just after shooting the sun, we spotted Tin Can Island in the distance, which was a welcome sight, as it confirmed the position I had calculated as being correct, despite that I no longer could see the sun clearly through the sextant as one of its mirrors had started to lose its silver. The rather strange name of the island is caused by the fact that all mail both to and from the island is brought in a watertight tin can. The ship then simply throws the can over the side into the sea, where it is grabbed by a native who has swum out from shore to meet the ship, as there is no port and not even an anchorage in the island. The outgoing mail is fished out of the water by the ship when at the rendezvous with the swimmer.

The 4th August was to last us only twenty-one hours, for we crossed the 180 degree longitude at nine o'clock at night, thus having to move the calendar forward one day to catch up the average of ten minutes a day we had been losing as we sailed westward. And 5th August was to be the shortest day in my life, as it could only last three hours, because at midnight a new day started as usual, this making it already the 6th.

In addition to the strange experience of jumping a day, the 180 degrees longitude was to have another significance to us, because the voyage had started at Birdham almost exactly on the longitude of Greenwich, on the zero meridian, so we now were crossing the half-way mark.

From the *Pilot* the island of Gaua in the northern group of the New Hebrides sounded particularly beautiful as well as unspoiled, so we had set our course for it, disregarding the fact that it was highly against the law to stop there without first sailing to the capital Vila in the south in order to let the authorities check our papers and generally waste both their time and ours. We figured that no one would bother us and ask for any papers in Gaua and that by the time the authorities in Vila heard that a yacht had entered the territory without checking with them we would be far over the horizon. In this case that reasoning was to become much truer than I had hoped.

On Saturday the 11th, getting closer to our destination, we kept a good look-out, as the visibility was rather poor and I had no great confidence in the sextant any more on account of the bad mirror. At 6.20 in the evening I just got a glimpse of Peak Star before nightfall. We kept careful watch all through the night and by 9.20 next morning we passed Star Island at a safe distance. That same afternoon we finally anchored in the bay of Lakona on the island of Gaua, where we expected to replenish the larder, which by now was very nearly empty.

The sweet smell of a tropical island came out to us where we were anchored and it felt good to see again palm trees sway in the breeze, but the village looked a lot smaller than we had expected from the description in the *Pilot*. The natives had already assembled themselves by the beach, watching us. Even at a distance they looked rather frightening, and even though several pirogues were lying on the beach none of them made any attempt to meet us where we lay at anchor, as the friendly Tahitians so often did. Through the glasses I noticed that they looked entirely different from the generally good-looking Tahitians, and cannot have had the same ancestry. The *Pilot* warns sailors against these natives as being not only unfriendly but until a few years ago still cannibals.

I paid not much attention to such warnings, probably because I had never so far been put into any native meat-pot and on the contrary only met with friendliness. Besides, we noticed that there were both women and children on the beach, and anyone who has read a few adventure books will know that when natives prepare for war women and children are hidden behind the lines in safety; so we ignored their rather gloomy looks and resolutely assembled our dinghy and launched it over the side. We had, however, just taken a few strokes with the oars towards shore when we heard a loud bell ringing frantically and immediately all the women and the children disappeared, leaving only the men on the beach. I hesitated an instant and most of all would have liked to regain *Dorothea*'s deck, but realised that if they wanted to they could easily overtake us with their much faster pirogues, so thinking that after all this is the twentieth century

The author sanding down the new deck before laying on the fiber glass. (Honolulu)

A native sailing sloop in Samarai. These boats were built by the natives under the supervision of British missionaries and to plans of old British workboats. They proved to be admirably suited to the local conditions and excellent sailers.

Some of the natives from neighboring islands who had arrived in their "Sunday clothes" to participate at a local festivity. (Samarai)

Dorothea on the slip at Belasana. The boat looks much bigger than she really is due to the optical illusion caused by the native's tiny size.

and that no natives ever used white men as meat dishes any more, nor were they likely to force Simonne to be their queen, I ignored my fears and rowed calmly towards the men on the beach.

As we pulled the dinghy out of the water and up the beach they all stood in a ring around us without saying a word and without apparently changing a single muscle in their faces, judging from their expressions. Only their eyes followed every one of our moves. I said, 'Good day, good day' to them in English, French, Spanish and Tahitian, all with the same negative response. I never thought also to try Norwegian, but I presume it would not have helped much either. In an effort to thaw the rather cool reception, I began shaking everyone's hand as a friendly gesture, starting with the oldest man, hoping that they would consider it proper to show respect to age, and just for safety I arrived last at the man carrying the lance and very last at the one with a shiny axe, while I had great difficulty in keeping up a rather forced smile. When that was done and had not improved our chances of conversing together, I stepped out of the circle and resolutely walked towards the village, closely followed by first Simonne and then all the natives.

As soon as we were among the huts I immediately realised that there were no hopes of any tinned food. In fact, except for a few worn-out European clothes some of the people wore, we could as well have been in the Stone Age. The huts were made of thin thatched branches with thatched palm leaves for the roofs and had no windows. The only opening was a door and that was so low that anyone entering or leaving had to crawl on all fours. But to our great relief we noticed some of the women getting out of the huts and watching us from the door openings. The men were not tattooed, but the women made up for them, for they had tattoos all over. Even their faces had geometrical designs around their eyes and following their noses and chins. At the sight of their pathetic arms and legs, their low-hanging breasts, round and protruding stomachs and their small, close-set eyes, I could not help thinking that not all South Seas girls are tempting. What a difference from the many beautiful girls in Papeete!

If there was no store in the village, the people there still must have had some food and we would have to be satisfied with whatever they would be willing to sell us, for we had to get food before daring to go to sea again with a very nearly empty larder. We saw some small pigs running about and as a start made them understand with signs that we were hungry and wanted one of them to take to the boat—a fact they really seemed to understand, but difficulties presented themselves when we tried to make payment. I offered both Tahiti money, French francs, dollars and pounds, but in each case the notes were handed from hand to hand while each man took a close look at them. At first I thought that they tried to evaluate each note, but soon realised that they just looked at them as they would have looked at a picture.

In turn they were all returned to me and I got the impression that they thought that I tried to treat them as fools if I hoped to get a good pig for some rumpled and dirty pictures. This was the first time in my life I had found a place where money had no value, and even seemed unknown. I should have been thrilled to have found such an unspoilt place, but at the time I wished it had been a bit more civilised. I could, of course, have tried to barter with something. Many white persons have made a fortune trading worthless mirrors and glass pearls for diamonds, gold and silver, but I am not very clever at such things. The only thing I could think of which would tempt them was old clothes, but after three years in the tropics, where everything spoils with mildew, I could do with some myself. I did have some paint, but as neither their houses or canoes were painted I rather presumed that they either did not know what a can of paint would be or that they would consider it highly unnecessary. As they did not seem willing to give us any food for free either, we thought that the easiest thing would be to sail to the next island north, which was only a few miles away, and where the *Pilot* promised several villages and an agricultural missionary school. I felt sure we would there find both a store, tinned food and people who would accept money as payment.

We shook everyone's hand and then turned back towards the beach the way we had come. We had hardly reached the path when we heard some wild shouting behind us; the man with the axe was running at full speed at us. We should have fled without losing any time, but we were both paralysed and frozen to the ground. Simonne clung to my arm and I did not feel at all up to the situation, unarmed in a very wild territory among unfriendly natives and out of reach of the *Dorothea*. Just a few feet from us the man slowed down and stopped, took his axe over to his left hand and stretched out his right hand: he just wanted to say 'good-bye'! Apparently he must have been away when we shook everyone's hand on leaving and now did not want to have been the only one we had not taken a formal leave of. Greatly relieved, we shook his hand heartily and then went back to the dinghy and *Dorothea*.

It might have been as well that at the time we did not know that just a few weeks before our arrival there had been a great feast in the village when the main dish consisted of an . . . old grandmother! Somehow the authorities in Vila had heard about the cannibalistic meal and had arrived soon after in the police boat and arrested a few of the natives. In court they readily admitted having eaten the woman, but strongly denied killing her. They on the contrary declared that they had been so grieved by her death as they all loved her so much that they could not get themselves to put her down in the cold dark earth and had preferred to eat her so she would remain more a part of them all. I never learned what the judge decided their punishment to be, but I can imagine that it cannot be easy to practise white man's law among such primitive people.

Next morning, after having done a couple of hours' repairs on the sails, we broke out the anchor and sailed along the coast and across the channel to the next island, the Vanua-Lava Island. It was to be a beautiful sail along the shore of tropical islands just like a story book, but when in the lee of Vanua-Lava we saw no signs of life and no signs at all of any agricultural missionary school. By sundown we had reached the northern end of the island, still without having seen any signs of habitation. Of course, even if we had not seen anything from our ship it did not mean that the island was uninhabited. In fact, if we went ashore and penetrated the bush we might well discover that the island was full of both natives and missionaries, but we still became discouraged with all these unforeseen difficulties in finding food, and wondered if the night would not be better employed in sailing towards the Torres group of islands farther north, rather than wasting the night at anchor waiting for daylight so as to investigate in the morning if there should be people here after all.

The Torres Group (not to be confused with the Torres Strait north of Australia) consists of five islands of which the northernmost was to have many villages, including quite an important one. By sailing during the night we should arrive there by morning and our chances should be better there than here, now that we had failed to see any villages along the coast. Thus we never stopped at that island, and after a couple of hours when we were well clear of land we went to bed while the ship steered herself towards the Torres Group. Next morning we awoke and saw the southernmost of the group, the *Dorothea* having steered a straight course during our sleep.

When in the lee of Hiu we sailed close to shore and had decided to stop in the very first village, even though the farthest one to the north was supposed to be the largest, for we had become pessimists and thought that that way would only increase our chances against a failure in purchasing the food we wanted. But the miles went by without us seeing a single village nor indeed any form of life whatsoever. Soon we arrived at the northern bay, where we anchored. We still could see no sign of any village, but through the binoculars a dug-out canoe could plainly be seen pulled up on the beach, and since the village was at 300 feet altitude it was only natural that it would not be visible from the sea, with the tropical vegetation growing everywhere. Assembling our dinghy and rowing ashore, we soon reached the spot where the native canoe was lying, but we were greatly disappointed to see that it was completely rotten.

However, we told ourselves there was no reason to become alarmed, for the very fact that the village was not lying by the beach but was built at a height only showed that the inhabitants were not too interested in the sea, but were probably farmers rather than fishermen, a fact we should be glad of. We also soon found the path described in the *Pilot* which leads to the village, but since they obviously had lost interest in the sea it was so badly overgrown that we made very painful progress. We had to climb over trees which had fallen across the path or under some large branches a few feet above the ground. We continually had to push aside new growth and walk through bushes as high as ourselves.

We were surrounded by the many strange sounds so typical in tropical forests and although we knew that most of the sounds were caused by the many animals living in the jungle, we saw no animal life of any kind except one large and colourful hen which crossed our path with fluttering wings. We felt sure by then that the village could not be far away, and indeed the jungle did thin out just ahead of us and then all of a sudden opened up in front of us to show us a wide-open place with no trees and hundreds of stone foundations on which a few broken huts still remained, while on most of the others the jungle undergrowth was already crawling: the village was abandoned!

On the way back to the beach we had only one thought: chicken hunt, now that we knew that they no longer belonged to anyone. But this time we saw nothing. To make matters worse, we lost the path and were unable to find it again, even when trying to retrace our steps. All we then could do was just to walk in the general direction which I checked with my watch each time the sun's rays became visible through the tight growth overhead, as I had not forgotten the simple rule taught me as a child in Norway that due south would always lie exactly halfway between the hour hand and the twelve sign when I pointed the hour hand towards the sun. Progress became even slower than when we were in the overgrown path, but after a couple of hours we suddenly to our great joy heard the sound of the surf and a few minutes later stood on the beach, blinded after the jungle's half-darkness. Our 'navigation' had been good, for we had arrived within a few hundred yards of where we had left the dinghy.

Exhausted from the long tiring walk, we sat down and discussed what to do. According to the *Pilot* the next group of islands up north sounded just what we needed, but by now we did not dare to trust it too much. Few ships ever came to these islands, and those which did apparently did not bother to notify the hydrographic office about the changes which had occurred since the original printing. As long as those offices receive no word to the contrary they will reprint each year the same information. At a time when we are exploring outer space and generally think that we know just about everything there is to know it comes sometimes as a shock to realise that the world's charts and the seaman's Bible, the *Sailing Directions*—also called the *Pilot*—are highly inaccurate and lacking in information.

Should we now be disappointed in the next group of islands also our situation would become worse and worse, for each day our food supply was diminishing. The nearest places I knew for sure we would find food was in Vila, but that was now more than 300 miles to the south and a great detour from our destination towards Torres Strait. The wind was very fresh and had been steady in the same direction for several days. It was a favourable wind for us if we sailed to New Guinea, where we also knew we would find towns and food, but it was about a thousand miles away.

A cruise of a thousand miles is a long cruise for a boat with an empty larder, but we then thought about the coconuts lying on the beach! They would keep us from starving. We filled the dinghy with as many nuts as we could find room for and then rowed happily to *Dorothea* just as night fell.

Half an hour later we were under full sail, headed for New Guinea in pitch darkness but wonderful trade-wind weather. By daybreak the island had disappeared and we were again alone on a lonely sea. The fishing line which trailed behind the ship for thousands of miles without ever getting a bite suddenly jerked tight: we got a large fish for breakfast. We ate what we could of it and salted down the rest. The days passed with the bow-wave steadily staying half-way up to the deck by the ship's great speed in the fresh wind, but I had no more luck with the fishing. On the other hand, I started to think about getting some of the many seabirds into our frying pan, or better still into our deep skilton. They often landed on deck just before sundown and I had the chore every night of chasing them away.

I never had had the heart to chase away any landbird which sometimes has landed in a more or less exhausted condition, but I have never had any sympathy for the seabirds, who in my opinion can just as well sit down and sleep on the water as they always do when *Dorothea* is not there. On deck they will make a terrible mess for me to clean up next morning when they leave without saying thanks, but worst of all, if I have any work to do on deck at night adjusting the sails they might fly up right into my face as I step on them in the dark, and on one occasion I very nearly fell over the side in the confusion. To chase them away is not as simple as one might think, because not knowing the meanness of man they are completely un-afraid. Shouting or waving my arms at them is rarely sufficient to get them to leave. I generally have to push them bodily away, only to have them circle the boat once and come right back, sometimes at the very same spot, sometimes just a few feet farther away, but also sometimes to the other end of the ship. Fortunately they never land after dark, and since they never seem to be interested in *Dorothea*'s comfort in the daytime, I only have to keep pushing them away during the ten minutes' tropical twilight to be free of them until next night.

But now as we were getting hungrier and rather tired of coconuts, I decided not to chase them away, but on the contrary get them into our galley. I tried at first to tell Simonne that food was her department and that therefore it would be her job to kill the next seabird landing on our deck, but I soon realised that her hunter's instinct was even less developed than mine, for she looked so unhappy at the thought as to almost fall into tears and absolutely refused to do any killing of any kind. So we compromised: I would kill the bird, but she would do all the cleaning, including taking off the feathers.

Just before sundown a very large bird sat down comfortably by the tiller. I could have used the gun, but its tiny ·22 bullet, I was afraid, might not kill it instantly, and should the bird just flutter his wings a few seconds it would be enough to lose him over the side, so I preferred to hit it on the head with one of the dinghy oars in a heavy blow towards the deck. Simonne hid herself down below while I was doing the killing. I raised the oar high in the air while walking towards the bird, expecting him after all to leave when seeing me in such an unfriendly posture, but he just sat where he was looking me into the eyes indifferently. Out of fear of only half doing a job, I struck with all my strength. The bird just collapsed without a sound and without moving its wings even once, but the oar was broken in two.

Simonne declared that it would teach me a lesson, but nevertheless prepared and cooked the bird as promised. A French 'gourmet' would probably have had poor thoughts of our bird's flavour, but for our hungry stomachs it seemed delicious. I decided to have seabird and coconuts every night for the rest of the trip, even if my oar was broken, but the extraordinary thing was that after that night not a single bird ever came to our deck for the rest of the voyage to New Guinea, despite the fact that we still saw as many flying around us in the daytime as before.

Pulling out what charts I had of New Guinea, I became rather apprehensive: I did have a very detailed chart of the Straits of Torres and also a chart of the land around Port Moresby, but I had absolutely nothing of the south-eastern corner of Papua where Samarai would be a perfect place for us to restock and which was several hundred miles closer than Port Moresby. To make matters worse, I knew that these were considered such dangerous waters that practically no yachts ever went there, even when well equipped with charts, crews and auxiliary motors and depth-sounders. According to the *Pilot*, the current rushed back and forth with up to eight-knot currents in some places, the positions of the many reefs were uncertain and the probability of many uncharted reefs made the waters sound rather unhealthy. Under such circumstances I would normally have made a big detour around that land, but we were getting hungry in earnest and I was fully determined to find Samarai if it was at all possible.

Reading carefully through the *Pilot*, I noticed that Samarai's longitude and latitude was given as well as the exact position of some of the islands around that part of the country. That gave me the idea of making a chart myself of as much as I could of the country from the information given in the *Pilot*. I started by taking out an old chart, laid it upside down on the chart table and drew the latitude of Samarai a little to the left of the middle, on which I wrote the longitude of the town. Then reading through the book I finally found how many miles the barrier reef stretched south of Samarai and converted the number of miles into degrees of latitude and then drew a line about an inch from the lower edge of the paper on which I wrote the calculated latitude. Then I had the desired scale for using the paper to best advantage and just divided the distance between the two lines in many lines equally spaced and wrote the correct latitude on each, then used the same scale for the longitude. (As one gets closer towards the poles the scale of latitude and longitude will become different, but close to the Equator the scale will remain almost identical.)

Then reading through the book again, I marked off all the points whose longitude and latitude were given, but when I had them all down, the chart was indeed only a succession of half a dozen points with their appropriate names, and of little help to navigate, but by reading again in the *Pilot* I would, for example, read that from one of these given positions the island would stretch in a north-westerly direction for four miles, so I would measure off four miles and mark off the other extremity of the island. A little farther on they might mention that the island's average width is $1\frac{1}{2}$ miles, so I would then make a very rough contour of the island, making it of that width. As they described the coast they would mention each bay by its name, of course presuming that we had a chart on which we could find the bay they had mentioned, but for me it was still of help, for I wrote down the names as they came and placed them where I thought proper with light pencil, until I could check them with later information, a little in the same way as we solve crosswords.

As I worked the chart became clearer and clearer, the islands showed up one after the other with all their attendant dangers and reefs, but it did take me three days of work in the rolling boat and it did give me a splitting headache which I otherwise never get, but when it was all finished and I

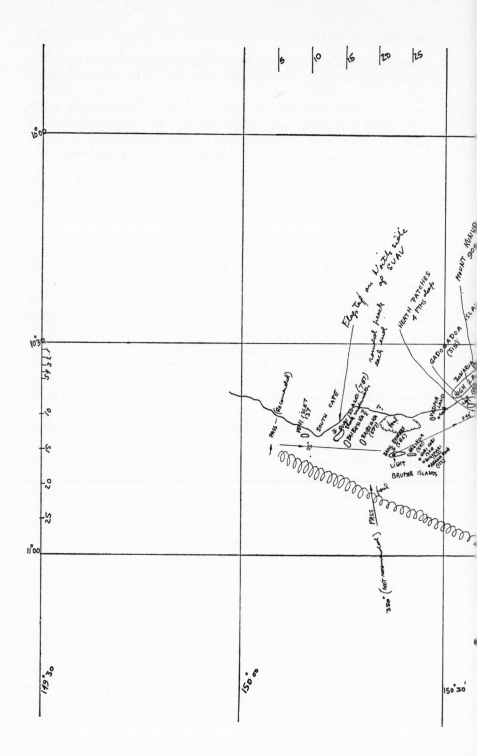

1. START FROM SAFE DISTANCE STRAIGHT NORTH AT LONG 150°37 E:-
2. Should sight Dumoulin first by its white cliffs and read 8-81 page 299 -
3. Steer straight North until lighthouse is at 245° then steer 41° about 700 yard north of Borerua Hillili
4. When western extremity of Doini Island bears 150° and is well open eastward of Rogeia, steer for anchorage -

to southeastern —

KWATO EINA KABA KWASI Rock with — 1 fm deep — A pile beacon with Triangular head stands on rock —

light from steel structure

41° lead through Anchor in 6 fathms bearing 1 at & close mud, West of Borerua Hillili

bearing 1st path, extremity of Rogeia —

KAWADO (20)

BASILAKI

SIDEIA

lowest in middle looks like a saddle well wooded

OBEIKA (30)

DOINI (510)

JEWADEKA 140

GUARA KABA OMANA (30)
OMASA RIRI (230)

CASTORI ISLETS

Doini

(sea cliffs)
DUMOULIN
OMIRI ISLET

AUA BARI BADILA
AUA WARAMA KIU KIU (175)
OMIRI (360)
AUA KARUKARUA (225)

BELL Rock (good landmark, dark colour)

WARI ISLAND (385)

BLIGHT PATCH 6 fms or less

reef

Sunken barrier reef

STUERS ISLETS (low wooded)
MARAI   TALLWEWAI

ULUMA reef

reef above water

151°00   151°30

reread the *Pilot*, checking off on my chart the route I should take to Samarai, everything seemed to fit as if the chart had been bought in a shop. I felt confident that we should be able to sail through all the reefs and safely arrive at Samarai.

On the seventh day after leaving Hiu the beautiful trade-wind weather changed to pouring rain falling so heavily as to cut visibility down to a very short distance. That was a great annoyance, because I counted on making land the following day, and it was therefore most important to get a sight that day. At ten o'clock at night I did not dare go on any farther for fear of running on to a reef during the night, as land could not be too far away. I reefed down and then hove-to until daylight. If we lost time, at least we gained on our sleep, for there is no sense in staying awake when the ship is not travelling, so we avoided that last strenuous night watch when closing up on land and when one cannot sleep.

Next morning the rain had stopped, but I was greatly annoyed to see that it was still completely overcast and there was no possibility of shooting the sun for a position line. But at least the visibility had improved sufficiently so that we would not have to be afraid of running ashore without seeing it, so I reset the sails for full speed ahead, while staying on deck and watching for land, and for discoloured water, different wave forms, breakers, or other signs of danger. At nine o'clock to my great relief a break in the clouds opened up and lasted long enough to allow me to shoot the sun. Calculating the sight it checked with my dead reckoning transferred from the last sight two days before and just two hours later I spotted land in the form of a small rock a few miles away. I did not get a sight at noon, but several other rocks and islets appeared and soon after, by taking cross bearings with the compass on the various rocks and islets, I recognised them on the home-made chart and spotted our position on the chart.

As the miles passed new islets appeared and they all checked with our chart, which was fortunate, because the sea was rough, the visibility rather poor, and among all these reefs this was no place to get lost. We crossed the sunken barrier reef with no trouble, but I soon realised that we would not have time to get all the way to Samarai before nightfall, and I had no desire at all to sail among all these dangers in the darkness, for here navigational dangers were not lit by lighthouses as they are in Europe or any other civilised places. As I steered the ship among the various islands, which became more and more numerous, I tried to determine from the chart which one would afford a reasonably safe anchorage for the night, and finally decided on one called Doini. Throwing the lead regularly over the side as we approached from the lee side, I let the sails fall on deck when I sounded six fathoms and was about 200 yards from the beach. As soon as the yacht gathered stern-way I let the anchor go, well knowing that it could then not get foul of its own cable, and after letting out slowly six times the depth of water prepared to go down below for a well-deserved rest.

We had sailed a distance equivalent from England to North Africa in just eight days, but with hardly any food. Now we had just a couple of hours' sail in the morning to get to Samarai and then we would eat and eat and eat . . . But before I had the time to get down below, an outrigger canoe paddled by one native forward and one aft and in which sat a very fat white man, came alongside.

'Welcome to Doini,' said the fat man. 'Where are you from?'

Simonne did not look a bit surprised to get confirmation that out of the cluster of islands in that vicinity we really were at the one I had said, but the fat man made no attempt to hide his surprise when Simonne said we were from Norway. Of course, Simonne with her pitch-black hair, dark eyes and gypsy blood did not exactly look like the big fair-haired girls of the North, but she felt so much a part of the ship by now that she had no intention of lying when saying it, even if the ship had not even been in Norway. We did fly the Norwegian flag and at the Antipodes, as we were now, the small distance between Norway and England seemed hardly even worth mentioning.

After recovering from his surprise he introduced himself as McGuinness, manager of the ranch and the only white man on the island. When he invited us ashore for a shower and dinner we had no greater desire than to accept gratefully, but hesitantly explained to him that we were not permitted to land before having had permission from the authorities in Samarai, and considering that we were so close they would be bound to hear about it if we landed now unlawfully. But McGuinness laughed it off, saying that the doctor, the immigration officer and the customs man were his friends, and assured us that we would get no trouble from them.

We needed no more reassurance and never regretted accepting the invitation, for even today we still remember it as one of the most pleasant evenings we have ever spent, the best meal we have ever had, and even as the most pleasant shower we have ever had, even if its plumbing was of the simplest kind, consisting of just a bucket with holes in its bottom, suspended over our head while one of the many male pareo-dressed servants poured hot water into it.

10

Papua

HERE in the quiet little bay in front of McGuinness's house the ship was well protected, the water calm, and we could sleep all through the night with no interruptions and no worries. No one who has not been at sea for weeks in a small boat can fully understand the simple joy of a restful night's sleep.

Next morning I had hardly got on deck to admire the beautiful anchorage when I saw an outrigger canoe pull out from the beach and steer for us. I hurriedly laid out my fenders for protecting my topsides. But it came alongside so carefully, without even touching them. He could hardly have been described as 'beautiful' by our standards, with his woolly hair, red-painted teeth, split ear-lobes 'decorated' with thin leather strips; indeed, the man's tiny size would have been enough to prevent anyone in our countries from considering him as handsome, for he must have been less than five feet in height. Nevertheless there was something attractive about the tiny man with his open smile, and I liked him instinctively.

'Good morning, Tabada,' he said to me.

'Good morning,' I answered, wondering why he called me 'Tabada'.

'Come in my boat, Tabada. Also Sinabada. My master wants you to have breakfast with him.'

We did not have to be asked twice, and sat down carefully in the narrow canoe. McGuinness waited for us on the beach and took us for a walk so we could have a look at his property before breakfast. He explained to us that 'Tabada' and 'Sinabada' were marks of respect a little similar to our own 'Sir' and 'Madame'. Simonne was so thrilled by the sound of the word that she called me 'Tabada' for a long time afterwards.

Among the many things our host showed us I was especially interested in what he told us when we got to his beautiful tomatoes:

'It is hard to see my tomatoes for all the bad grass growing around them and you must wonder why I don't give them more care. When I first came here to take over this plantation that was my first reaction. I therefore ordered the workers to pull up all the bad herbs despite their protests, which I thought was only caused by their laziness. Much to my surprise the tomatoes which had been beautiful became small and with many faults in them and looked rather miserable. My workers declared that it was quite natural that the tomatoes were "unhappy" and showed it when they no longer were protected by the underbrush from the scorching tropical sun. Rather as an experiment, I let the natives have their way. The jungle soon got its underbrush back and the new tomatoes were healthy-looking and of the best quality. I realised that the underbrush must indeed have protected the fragile tomatoes and held on to some of the earth dampness against the too-hot sun. Little by little I have discovered that what is true for us in our countries is not necessarily true under new skies in different climates. Now I often ask my workers for advice before taking any decisions and this habit has saved me from making many mistakes.'

I wish a man of McGuinness's experience and with his philosophy could work as a missionary instead of the narrow-minded kind which generally seem to be thriving in the tropics.

Breakfast customs vary from country to country, so we were wondering whether he believed in good heavy breakfasts or toast and coffee like the French, for we were still feeling starved despite the huge meal of the night before. We both did have a bad stomach-ache for some unknown reason, but thought that it would pass after a new good meal. We were soon reassured about the breakfast when we were led to the table, for I have rarely seen a more complete breakfast table. There were in addition to the coffee and toast, large dishes of smoked fish, fried fish, bacon, many kinds of cheeses, jams, jelly, bread and even a large plate with all kinds of fruits. As if all this was not enough, McGuinness called his servant and told him:

'Bring four eggs to Tabada and to me. Bring three eggs to Sinabada.'

We made wild protests against the order, for by now we had already had so much of all the other good things on the table that we did not think we would be able to get down that many eggs, but our host assured us that no one was ever going to leave his table hungry—a statement we easily believed. When the eggs arrived we really wondered how we were going to get them down, for never had we seen such huge eggs. At our obviously surprised faces, our host explained that they were not chicken eggs but goose eggs!

McGuinness showed us such attention and friendliness that we had the impression that we were lifelong friends who had just been reunited rather than perfect strangers at their first meeting, but nevertheless we had to say good-bye just after leaving the table, for I did not want to wait too long before arriving at Samarai for checking with the authorities, as I would run the risk that they had already got the news of a strange boat in their waters which had not checked in with them.

While we sailed towards the little town which was the port of entry for that vicinity I came to think that Simonne, who is French and never ate more than toast for breakfast, had consumed an amazing amount of food. Only then did I finally realise that her 'poor appetite' during the last days of the trip when the food supply was at its lowest had only been pretended so I would have that much more food. I was conscience-stricken at the thought that I had without thinking any further taken the greater part of the food while she had had that much less. I also had to admit that she had lost a lot of weight, but she just laughed it off when I told her of my thoughts.

'You know very well, Tabada, that I have always wanted to lose a few pounds. What better occasion could I have had?

It was just a short sail to Samarai, so soon we were dropping anchor in front of the beautiful little island, waiting for the authorities to spot our yellow flag, which did not take long. They came alongside in a little motor boat and soon fixed up the paperwork. Especially the customs officer's job was quickly done: no cigarettes, no alcohol, two sardine cans, two packages of tea, half a pound of sugar, one pound of salt and six small cans of tomato paste. Nothing more. We really had arrived at our last gasp.

We rigged up our collapsible dinghy and rowed ashore. On the dock stood many men watching us, and obviously commenting about us to each other. Some of them were dressed in European clothes, but most of them were in pareos. These pareos were, however, different from those in Tahiti, as they were each a single colour. Some were all red, some all green, and we saw many blue and even a few all white. Even the fabric seemed different from those in Tahiti, where they were always of very light cotton. These were rather thick and almost like wool. All the men were very short, and Simonne, who on high heels hardly came up to my shoulder, felt a giant for a change when standing next to them.

'It is not very often that I can look down on a man,' she declared, 'but I must say it is rather a strange and pleasant feeling for a change.'

In one of the town's two large and well-equipped shops I suddenly bumped into a practically naked woman: absolutely all she was wearing was a cute little grass skirt around her hips! She had the same woolly hair as the men, and Simonne declared on the spot that she was even more unattractive than the men, but I disagreed completely with her. In fact, I thought her rather cute. She had small, nice round shoulders without a blemish and even a Hollywood star would envy her breasts. Her face was tattooed with geometric designs going around her eyes, nose, down her neck and around each breast. I stared at her unashamedly and before Simonne had the time to announce that she thought her tattooing most ugly, I declared that it was rather attractive and certainly had the great advantage of not rubbing off on a man's shirt like a white woman's lipstick, powder and eyeshadow would.

Samarai is the only town in that part of New Guinea, so it was an important trading centre. Since there were no roads in the area, everyone travelled by boat, and most of the natives used their dug-out canoes, in which they paddled great distances. Some had as much as seven days' paddling to bring their copra or other merchandise for sale.

When the Sunday arrived we went to look at a babies' beauty competition. The children of primitives are nearly always pretty with a natural charm, but this time even with our best will we could not consider the long row of babies as pretty. In fact, neither of us could remember ever having seen such a collection of unattractive children. When the first one was presented in front of the judges Simonne had great difficulty in refraining from giggling, so ridiculous did it appear to her to present such babies in a beauty contest. But as we saw the hopeful and proud expression on each mother's face and realised how obviously proud each mother was of her child, I could see all desire to giggle had left Simonne and she even had tears in her eyes. We clearly saw and were reminded that everywhere in the world each mother always considers her own child to be the most beautiful of them all. And perhaps she is right, for what is really the definition of beauty?

There were several churches on the tiny island, and we were very surprised to see some of the natives walking in in the nude except for their grass skirts. In most of our countries women would be refused admission to churches if they were improperly dressed. Different countries, different customs. For once I witnessed priests who were broadminded enough not to try to change the local customs which had been handed down through centuries and had proved suitable for these local conditions.

In addition to the many dug-outs there were also in the harbour many native sailing ships ranging in size from just barely 20 feet overall to quite large schooners. I noticed they all had one thing in common: they were all copper sheeted. When I heard that a Norwegian was operating a shipyard just a few miles away from Samarai on the mainland, I thought it was about time I changed the old worn-out copper of *Dorothea* before the worms got into her and sank her, as has been the fate of so many wooden ships.

The slip lay in a very beautiful little bay where the jungle came right down to the water's edge. The Norwegian proved to be a Swede, but I was not too disappointed, and when the Swede told us he had to leave for a couple of months and that we would be welcome to move into his house while he was away, we made up our minds on the spot, for there is nothing we hate more than living on the boat when on the slip. The first thing we did when the Swede had left was to move all our things into his house, emptying the ship completely. We intended taking the opportunity to scrape down the wood on the inside and revarnish.

It is almost unbelievable seeing all the gear which can accumulate in a ship after a few years. It took us two days of work to carry everything up to the house half a mile away from the ship, and finally when it covered the floor of his bedroom and half the living-room we could hardly believe we had had room for it all in our little boat, yet when everything was stowed away in the ship it hardly even showed, as it was fitted so neatly. We just hoped that the Swede would not return before schedule and before we had had the time to get it back on board, for it was a sight which would have discouraged less fussy persons.

The house consisted of two bedrooms, bathroom, kitchen and a very large living-room with a corner arranged as a dining-room. That room had windows all around, and had a beautiful view all over the 'China Straits'. This was the rainy season and never have I seen so much rain in my life, except perhaps in the movies when describing a tropical rainstorm. For once the movies did not exaggerate. The rain poured down so heavily that I often preferred taking my shower in the rain rather than in the bathroom, where the water pressure was not so strong. I stood under the roof when soaping myself and only stood out in the rain when waiting to rinse off. Had I stood in the rain while trying to soap myself, it would have been rinsed off quicker than I could get it on!

It kept on raining like this day and night for as much as a whole week without stopping. Then perhaps the sun would appear, making all the water on the ground steam up like in a steam bath, so we were almost glad when after a few hours of sun the rain started all over again. These conditions did not stop the work going on. The workers kept on the job eight hours a day half nude, for no raincoat would have been any use. The rainwater was lukewarm and did not feel uncomfortable, but nevertheless I did feel a bit sorry for the men, so I rigged one of my sails over the ship and stretched it towards some trees on either side to give them a bit of protection.

The work started by stripping off all the old copper, which was quickly done, as it took only one day for four men; then the bottom was scraped down to bare wood, but then started the slow work: about 5,500 tiny nail-holes to be plugged where the old copper nails had held the old copper. It is quite common to fill the holes with just a coat of tar which is applied under all copper sheeting, but in a really good job every one of the tiny holes should be plugged with small wooden plugs which have been dipped either in glue or in paint. I insisted on this and it took two men a whole fortnight to plug the holes. When this was done the bottom was sanded down and then a thick coat of hot tar was applied while a heavy felt was stuck on the tar while still hot. Only then could the actual coppering be done.

While the men had been plugging the holes I had tried to unscrew the toilet's skin fittings, so the copper could be put under them, but much to my horror as soon as I tried to turn the bolts they snapped off at the very first try and without my applying the least force; the bolts which had been fitted just before I had bought the ship and supposedly of gunmetal were completely 'rotten' and had no more strength than if made of cardboard. Evidently they cannot have been of proper bronze, but probably just plain brass, which, of course, is no good in salt water.

I really got scared at the thought of the rotten bolts which so easily could have broken at sea, leaving nothing to hold the skin fittings in place. It would only have taken minutes to sink the ship through the huge holes which would have been left after the skin fittings had fallen off. The toilet had long annoyed me with all the trouble it had given me, and I hesitated no longer: I took out the skin fittings for good, plugged the holes securely and permanently, and took out the toilet, which I put on top of the yard's large junkheap. While I was at it I also did the same with the salt-water pump for the galley, so when we laid on the new copper I had the great satisfaction of being able to admire a perfectly slick bottom without a single hole or skin fitting to mar its continuity. Not many yachts today can claim such a beautiful feature and the safety that it means is worth more than the possible disadvantages. Now the men use the lee of the sails and the women use the plastic bucket, and I have no more worries. Simplicity is the key to peace of mind.

The tropical fever I had had off and on at regular intervals the past few years had come back, but this time it did not come in the usual violent attacks which only lasted a few days, but seemed to remain chronic and permanent, although fortunately in a much milder form. But eventually it drained my strength and I felt weak and sick. Despite my great love for the tropics, they do not seem to do me much good in the long run. The doctor told me that since the medicine did not seem to cure the fever, the best I could do was to get into another climate as quickly as possible, before it was too late. On the other hand, the port captain recommended me staying for another six months for the good season to return, for now the hurricane season was starting all over the Indian Ocean on my route to Europe, where I would get the right climate to bring back my health. I was more afraid of the sickness than of the hurricane, so I did my best to speed up the work so we could leave as fast as possible.

As much as my strength permitted, I worked with the slipworkers. They were very small men and could almost be considered pygmies. They were rather thin and had very little muscular strength, but on the other hand they seemed impervious to fatigue and worked all day long without ever slowing up in the exhausting hot and damp climate. The little man who, for example, was sandpapering down the interior to bare wood was vigorously sanding all day long without any stop whatsoever except for the hour's lunch break they had in the middle of the day. He had had a bad attack of malaria the year before which had left him 100 per cent deaf. This deafness, which prevented him from even hearing his own words, resulted in him gradually losing the use of his voice, as he could no longer correct it. When sometimes he tried to talk it was extremely difficult to understand him. He was, of course, also unable to hear my footsteps when coming on board to see how his work was getting on, and yet not once did I catch him taking a rest, while I know that I would have been exhausted within a couple of hours.

I had originally intended doing the varnishing myself, but knowing how rewarding it is to put on the shiny varnish after having done all the sanding I thought it unfair to deprive him of that pleasure and so let him do it. When it was all finished he called me over with big hand signals so I could come and admire his work. After working hours, I was much touched by seeing him call over all his fellow workers so they could also admire his work from the open hatch, for he explained to them in no uncertain terms with his gesticulations and hoarse voice that they could not go inside. When the varnish was completely hard I showed him by signs that he should rub it all down and then put on a second coat.

When I saw his face drop I realised that he thought I did not consider the job well enough done, so it had to be done all over again, and I was very upset not to be able to explain to him that the job was, on the contrary, very well done, but that it was customary always to put at least two coats of varnish on bare wood, and that a light sanding had to be done not because the first job was poorly done but because the second coat would not stick on properly unless sanding was done again. When he called me over again after the new coat had been applied he did not look exuberant like the first time, but rather almost fearful. I had intended to put on a third coat, but just did not have the heart to let him think once more that he had to do it all over again because it was not good enough, so with a big smile declared it as A.1, and only then did his eyes change from fear to overwhelming joy.

The Swede's leadman was called Jack, a most cheerful man, and it was thanks to him that all the work on the *Dorothea* was first class, for there was little Jack did not know about boats. I consider him as good as the best European craftsmen and probably a lot faster. In addition to really knowing all about small wooden craft, he also taught me a lot about the native customs. He explained to me among many other things that although most Papuans are Christians now, few of them marry legally as we do. The Papuans prefer to give some present to the girl's parents which represent our marriage ceremonies, whereupon the girl will be considered his wife. Sometimes the 'marriage' will last a lifetime, but sometimes just a few months or even just a single night. No divorce is necessary. All the man does is to leave the house and all they might have owned together, including any children which might have arrived. The man thus loses everything he might have accumulated during his marriage, but on the other hand has no further obligations for the future. The woman has a house, probably some cultivated property and whatever else they had accumulated. It will probably be enough to let the family live reasonably well and might also be more than enough to attract another man, who can then just move in without going to the effort of building a new house, and so forth. I think the system is very wise and fair. Probably the only people who would really lose on such a system in our society would be the lawyers, judges and our other society parasites.

The stay on the slip took much longer than anticipated, as it always does on slips, and almost two months had gone when all the work was finally finished, but the ship was really greatly improved, for in addition to having refastened the bottom, with huge copper rivets, recaulked her, revarnished the inside, I had also made an entirely new improved self-steering windvane, moved the chain-locker and the chain-brake to a more convenient place; I had made a combined staysail traveller and foredeck guardrail of immense strength, I had improved the galley, scraped down the mast and re-oiled it, sewn a new running sail of a strange design of which I expected great things, improved the running rigging, painted the topsides, bored the rudder's pintles oversize and then fitted a new bronze rod, as the old one had got too much play, and another thousand small jobs which all take up so much time, but which are important if one wants a comfortable and safe ship.

So when we finally hoisted the sails the season was really too far advanced to hope for favourable winds and an easy trip, but I did not want to wait in that unhealthy climate, so after a day's stay off Samarai for replenishing our stores and visiting the friends we had made there, we set sail for Torres Strait, despite it being a Friday—Friday, 19th October 1962.

11

On to Christmas Island

I DON'T know whether it was a sudden urge not to leave Papua without having seen some more of its primitive villages or whether it was just to break the bad luck likely to overshadow the voyage of a ship leaving on a Friday, but the fact is that just a few hours after having waved our friends farewell in Samarai we were dropping the hook off Suau, a small village protected by a beautiful bay.

Ashore we were met by a dozen bare-breasted women, some children and a few men, who insisted on guiding us to the top of the hill, where we met an English-speaking native who seemed to have a lot of authority and announced that he was the missionary. His house was very large and almost luxurious compared with most of those in the village, and was certainly very agreeable, with a fresh breeze blowing straight through the living-room, where he invited us to sit down. After a long talk which was most concerned with letting us know how beloved he was by everyone, he took us around for a walk to see the village and to act as sale promoter for the various items the natives wanted to sell us. I do not like high-pressure salesmanship any more in primitive places than when I lived in the States, so they soon realised they were wasting their time. I became, however, very curious about an aluminium seat which one of the natives used as an easy-rest outside his hut. When I enquired how they had acquired such a chair he explained to me that they had salvaged it from an American plane which had been shot down by the Japanese not far from the village during the war.

I would have expected people who lived so primitively and whose women even wore grass skirts not to understand anything about our wars, even if it had happened on their threshold, but I realised that on the contrary they knew very well what was happening and seemed in no doubts about which planes were Japanese and which were American.

Next day being a Saturday we thought it safe enough to start our voyage through the Torres Straits, which has such a bad reputation.

The seventh day at sea after our departure, over a sea which constantly had changed from flat calms to squally weather, the wind finally seemed to become constant and freshened more and more, while the small cumulus trade wind finally appeared. We were not too far from Bramble Island, so at the rate the ship now moved I expected to see it before nightfall. When the night fell without any land being seen, I consoled myself that we would see the light and that we had not seen the island because it was so low.

But when the full darkness had arrived and we still did not see land I was seriously worried, because if we were not in the immediate vicinity of that island, then I must have made an error in my calculations, and in this case it meant that I could just as easily be in an entirely different place among the reefs and underwater rocks the Strait is so notorious for. The currents are also both strong and irregular in this part of the world, so I was far from happy as the ship raced on in pitch darkness. Had we, on the other hand, seen the lights of Bramble Island, we would have found the entrance to that dangerous passage. Not knowing where we were, all I could do was to heave-to and hope that no current would sweep us on to some rocks during the night, but before giving up I went down to recheck my old figures, when I heard Simonne's happy voice call me from deck:

'*Viens vite. Je vois une lumière juste devant.*'

And indeed just ahead of the ship was a bright light flashing in the dark. Simonne had been both surprised and upset when the light had not at first appeared as I had said it would, for she had so far considered my sextant as a foolproof gadget, so she now seemed at ease again, and I must say that I was greatly relieved. We steered for the island, sailed around to its lee side, and then carefully approached in the black night, sounding the lead continuously. When I had eight fathoms under the keel I did not dare approach any closer in the swell, and so I let the anchor go. Less than an hour after first seeing the light we were at anchor and in bed. We had not been far away when we finally saw the light and I really cannot understand why we did not see it long before.

The next day it took a few hours to reach the next island, but from there on I had the feeling of almost being on a slalom run: to the right of that island, to the left of that one, then between those two. I had to follow closely on the chart so I would not mistake one island for another one, for it would not take a big navigational error in waters like this to wreck the ship. Though the very fact that there were so many reefs and low islands which made navigation dangerous also made it easier, for all those reefs and islands were sufficient to prevent any sea forming, while they were low enough to let the wind blow uninterrupted across them, thus we had that dream of all sailors—a fresh breeze, yet a flat sea.

In the afternoon we were outside Coconut Island, which Alain Gerbault and also Harry Pidgeon had chosen for a night anchorage, so thinking that if they had judged it safest to stop there for the night I saw no reason to tempt fate by continuing in the darkness. The island was inhabited and the natives seemed friendly, for a dozen of them or so stood by the water's edge and made big signs for us to get closer to them. Their signs were eloquent enough, but I just could not understand how it could be safe for me to get as close to the beach as they seemed to want me to, because the water looked to me at the distance I was to be rather shallow there. I always like to listen to people's advice, but I never follow it unless it sounds true and logical to me, so despite their shouts I let go the anchor at a safe distance from the beach. When I rowed ashore with Simonne I noticed that the water was indeed very shallow close to land, but soon got the explanation of their advice to get closer: they had intended to help me pull out my ship on the beach! Evidently they had no experience with keel boats.

I cannot blame them for not understanding a foreign boat unknown to them, but this did serve me as a reminder to always listen to local advice with caution. One of them, a tall negro who seemed to be a chief of some sort, took us under his protection and showed us the village. We were greatly amused by the straight and wide streets, obviously modelled on European lines, with the exception that they had not removed the trees growing in the middle of the street, which made it look rather peculiar, especially since they had even made sidewalks and we wondered how any cars could pass. The explanation was simple: there were no cars on the island! The sidewalks seemed rather superfluous, but it was just another example of the ridiculousness of importing our customs to different civilisations.

Leaving Papua we had forgotten that little item which has been the cause of so many jokes: the tin-opener. And to some people the idea that it would be possible to starve to death surrounded by countless cans of food just because of not having an opener is rather hilarious. We did not find it all that funny, but we did not starve on that account, because with a well-assorted toolbox it was still possible to open them, but I longed for a regular opener which would do the task much easier. We therefore asked if there was a store on the island and whether it was open. Our guide answered, a bit hurt, that of course they had a store. It was closed at that time of the day, but he added very chivalrously that for us it would be opened. There we did get our can-opener, and since we thought it rather embarrassing to have had the store opened just for such a small purchase, we bought a few more items like soap and more tinned food, despite the price being surprisingly high. The prices were written on each box, so I am not insinuating that we were overcharged, but we instinctively expected prices to be lower in small places, while the opposite has to be true for imported things, since, after all, transport has to be paid by the consumer.

Next morning at daybreak we continued the passage of the Strait with the same good speed and the same flat sea and enjoyable sail. By early afternoon we anchored in front of Thursday Island, with our yellow flag, awaiting the authorities, for this was a port of entry to Australia. We did not have to wait long before we were approached by a small native motor boat with an immigration officer on board who was in company with a jovial-looking man in a blood-spotted apron. They both came on board and I was much surprised to realise that the man in the blood-spotted apron was the doctor. I was to be told that he was an exceptionally capable surgeon and had come directly from the operating-room without taking time to wash up, in order to save us waiting too long for him.

The papers were soon fixed up, despite their impressive sight, but they recommended us to move a little farther over where all the native pearl-fishing boats were anchored, and added that they would be only too glad to give me a hand if it would be of any help. The wind was strong and we were pitching heavily to the anchor line, so I gladly accepted their offer, and for the first time I thought that red-tape officers could have some justification as I saw them sweat pulling in the anchor line while I sat at the tiller. After having dropped anchor at the new safer place, I rowed them ashore one at a time in the little collapsible dinghy, and Simonne was extremely satisfied to see that they looked even more insecure in the tiny dinghy than she had ever done.

Thursday Island, or simply T.I. as seamen call it, is the centre of Torres Strait and a rather important place despite its tiny size. It is considered the separating-point between the Pacific and the Indian Ocean and was therefore for us an extremely important spot: we had crossed the immense Pacific; now an entirely new ocean was ahead of us—the mysterious-sounding Indian Ocean!

Once the formalities were all completed the first thing Simonne asked me to do was to take ashore a large bundle of clothes which had had salt spray on them and which had to be rinsed in fresh water, for clothes which have been wetted by salt water will never dry unless the salt is rinsed off. Even before reaching the dock I was hailed by a tall slim guy who introduced himself as Len Foxcraft and invited me on board his 36-foot ketch *La Mouette*, where he also introduced me to his wife, Carol. He told me that he had sailed up the coast of Australia with the intention of sailing around the world. But here in T.I. 'came that thing along', he said, pointing to the floor, where a completely nude child crawled on all fours. Now they just lived on board and he had a steady job ashore. He had given up any idea of a round-the-world cruise now, he said, in a resigned voice.

When talking about common friends, about sailing and good times, the hours passed unnoticed. I suddenly realised that I had been there over two hours and hurried back to Simonne, who sat alone on the ship, waiting for me.

'But you haven't rinsed the clothes!' she exclaimed, rather surprised, as I pulled alongside. She laughed, half annoyed and half amused, when she realised that I had completely forgotten my original errand ashore.

Thursday Island proved to be a very cosy little place, with a strange Wild-West atmosphere, and we would have liked to have spent some time there, but when next day the port captain told us that it was extremely rare to have any east wind so late in the season, and that the fresh easterly now still blowing could drop any moment and would then be replaced by either calms or very strong westerlies, we decided to leave immediately. He also said that it was impossible to sail against the north-west monsoon north of the Indonesian Islands and considered it a better route to sail on the west side of Indonesia. But best of all he considered we should stay for about six months, waiting for the good season, as he had never yet seen any yachts leave this late in the season, and told us that he even doubted whether we would be able to get out of the Arafura.

Six months is a long time, so we preferred taking a chance of being able to pass despite the unfavourable time of year. I hurriedly traced off the map of the north-west corner of Australia which was nailed on the wall in his office, and as soon as it was done we rushed back on board and started to haul in the anchor, less than twenty-four hours after our arrival, in an effort to get as far as possible while the wind was favourable. We had hardly started to pull in the warp when Len came alongside looking worried and asking us if we really believed we would be able to get in the anchor and sail out of the crowded harbour in that strong wind without hitting any of the native boats all around me. I replied, as I knew he hoped I would, that it would indeed be much easier if he came on board and gave a hand. I did not have to ask him twice. Almost instantly he was on board with his dinghy made fast aft.

I knew instinctively that he was a first-class sailor, and we worked silently together as if we had been on the same sailing team for years. The sails came up and we broke out the anchor in an elegant manoeuvre between the pearl-shell fishing-boat fleet while we were watched carefully by the many crews. In short tacks we zigzagged out of the anchorage with the bow-wave high on both sides of the ship. Len's eyes shone with pleasure as I gave him the tiller and he steered for the dock where he had his boat. As *Dorothea* came close to his boat he gave me back the tiller and jumped into his dinghy, while Simonne held her breath for fear he would capsize the little dinghy at the speed we were going.

Most good-byes sound much alike: 'Good-bye and have a good sail' or something like that, but Len forgot these conventional phrases. He just mumbled: 'Damn lucky fellow . . . I wonder if I will ever get the sails up on my own boat . . .'

More I did not hear as the *Dorothea*, heeling over in a squall, shot away in a spray of water. Soon we were far away, but turning back I still could see Len standing up in his dinghy, watching us fade away in the distance.

In the very fresh following wind it did not take us long to pass the last of the Torres Straits Islands, and already I had visions of a record-breaking crossing of the Arafura Sea, but unfortunately by midnight the wind weakened and by next morning we were in an absolute calm on a sea which seemed never to have been disturbed by any wind whatsoever. For the next two weeks the flat calm was only interrupted by very light breezes which lasted a few hours each time, permitting us to coast along on the flat sea, and was surprisingly enough to give us more than fifty miles a day average speed.

The heat was absolutely scorching and it was impossible to walk on the deck without burning our feet unless we wetted the deck first. In the middle of the day, when the sun was directly overhead and the sails did not give us any shade, we had to stay below, where the heat was indeed bad enough, but where we did at least have protection from the sun's rays. We did not lie on the bunk, as our sweat would soon have transformed the mattress into a soggy mess, but lay on the bare wood of the cabin floor, which anyway felt cooler than any mattress or cushion could have done. The sea was so flat that we left all the hatches and portholes wide open, which is contrary to our habits, as we consider it too dangerous should a sudden squall arrive, but here in the Arafura the thought that it could ever blow seemed impossible to us.

The sea was strange to us in this area: the water was covered with a thick layer of dust as if dirty, but was probably due to the vicinity of the Australian desert and previous winds blowing from that direction. We also saw for the first time in our lives sea serpents, which were lazily undulating their way on the surface, but we saw that when they wanted to they could also swim below the water. We later heard that the bite of one of these serpents was so poisonous as to cause death. We were glad we had been sufficiently scared of sharks not to have swum in those waters, but just contented ourselves throwing buckets of sea water on each other.

Around Arnhemsland and through the Gulf of Van Dieman our lead showed on many occasions just a few feet of water under our keel. Since the water there most of all looked like mud, I sorely missed a more detailed chart and also a tide-table but we finally arrived safely at Darwin seventeen days after leaving Thursday Island. It had not been a fast passage, but considering the flat sea and the lack of wind it was rather surprising that we are not still there.

When thinking about Australia I always imagined a temperate climate, but I forgot about Australia's huge size, which allows the southern end to be in a rather cool climate while the northern end of the country is very much in the tropics. Neither of us had ever felt a land with such terrific heat or with such a scorching sun, but then we had also arrived in November, which is the warmest time of the year. But even if the heat was terrific at least it was not raining and the air seemed dry and healthy, which was more than could have been said about Papua. Next day when I rowed ashore my clothes were soaked by my sweat even before reaching the dock.

The Australian aborigines are not very highly esteemed in Australia, despite the fact that they were the original inhabitants before the white man came and stole their country, and it is the same problem as it was in the States with the Indians. A new-comer is a foreigner only as long as he is in the minority. As soon as he gets so numerous as to leave the original inhabitants in the minority, he will not only feel at home, but even consider the original inhabitants as a nuisance and undesirable. '*La raison du plus fort est toujours la meilleure*', said La Fontaine a long time ago, and those words will always remain true.

One of the laws discriminating the natives made me rather mad, as I thought it an outrageous restraint on personal freedom: any white man caught alone with an aborigene woman is liable to a year's imprisonment! But after having seen a few native women (at a safe distance) I thought that the temptation must be rather easy to overcome, for they were really not much to look at.

We soon made friends in Darwin, and one of them who had a vacation village on the other side of the fjord invited us to spend twenty-four hours with him, as it was the off season and he had not a single guest, so we could choose any one of the bungalows for ourselves. We do not as a rule like leaving the ship alone at night, but we made an exception, as we thought it would be fun to see how people spend their vacations on this side of the earth, and we also liked Karter, our proposed host, so we accepted with pleasure.

We chose a bungalow about two miles away from the main building, and since the place was deserted and we were practically in the bush we had no hesitation in this terrible heat in sleeping in the nude with all windows and doors wide open.

At three o'clock in the morning Simonne got up to pay a visit to the little house which was about fifty yards from our bungalow. She saw no reason to put on any clothes in this wilderness, and since the moonlight was bathing the whole landscape in its light she felt sure she would not lose her way, but hardly had she taken a few steps outside the door when she turned around screaming with fear and slammed the door behind her. Begging me to lock all the windows, she sobbed, almost hysterical with fear:

'There was a horrible-looking man standing just outside the door. I almost ran into him. Oh, he looked like a monster and must have been abnormal . . .'

When she had calmed down a bit she admitted that he could not have been a dangerous man, for he had fled in the opposite direction as soon as he had seen her standing in front of him, but nevertheless we found it safer to sleep for the remainder of the night with everything shut and locked, despite the terrific heat and the sensation of choking from lack of air. Simonne was unable to describe the man any further, for she had turned around the very instant she had seen him in the moonlight and she had in addition only been half awake. We were rather intrigued about who that Peeping Tom could have been, for Karter had assured us that absolutely no one lived on this side of the fjord except him and his wife. The only thing Simonne was sure about was that the man had had some sort of infirmity and she also remembered clearly that his footsteps had made a peculiar rhythmic sound as he had run away.

Next morning at the breakfast-table we told our hosts about the night's happenings. They listened carefully to our tale until they suddenly both burst out laughing. Simonne and I looked at each other a bit surprised and almost annoyed, as we could not see what was so funny about having a man looking at us in our bedroom. After a while our hosts' laughter calmed down and they explained, still frequently interrupted by fits of laughter when they were unable to speak, that it had been no man outside our windows, but just a kangaroo, of which there were many in that region!

The fifth day after our arrival in Darwin we hoisted sails again despite the harbourmaster's protests, who told us that the hurricane season along the north-west coast of Australia had begun and we would be wise to hole up right here in Darwin during its duration. Maybe the gods agreed with him, for no matter how hard I sailed over the anchor it refused to come up. I finally had to lower the sails again and dive down to free the anchor.

The water proved to be so full of mud that I could only just see my own hand when I held it about ten inches in front of me. Anything farther than that disappeared in a thick fog. By putting my face just inches away from the rope I was able to see where it was caught, so I could undo it around each sharp piece of wreckage, but even though all the time I expected the rope to come completely free, there was always another snag a few feet farther on. I finally did get the anchor freed, but more than an hour had elapsed since I first started. It was with great relief that I got out of the water and finally set the course for Christmas Island in the Indian Ocean on our way to the Red Sea and Europe.

It was only the following day when land had long since vanished below the horizon that Simonne confessed to me that one of my new 'friends' had tried to persuade her to leave me and to marry him. I should probably have been mad, but I could not help laughing when I heard that he had proposed to her while I was at the police station making a complaint about my bicycle which had been stolen, and while he had waited for me in his car with Simonne just outside. I still remembered how much I had thanked him for driving me to the police station and giving us the ride and how nice I thought it had been of him to suggest it when he had heard that my bike had been stolen. I had been so annoyed about having my dinghy's rowlocks stolen the very first day we left it ashore, and then two days later having lost my bicycle despite the heavy chain I had used to attach it to the dock, but I realised now that I could have lost a lot more. The fact that I had saved my anchor and my crew made me almost laugh about the loss of the rowlocks and the bike.

When Christopher Columbus finally had seen land come up over the horizon he thought he had arrived in India. Even today the land he came to is called the West Indies. Many will smile over his mistake and think that he was very naïve to underestimate the size of the world to such a degree, yet it was far more excusable than most of the people who criticise him, for most of them also grossly underestimate the size of our world, despite the fact that today we have accurate globes for sale in almost any paper store. Many people think that once we have crossed the Atlantic Ocean we are about half-way around the world, and would be surprised to see that the Pacific Ocean is more than twice the size of 'our great Atlantic', and that it is not until we are on the opposite side of the Pacific that we have finally reached the half-way mark around the earth! Those who claim that the earth is small can never have tried sailing around it in a small boat.

We were now on our way from Darwin to Aden and the Red Sea. That is a distance equivalent to from England to the Galapagos. I doubted if our forty-five-gallon water tank would be sufficient for such a long trip, and that had made us decide to make a stop at Christmas Island on the way for replenishing our water stocks.

The hurricane season had started, but while a tropical hurricane is to be regarded with great respect when in any ship, and particularly so when in a ship of *Dorothea*'s size, I still was not too worried, because I considered that the danger was in this case very small, thanks to the accurate charts I had of the hurricane tracks which would enable me to avoid all of them by sailing a few zigzags over the ocean and thus lay my track where the hurricanes never blew. All but one of them could thus be avoided, the hurricane blowing along the north-west coast of Australia and just about where we now were. But after all, hurricanes do not blow all the time even at the height of the hurricane season, so I thought it would be exceptionally bad luck if one blew just during the two days it would take us to get through the danger area, given a good wind.

But despite all my logical reasoning I started to worry when I saw the barometer falling, the clouds getting blacker and blacker, while the wind picked up an alarming strength just while we were in that one dangerous spot. When the sea got white from the breaking seas I cursed my bad luck while reefing down the sails and wondering what steps to take when the full force of the approaching hurricane would be upon us. I recalled with awe the only hurricane I had ever been in before, and had never forgotten how close to foundering I had been, yet then I had been in *Windflower*. I wondered if this hurricane would be the end of us.

Simonne, who is a fatalist and firmly believes that no one can escape or change their destiny, had calmly gone to bed, which was the only place we felt reasonably comfortable when the going got rough, and had taken the transistor with her for listening to dance music. Suddenly the music was interrupted by the news. It was the station at Darwin. Among many other things they announced that two of the ships in the harbour had dragged their anchors in the morning's violent squall, but not a word was said about any hurricane! So it was certainly the same squall we were getting now. My spirits soared and I hurried up on deck and shook out one of the reefs, thus carrying the maximum canvas I dared in the strong wind in an effort to make the most speed possible while the squall lasted, and get as far as possible out of this critical region before we risked being becalmed and thus 'sitting ducks' for a real hurricane, which, of course, would come sooner or later. Two days later we were indeed becalmed, but by then we were out of danger.

The rest of the trip to Christmas Island went with light breezes and variable winds, often interrupted with calms. The sea stayed calm and life on board was agreeable. We had returned to our habits of the sea. Every morning I read the day's paper on the veranda—that is, I sat in the cockpit while Simonne prepared breakfast, and she handed me the two pieces of newspaper which had served to wrap the eggs and I always read wnat was on them before finally throwing them over the side. When I was ready to throw them I would always call Simonne so she could also see them dis-appear behind the ship. It sounded strange that that should be of any interest, but in an empty ocean, where the eye has no real point to rest, to prove for us that we are getting anywhere it is a most satisfying feeling to see the two small pieces of paper being left behind while the ship definitely moves away towards a new horizon. It also helped us to estimate our speed, which we could check with the noon sights when the wind was constant for a twenty-four-hour period.

'Five and a half knots,' I would declare.

'Five and a quarter,' Simonne would argue, and surprisingly enough our estimates were often within a quarter of a knot from the real speed, which is as good as any log could have told us, so we never missed not having such an instrument.

In addition to cooking, Simonne read many books and magazines; she played solitary card games and slept about twelve hours a day. I took care of the sail trimming, adjusting of the pilot, the celestial navigation, sewed a few feet each day on the new jib which I had cut and marked before departure, read travel stories and worked on the design of the new boat I planned to build after my return to Europe. If I did not sleep twelve hours a day like Simonne, I slept at least eight, but it was generally an interrupted sleep, for I often had to go on deck during the night to trim the sails or for taking in reefs when weather conditions changed, but I found that it did not matter too much if sleep was frequently interrupted as long as the total amount of sleep in any twenty-four-hour period was sufficient. The days passed rapidly and we were never bored at sea, contrary to what most people seem to think, as so many have asked us: 'But, dear, what do you do with yourself all alone in that little boat?'

The sixteenth day we saw the island creep out of the horizon in the sunset. Next day we sailed into the open bay which is the harbour of Christmas Island. Six jolly fellows came towards us in an open motor boat while waving beer cans and shouting 'Skaal' as soon as they saw our Norwegian flag. This, however, proved to be the extent of their Norwegian language, so it was in English that they suggested helping us tie up to one of the huge buoys which served to make the steamships fast. This is one of the world's deepest harbours and no ship can anchor on its own cables.

The harbourmaster soon came over to check our papers. When I saw him react about my name I knew that he must have known my uncle, who is a ship's captain and often sails in the Indian Ocean. And indeed as soon as I had told him that I was a nephew of Captain Lyder Tangvald there were no limits to his friendliness and he even invited us to dinner in his home. But he did also advise us to leave the island as fast as possible, for soon the hurricane belt would stretch all the way to the island and the port was far from safe. He added with a smile that had the port been safe he would on the contrary have forbidden us to go out to sea at this time of the year. We therefore were to stay only three days on the island despite the fantastic hospitality shown us during our stay. We were invited from one house to the next for dinner, lunch, tea, and to look over their houses. We were taken to the fascinating native restaurants and to picnics on the beach. In fact, the only meal we ate on our own in the boat was breakfast. There were many Indians and Chinese on the islands and they had strongly influenced the food in the restaurants, which to us seemed very strange and foreign. They had also brought their customs of dressing themselves, so we almost had the impression of being in the Far East rather than in Australian territory.

Three days went by fast, and soon we were standing on the pier among our new friends, saying good-bye. Only then did Simonne suddenly think about sending a letter to her parents, and therefore she asked me to row her on board so she could get it written. I had long thought that it was rather ridiculous that a girl who was sailing around the world could not even row a dinghy, so I took advantage of the situation to force her to try on her own for once. Very unwillingly she finally stepped down in the dinghy all alone, after I had promised to keep an eye on her in case she should drift out to sea. The sea was perfectly flat that day and she finally managed to get alongside *Dorothea*. But much to my horror I saw that as she stood up in the dinghy to get on board she lost her balance, capsized the dinghy and fell in the water.

She is a very good swimmer, but in common with most girls she is quite unable to hoist herself on board alone from the water, so since these waters are reputed to be very dangerous on account of sharks, my first thought was to swim over to the ship without losing a moment in order to help her quickly on board, but when I saw that an outrigger canoe near by *Dorothea* was rushing over to her I calmed down, as I knew that they would be there much before me. But much to my surprise, when the canoe came close to her it just stopped, and from where I stood it looked as if the two men on board the canoe just sat there and stared, making no effort to help her. Later, when it was all over, Simonne told me what had happened:

'Can you imagine anyone but Englishmen being so formal! Here I am in the water with my skirt and petticoat around my ears, hardly able to keep afloat, my high-heeled shoes floating away, also my bag and both oars, the dinghy is turned upside down and everyone knows that the sharks are dangerous here, but do you know what those two men asked? They just said, "Is everything all right, mad'm?" '

Simonne, who laughs easily, had so little expected such a question that she had laughed and had swallowed water before she had been able to tell them that everything was not at all all right and that she would very much like to get on board before the sharks spotted her. Only then had the men felt entitled to go into action (with a woman they had not been introduced to). In a flash one man jumped on board *Dorothea* and soon had pulled her out of the water, while the other went hunting for all the things which had drifted away.

The French speak as much with their hands as with their tongues, so I had no difficulty in understanding Simonne's signs of despair all the way from the dock as she stood soaking wet on *Dorothea*'s deck, that the row-locks had been lost as the dinghy had capsized. It was indeed rather annoying, as it was our last pair, and I felt sure it would be impossible to get them replaced until we returned to Europe. Her gesticulations were also understood by a man standing next to me, whom I had never seen before and who showed such an interest in the happening that he even wanted to know what size they had been. A couple of hours later we stayed on deck saying good-bye to the friends who had come alongside with their small outboards. Among them I recognised the man on the dock, who silently handed me a brand-new pair of rowlocks which he had just made specially for us in a metal shop!

And he was not the only one to show us extraordinary kindness: on deck were bags of fresh fruit, home-baked cakes, a ten-gallon can with kerosene and even a very large bottle of water which must have held about twelve gallons. They were worried about us getting becalmed in the notorious horse latitude where the old square riggers sometimes laid so long waiting for wind that they more than once had had to jettison all live animals for lack of fresh water to give them. From all the dead horses floating in the wind-still belts around the Equator had come the name 'the Horse Latitudes'.

Despite all the tragic stories dating from the square riggers, I was not particularly worried, because I knew that a small boat like *Dorothea* needs so much less wind to get moving than the larger boats, and as long as we moved at all it would only be a question of time before we got through the doldrums and to the trades on the other side.

The daily average close to the Equator would certainly be very modest, but then I counted on perhaps as much as a steady 145 miles in the north-east trade, so I thought a total average of 100 miles a day would not be too optimistic, or in other words about forty-four days. But I was soon to regret such a prophecy, for we had hardly come out of the bay when the wind fell completely and left us standing absolutely still, hour after hour, still well in sight of all our friends on shore. What I did not yet know at the time was that the postmaster was adding on the back of my letter to my parents: '*Dorothea* is leaving today the 11th December for Aden. If she continues at the same speed she will arrive there at Christmas . . . next year.'

One of the native fishing boats which passed us by Minicoy Island. (Indian Ocean)

The paint was worn down upon our arrival in Aden.

Dorothea under full sails, steering herself while the Skipper watches his landfall. (Among the Greek Islands)

The Skipper displaying the flags of the many countries visited, as *Dorothea* is sailing into Chichester harbor after having circumnavigated the world.

By midnight I started to worry at the thought that we would still be lying there next morning when everybody woke up for a new day, but fortunately a breeze finally came, as it always does if one just waits long enough, and by sun-up we were far on our way and the island had disappeared below the horizon.

12

Across the Indian Ocean

THE first few days after leaving Christmas Island we covered between 128 miles and 140 miles each day, measured in a straight distance from noon to noon position, but on the fifteenth we made less than 100 miles. The trades were dying down and we were approaching the doldrums which circle practically the whole world close to the Equator.

It was the following night that we were struck by a strange perfume. I thought at first that Simonne had opened some unknown perfume bottle, but she was just as surprised as I was. The wind had moderated to a very light breeze. We both were sitting on deck discussing how fast the stars' position had changed in the sky as we had moved north when the strange perfume enveloped us. We were several hundred miles from land—no smell could possibly reach us from there. A little later it disappeared and we would probably have forgotten about it had it not been that on the next day, when looking through one of the many books we had on board, we read about the valuable ambergris which floats about the seas and which under some circumstances can emit a wonderful perfume, and that it is this very smell which leads to its discovery.

We read further that even today its value is about the same as for gold and that one single piece of ambergris sometimes weighs several hundred pounds. The substance is ejected from sperm whales under certain special circumstances and its rareness causes its value, because it is much used in the perfume industry. We quickly estimated that it must have been a whole fortune we had by-passed in the dark without having had the sense to pick it up; our immediate reaction was to turn around and search for it, but we soon realised that the chances to hit its exact spot were practically nil, so we just sailed on with no new fortune, but on the other hand not any poorer either.

We have since learned that in the old time of sailing ships ambergris was often found just where we had been. The fact that it was rarely found today in that part of the ocean or any other ocean did not mean that it did not exist any more, but it merely stands to reason that from the deck of a fast-travelling and ill-smelling motor ship the chances of picking up ambergris at sea would be rather slim. Ambergris is frequently found washed up on the shores of the Maldive Islands, where at certain times of the year the currents bear it right across the ocean and on to those islands.

We now came to the dreaded doldrums, which had to be crossed before we got the north-east monsoon. The calms would be interrupted by the violent squalls which sometimes could heel the ship far over, even with all canvas lowered.

On an average we covered about seventy miles a day, except the day before Christmas Eve with only forty-eight, and Christmas Day with fifty-one. But if the speed went down on those two days we made up for it with the wonderful home-baked cakes Simonne specially made in her small bouncing galley. I thought it strange to think that in the same moment back home in Norway my old friends were also having home-baked cakes for the holidays, but there they would be muffled up in woollens at exactly the same time as we were perspiring, dressed pretty close to what Adam and Eve are claimed to have worn. It was indeed even a bit too hot for comfort, but then we were very close to the Equator, which we crossed on 26th December to be exact. However, we did not complain about the heat, for we knew that we soon enough would be out of the tropics and home again, when we would be missing the tropics' warmth.

A few days later we saw the Stella Polaris, the North Star, low over the horizon and not at all at the great height I had seen it in Norway or even in France, but nevertheless it was as if we were already home again. At least we had proof that we were home in our northern hemisphere.

If we were rather lucky in our passage through the feared doldrums, we were rather out of luck with the north-east monsoon. We encountered instead the outer edges of a large cyclonic disturbance which was to last for a full ten days, with miserable black skies, pouring rain and gale-force winds from the direction in which we wanted to go. The ship's motion became very tiring, as we were plunging closehauled through heavy seas whose crest came on board and washed across the decks from forward clear aft, so everything had to be kept closed. Only when we approached Minicoy, an island south-west of India, did the weather finally improve and even let me get a shot of the sun between two clouds so I could verify our position, before running on to any of the Maldive Islands, which I knew we were approaching.

By eleven o'clock on 9th January we spotted land in the distance and a few hours later we sailed through a small armada of native fishing boats which could as well have been cut out of a book from *The Thousand and One Nights* with their two-masted Lateen rig and their striking colour combinations. And these strange craft which have probably not changed much for the last thousand years or more were far from slow. They were faster than *Dorothea*, which with her high freeboard, short overhangs, and single colour did not come out to best advantage among these much slimmer and lower craft. They were crowded with men who stared as much at us as we on them, for if they presented a strange sight to us we must have looked no less strange to their eyes, as these islands were indeed off the beaten track and they might never have seen a yacht there before.

I longed to sail into the lagoon through the pass and visit that little-known island, which to us would have been doubly fascinating, because we had never seen any Oriental islands before, but unfortunately the only port of entrance was in Male, several hundred miles farther south, and I had heard that written permission had to be obtained from the Sultan in Male and shown to the authorities of any island in the group that we visited. Not daring to risk trouble with authorities in such strange countries, we thought it wisest to by-pass the island without stopping. We just hugged the beach and the coast as far as possible and I climbed into the rigging with my binoculars in an effort to see as much as possible of the village by the lagoon.

The island seemed to have been the turning-point for all our bad luck with the weather, as it continued to improve, and soon we got back our lovely small cumulus clouds, steady and strong following breeze which was to last for the rest of the trip. With almost dry decks we raced ahead of the large ocean swell and covered between 145 and 155 miles each day without having to touch either tiller, self-steering gear or a single rope of the rigging for many days on end.

Very often porpoises would keep us company and they seemed to like jumping out of the water just ahead of the bow-wave, and just a few feet below me, which gave me a spectacle of more grace and beauty than any grand orchestra seat could ever have offered. They were always two and two together—man and wife, I suppose. They jumped always together and always re-entered the water without making the slightest splash. While it was easy to feel that *Dorothea* was going at her top speed and that it took great forces accumulated in the sails to drive her as fast as they did, the dolphins seemed just to be cruising effortlessly without expending any energy at all. On a few occasions I saw some of them take off in a burst of speed so great that it was almost unbelievable had I not seen it myself in real life. They certainly have adapted themselves nicely for life in the water, even to the extent of having a most convenient breathing hole in the top of their heads of the same kind as the one I have always wished to have whenever I swim. They even have a valve fitted to its orifice and I could easily see it getting opened and closed the very moment their heads came out of the water and dived in again.

As usual it was through our little transistor radio that we got our first contact with a new continent. For the last few days all we had been able to get was the strange Arabic music, but while we would have preferred something from Armstrong, we did not complain for this music promised us a new land with new customs and for us a new civilisation.

On 24th January we spotted land and soon we were entering the large bay leading to Aden harbour. A slim motor boat of typical English design came towards us with half a dozen white-clad officers on board. In the still heavily running swell I hung out my two big aeroplane tyres which have saved me from damage many times before, but I need not have worried. Immigration officers in British-run countries are the most polite and have the minimum of red tape. The motor boat just made a large turn next to us and then followed us, keeping safely at a few yards' distance while the following conversation took place:

'What is the name of your ship, sir?'

'*Dorothea*,' I called back.

'What was your last port, sir?'

'Christmas Island.'

Christmas Island was pretty much on the other side of the Indian Ocean and about 4,400 miles away, which would be the equivalent of a non-stop round trip from England over to Newfoundland and back again, but had we expected any of them to show any surprise we were disappointed. Not one of the phlegmatic officers showed the least reaction, their faces remained as impassive as if they had been told we came from the neighbouring town.

'Is anyone sick on board?'

'No, we are fine.'

'In that case you may take down your yellow flag, sir, but would you please check in at the harbourmaster's office at your earliest convenience. You will find a good place to tie up down there.'

When I promised to go to the port office they wished me a 'Good day' and were off to more important matters. If all countries were as easy on visiting yachtsmen, cruising would indeed be even more pleasant.

Aden was indeed a new world for us. The tropical vegetation we had become so used to had disappeared. The country was like a desert—only rocks and sand. It was scorching hot, but it was a dry heat which did not feel as tiring or as unhealthy as the damp heat we had known. Ashore the formalities were done with a friendly smile in a matter of a few minutes; we were thrilled with this new world.

On the street itself we saw several men prostrating themselves with their foreheads to the ground, saying their prayers, while paying no attention whatsoever to the people or the cars around them. Others lay asleep on narrow beds placed alongside the outside walls in the streets. The crowd in the street walking past their beds did not seem to disturb them. The women were mostly wrapped up in dresses which reached all the way to the ground, and they had large veils around their heads and faces, leaving only their eyes visible. But contrary to what one might suppose, it is still easy to distinguish between a plain woman and a beautiful one. The dresses might have covered most of the woman's skin, but its light weight did not prevent a man from evaluating a woman's figure through the thin fabric which moulded and followed the contours of the body. Nor did it hide the grace of a woman's walk. Some of the men were also in dresses, but these were of an entirely different kind and there was nothing feminine about them.

We tried to find a restaurant, for after so many days at sea we were anxious to have some fresh food again, but as we tried to open a restaurant's closed door we were sharply told that this was Ramadan and no one was supposed to eat before sundown. Fortunately the food stores were open, so we bought the fruit and vegetables we wanted to eat on board. Meanwhile, I sent a postcard to our friends at Christmas Island telling them that we had 'arrived on schedule'. It was, of course, an almost unbelievable coincidence that it should have taken us exactly the forty-four days I had told them it would.

The boat had been completely painted in Papua, yet now, hardly three months later, the paint was so badly worn that the bare wood showed through in several places on her topsides, having been worn down by the constant friction of the waves against the boat for many thousands of miles. Fortunately, painting a ship's topsides while afloat is very easy when the bottom is coppered and ends well above the waterline. Thus a harbour's wavelets will not reach as high as where we are painting and there is no difficulty in getting a straight waterline: all we have to do is to paint down to the copper.

While I was busy with this work a white boat appeared from among all the colourful native boats at anchor: it was a yacht! The first yacht we had seen since leaving Bora-Bora, if we discounted Len's boat in Thursday Island, which in any case had almost become a houseboat. When we consider that Bora-Bora was by now almost on the opposite side of the world, it can be understood that we were rather excited. I laid aside the paintbrush and watched them. She was a 44-foot Bermudian ketch called *Betina*, and she proved to be the American yacht which had left for Suez the day before my arrival, after having had a three weeks' motor overhaul in Aden. Two days after her departure her stern bearing had become so loose that they had considered it safest to turn back to Aden for a new repair.

Together we were to study the charts of the Red Sea and to discuss its problems with the many submerged reefs, some of them out of sight of land and most of them unmarked by beacons or lighthouses, its constant north wind which for us would be a dead headwind, and its unfriendly coast where lately several yachts had been shot at from shore when trying to anchor. I even remembered that in one yacht several people had been wounded by gunfire from shore and the story had been published in *Life* magazine. *Betina*'s skipper told me about a friend of his who just a few months earlier had gone aground on one of the treacherous submerged reefs in the middle of the night about eighty miles south of Suez.

They also showed me a couple of newspaper clippings about two other yachts which had been wrecked within the last twelve months, and when they finally reminded me that no yacht had ever done the voyage without a motor I almost regretted not having chosen the route south of Africa; but I consoled myself by recalling that no matter from which port I had set sail before, people, friends and the authorities had nearly always tried to discourage me for one reason or another. I told myself that if there was a risk of being shot at, all I had to do was to stay away from the coast; if there was a danger with underwater reefs, I should be extra careful with my navigation, and since they are most of them on the charts there should be little danger in that respect, since I had invested in very detailed charts for this voyage. The north wind really seemed to be constant, judging from all accounts, but then *Dorothea* is an unusually good boat to windward, and after all, didn't the natives of those shores navigate even in antiquity, so why shouldn't we also?

On 30th January we took on stores for the voyage, filled the water tank and made the last preparations. The next day, seven days after our arrival, we sailed out to sea again, little knowing that all the dangers we had foreseen were to be insignificant compared with the calamity which was to strike us on the way to Suez.

13

Red Sea Passage

THE wind was good and we could not have hoped for any better weather in which to start our voyage. I kept watch most of the night, as we were hugging the coast towards Perim, the actual entrance to the Red Sea, and Simonne did not trust herself in judging distances in the dark should the ship have approached land dangerously. Next day we entered the Red Sea by Perim by ten o'clock, pushed by a very strong following wind from the south.

We were overjoyed at not getting the north wind we had expected and did not take in any reefs in the sail, in an effort to make the best use out of the favourable wind.

The sea became, in fact, very rough and we were carrying so much canvas that the bulwarks were rolled deep under the sea. When the port navigation light was washed away I finally came to my senses and reduced sail. I only wished I had done it a little earlier, for the loss of a navigation light in such crowded waters is a serious handicap. All I could replace it with was the all-round white paraffin pressure lamp we had on board, but as dinner was just ready by then I decided to light it afterwards, and to guard against our being run down during our meal I would take a quick look around from the hatch every ten minutes.

I don't know whether I had not looked properly the time before or whether a local fog patch had hidden its lights from me, or whether a good deal more than ten minutes had elapsed since my last look-out, but when I got my head out of the hatch, still with my fork in my hand, I was horrified to see a towering wall alongside, and almost in the same second a man leaning over the side from the bridge, immediately followed by several others at his shout of 'There is a boat down there'—which we guessed at more than heard in the whistling of the wind and the roar of the waves.

We had not been aware of each other's presence until just a few yards apart. Fortunately we were on parallel courses and did not touch, but nevertheless it showed me once more that a few minutes' carelessness at sea is sufficient to cause accidents and even death. Needless to say,

I lost no more time in getting the pressure lamp lit and hung in the rigging.

Next morning the wind moderated, so I shook out one of the two reefs I had tied in the previous day and a few hours later I took out the remaining reef. It was pleasant sailing, but not for long: soon the wind died down completely and left us bouncing in the choppy sea, which was still running high from yesterday's strong winds. Next morning the wind came back, but this time from the north-north-west, or in other words, dead against us—and there it was to remain for the rest of the trip to Suez. We tacked back and forth across the Red Sea I don't know how many times. Crossing the steamship lane I worried about collisions, and I could not sail many miles either side of the lane without worrying about the many submerged reefs.

Sometimes the wind was light and pleasant, even if it was against us, but very often it was strong and made such a steep uncomfortable sea that life on board became extremely tiring, due to the violent motion of the ship plunging through the seas which washed clear across the decks from stem to stern. We had to keep all the hatches closed, which at first in the hot climate made us feel as if we were suffocating inside the little cabin, but as we moved northwards the lack of fresh air was not felt as much, as the climate was cooling considerably, and we were, in fact, freezing miserably at the end of the voyage, for this was mid-winter and the wind was blowing straight down from Russia.

All this, however, we knew that we had had to expect before even starting. What we had not expected was that Simonne was to become seriously ill. Women in the tropics often experience feminine troubles, so we did not worry too much at first, but she became so weak that she stayed in bed most of the time. I decided to steer for Port Sudan and let the doctors there have a look at her. On the way to that port the wind stayed very light and the sea became smooth and pleasant. *Dorothea*'s motion became smooth, and perhaps this was the reason for Simonne getting better. In any case, when we were ready to sail into Port Sudan, Simonne assured me that the crisis was over and that she would soon be fit again. So we by-passed the only place with a hospital before Suez.

The wind stayed light and pleasant for a few more days and we made as good time as we could expect when beating. We covered about 120 miles each day through the water, but due to the tacking we made only about 60 or 65 towards Suez, which was still very good under the circumstances. Then the wind increased, I had to gradually reef down in the quickly rising sea, the motion became violent and was to stay like that for the rest of the trip.

When we were about half-way between Port Sudan and Suez, Simonne had a relapse. Now I know that I should have turned around and in the strong north wind we would have made good time back to Port Sudan, where its hospital would have been welcome after all. It is so easy to be wise afterwards! At the time I did not know that it was to be any more serious than the first time, nor could I know that the wind would not turn sufficiently to let us lay our course for Suez. Indeed, for all I knew, if we did turn around, counting on the north wind, it could even die down and be replaced with a southerly wind. Northerly winds were strongly predominant, but if we count on a predominant wind it will often fail us.

In any case, I did not turn around and thought that the best thing to do was to let Simonne rest as much as possible and drive *Dorothea* at her greatest possible speed for Suez. Two days later Simonne was so weak that she was unable to get out of her bunk at all and had to be nursed like a baby.

I was terrified, and from then on the voyage was to become a real nightmare. Simonne was rapidly getting weaker and could hardly talk. I was afraid that she would die, and once I even thought that she was dead. While trying to talk to me her eyes closed in the middle of a word and her head fell on one side; I could not feel her breath and I was near despair when she finally opened her eyes again—she had only fainted. I was considering stopping a steamer and getting her transferred to it, but most boats—if not all—were tankers, and there would be no doctors on board; but perhaps a north-bound ship would get her to Suez quicker than I could.

By staying in the middle of the shipping lane with the appropriate signals a ship could not fail to stop for us. Lying alongside in the choppy sea *Dorothea* would almost certainly be stove-in and fatally damaged, but under the circumstances I only considered that a minor detail; what worried me, and finally made me give up the idea of stopping a steamship was that I doubted very much if Simonne could survive the rough transfer up the sides of the steamer. In fact, I did not even know how I could get her up on to the deck of the bouncing *Dorothea* through its narrow hatch without causing her a fatal injury in her weakened condition. I saw no other solution but to rush to Suez.

Later Simonne confided to me that during that time she had really thought she was dying and had worried so much about all the troubles I would get into because of her, when arriving in port with a corpse!

The medical books I had on board were all as useful as usual: 'Call the doctor' was their advice!

I kept watch all through the nights, as the lamp was often being blown out by the strong wind and the spray, despite the manufacturer's claim that it was a 'hurricane' lamp and would not blow out in any wind. I slept during the day-time for about half an hour at a time, as I did not trust the steamers even in broad daylight, after having seen on two occasions tankers cut my route less than a hundred yards ahead of my bow.

As we entered the very narrow northern part of the Red Sea which is called the Gulf of Suez, I was near exhaustion with worry, lack of sleep and navigational difficulties, and the five steps I had to take on the ladder in order to get to the deck seemed a terrible effort. Had I been alone I would have looked for a quiet bay in which to anchor and get some rest, but it seemed obvious that Simonne would die if we did not get to a hospital soon.

I will never forget the night we entered the narrow Gulf. The traffic was so heavy that I sometimes counted as many as twelve ships at a time coming in a long line, one after the other. The wind had increased to near gale force and the motion was incredibly rough. I had given up keeping the light burning, as the solid spray coming continually on board would blow it out even before I could hang it in the rigging. With no light to show *Dorothea* I did not dare cross the shipping lane, so I always came about before reaching it. In the rough sea and in my exhausted condition it was no child's play to make the manoeuvre. It was blowing far too much to be able to come about head on to the wind, for, even admitting that the ship would not refuse to tack in the steep sea, the sails shaking into the wind would flog themselves to pieces long before the ship had steadied herself on the new tack.

Contrary to the general belief of the smooth-water sailor, coming about with the wind astern and jibbing the sail over is a much safer manoeuvre and it will put much less strain on the rigging if it is done correctly. However, the disadvantage about that manoeuvre was that I was losing a couple of hundred yards each time, which in narrow waters will add up to a considerable loss. I had to make the tacks as long as possible if I wanted ever to get out of these very restricted waters where sleep was absolutely impossible. On the tack toward the shipping lane I could visually estimate when it was time to come about, but it was much more difficult and uncertain when on the tack towards the reefs.

According to my charts, this part of the Red Sea should have many lighthouses, but I could see only one at first. Only when using my powerful night binoculars did I finally spot the faint flashes of the other lighthouses. With two or more lighthouses in sight at the same time it is theoretically easy to determine the exact position of the ship without having to come about unnecessarily soon, but in practice it is not so easy. The flying spray soaked the binoculars, making them useless until I had dried them again; then I had to find a flash of light in the pitch dark and from the heaving deck take a compass bearing which had to be plotted on the chart. When those lines showed that we were near the reef, then I would come about. All this time I had to force my eyes to see straight, for if I relaxed I could get a double vision, as drunken men are supposed to.

The wind had by now increased to what I estimated to be Force 9, and I knew that I was carrying too much sail, even though I had just the small staysail and the main reefed down as far as it would go and had taken in the jib long ago; I should have changed to the heavy flax storm sail, especially as I was using the spare machine-sewn one which I had purchased in Tahiti. I knew I should change to the storm sail, but I had not the strength to do it. Besides, I considered it too dangerous in those restricted waters and in the dark, so I decided to wait till day-time.

Each time I went below I looked at Simonne, hoping for a miracle, but she stayed in the same state of half-consciousness. I was in despair, but our troubles were far from over. The next time I went about I sensed rather than saw that the mainsail had split from leech to luff, probably along one of the seams, just like a zipper. Before I even got half-way to the mast to lower the sail a vicious shaking made the whole ship vibrate. It lasted just a few seconds, but when it was over I knew that the sail had gone. It was easy to lower the little that remained still hanging to the bolt rope. The remains went over the side as the ship drifted to leeward under her staysail. I now had to get the storm sail up.

I staggered down below to get it out of the sail locker, and I still today remember that when I arrived at the main hatch, having dragged the heavy sail after me on the floor, I was so tired that I doubted if I could ever get the sail up the ladder and then to the foot of the mast to bend it on. But I did get it on after a long struggle, frequently interrupted by the necessity of taking bearings and for veering the ship as she drifted back and forth between the reefs and the shipping lane.

Daylight came at long last. I saw then that the sea looked even nastier than I had expected. No wonder the old sail went to pieces! When close to one of the north-bound steamers I saw that she was throwing spray clear up to her main bridge. I kept sailing all that day and finally got through the narrowest part of the Gulf. As another night approached I realised that I would not be able to control the ship until morning. If I did not fall asleep, I would just collapse. I was not far from a little bay which on the chart seemed to afford reasonable shelter. I could see two small steamships at anchor there, apparently waiting for the gale to moderate. I steered between them and dropped the hook. As soon as the sails were securely lashed I went down below and practically collapsed next to the near-lifeless figure of Simonne.

It was late afternoon when I woke up. I had slept about eighteen hours! But before realising that I had slept that much and while still half asleep, my first thought was for Simonne: she was awake and turned her head towards me, smiling. Thank Heaven, she was still alive. My second thought was to rush on deck and see if we were not getting too close to reefs or steamships, but as I got up I suddenly remembered that we were at anchor. We were, in fact, fairly well protected.

The two steamships had gone and the weather seemed to have moderated considerably. Simonne was able to talk again and looked much better. She even thought that the haemorrhage had stopped or at least considerably calmed down, and felt confident that she was no longer in danger. But I was sure that the sooner she could get a blood transfusion the better it would be.

Since the beginning of her sickness she had not wanted any food. I fed her a cup of soup with a small spoon, as she was too weak even to sit up in her bunk. I then made a hurried dinner for myself, but when it was finished and I intended to set sail again Simonne begged me to wait till next day at least. If we waited till next day, the sea might be flat and smooth and she would be more rested and better able to withstand the remaining voyage to Suez.

I suspect that the real reason was her desire to let me get some more rest, as she must have understood how near collapse I had been from lack of sleep. In any case, it was easy for her to talk me into delaying the voyage, because I was indeed far from rested and had already worried about the long watch during the coming night. And perhaps it had been for the best to have waited, because the next morning she looked a lot better and had no longer that terrible look in her eyes of people very near death. As for me, I no longer had the feeling that my legs were not strong enough to carry my body. And even the sea was as flat as a pond, but we still had enough breeze to make good speed.

It blew, however, still from the north, so it took us until the following day to get in sight of Suez. The flat sea had been a blessing for Simonne, for far from getting worse after having left the anchorage she steadily improved. As I made ready to enter port she begged me not to call a doctor, as she felt absolutely sure that this time it was all over and that the only thing she needed was rest. I have the same dislike that she has about calling a doctor, so I could well understand her desire to avoid one now, and I therefore decided to respect her wish, but she did finally have to have an operation when we arrived at Rhodes four weeks later. After the operation the doctor told me that we could not possibly realise how near death she had been. 'In fact,' he added, 'technically speaking, from the way she looks inside, she should be dead. That girl must have an iron constitution.'

As I sailed past the lighthouse by the entrance to Suez harbour its crew rang the bell and waved to me, which I thought a rather nice welcome gesture. In a freshening breeze I entered the inner harbour, which was rather crowded with craft of all shapes and types, but I found a vacant berth where I made fast as the ship came gently alongside. Twenty-four days had gone by since we had hoisted sail in Aden. It had been a fast voyage, yet to me it seemed like the longest voyage I had ever done. As for Simonne, I suspect that time had ceased to exist altogether.

Before arriving in a new country one generally has already some idea of what one expects to see. However, very often reality does not fit the mental picture which we have formed before arrival. Simonne, who improved rapidly, soon foresaw the day she would be able to walk ashore and see the Pyramids, the Sphinx and Cairo. She was greatly disappointed when we learned that we would not be permitted to leave the harbour district. Diplomatic relations between France and Egypt had been broken, the French Embassy and Consulates closed and French people were on the whole unwelcome.

Personally I did not care about either the Pyramids or the Sphinx, but I did get annoyed with the many teenagers who frequently threw stones at me, with the many beggars who did not take 'No' as an answer, with the storekeepers who hardly ever gave me the right change, and perhaps most of all with the endless red tape which never seemed to end despite the services of an agent. We had originally planned to stay several months in Egypt, resting and waiting for spring, as March is still winter in the Mediterranean, but with common accord we soon decided to brave the cold weather and sail the 360 miles to Rhodes in the Greek Islands, where we felt sure we would find a more pleasant atmosphere. It should be an easy trip except for the cold, and with luck should take no more than three days.

I usually never hire the services of an agent, as I prefer to avoid the expenses of middlemen, but as I had been told that Egypt was the one place where I would never be able to get through the red tape on my own, I had made an exception and had called up a reputed firm which had been recommended to me by a friend. We agreed on a total fee of £5, which I thought well worth the trouble it would save me. I gave the agent all the ship's papers he asked for, including the ship's log, but far from relieving me from all work I still had to wait endless hours in various offices to give my signature. When permission to use the Canal was finally granted I was presented with a bill for £58. I thought at first that it was an error and pointed out that we had agreed on a total fee of only £5.

'Certainly, sir. Five pounds is all we are charging you in fees. The rest are expenses,' said the man with the most charming business smile.

In addition to this I had to pay £14 for a tow through the Canal which I did not want but had to accept because recent changes in the regulations forbade sailing in the Canal. The tug proved to be an old dilapidated barge barely able to pull us at four knots in still weather, and when it started to blow from forward of the beam the speed dropped to barely two knots. The skipper made big signals over to us from his barge, clearly wanting me to hoist my sails in order to help. I hoisted the staysail, but could only hoist a small part of the main, as otherwise I would have either rammed him in the stern or passed him and taken him in tow. As it was, we were up to the original speed of four knots, but I thought that I was getting rather poor value for my money, because I could have sailed much faster on my own and it would have been a pleasant sail on that still water.

It took us three days in transit, as we anchored at night. The second evening we anchored off the Ismailia Yacht Club, where we were promptly invited to have dinner as the President's guest, and he proved to be a most charming host.

Behind the club were moored several yachts, and to our great surprise we recognised the *Svea* amongst them. Nearly two years had passed since its owners, the Kittredges, had waved us good-bye in Bora-Bora. They were just as surprised as we were and we chatted till late into the night.

Nineteen days and twenty-two hours after having dropped the sails when entering Suez we sailed out to sea again, passing close by the broken socle on which the statue of Ferdinand de Lesseps had stood until the Egyptians took control of the Canal and demolished the statue of the man who had built it.

The wind was cold and forced us to lay closehauled, but it did not prevent us from laying our course, and we made good speed. We were glad to get away from Egypt's police state and we were already reading travel folders about the Greek Islands and looked forward to a long stay in that beautiful archipelago.

Right after dinner Simonne felt seasick and vomited her food, which did not really surprise us too much, because even after a fairly short stay in port she would be seasick the first two or three days at sea before regaining her sea-legs. However, we did find it very strange when I also felt rather sick, as I had become very resistant to seasickness. I very nearly vomited, but was just able to keep down my food. Had we then understood that it was not seasickness but food poisoning, we could have avoided most of the ensuing miseries by vomiting, then drinking a lot of liquid and by putting a finger down our throats to make us vomit again until the stomach would be washed clean. Unfortunately we did not understand what was happening to us until it was too late.

During the night Simonne complained about having terrible pains in her chest and arms and as the night went on it became obvious to me that she was indeed very sick. She could hardly talk and seemed to have great difficulty in breathing. When I counted her pulse I was horrified to find it was 110. According to the medical book I had on board, pains in the chest and the arm could mean a heart attack, even though unusual in a young person, and all I could do was to help her rest. Next morning to my great surprise I started to get the same pains and my left arm, in addition to being extremely painful, became almost paralysed. The chances that we at our age should both have heart attacks at the same time was highly improbable and I wondered what other sickness it could have been, when it dawned on me that it could only be some kind of food poisoning.[1]

Almost twenty hours had elapsed since the meal which had made us feel seasick, so I considered it was too late to be any use vomiting. All I could do was to wait and hope that the poisoning would not be too serious. During the afternoon Simonne felt a little better and her pulse went down to a hundred, but I was feeling gradually worse. When sick at sea good weather would be a blessing, but our luck was not with us, and perhaps we had no right to expect any in that respect, for this was the equinox. During the afternoon the wind gradually increased and forced me to reduce sail, despite the pains which made every movement an agony. By evening it was blowing Force 7 and seemed to keep on increasing, while the barometer kept on falling. Not knowing how much worse I would become, during the night I thought it would be wisest to reef down completely and heave-to the ship.

It sometimes pays to be pessimistic, because the wind did indeed increase and I was to become so sick as to be unable to do any work on deck at all. The wind increased to probably a Force 9 and possibly more during the night. Breaking seas crashed on deck and against the coachroof with such violence that we almost expected the roof to fly off and let the ocean fill the ship. The ship heeled over steeply despite the tiny size of the reefed-down sails. Yet the gale seemed a minor drawback, especially since all precautions had already been taken and no further work was required. On the other hand, we worried about being so sick alone at sea. In the early morning before daybreak, my pulse was 110, my head ached terribly, the pains in my chest were unbearable and I had great difficulty in breathing. By daybreak Simonne was feeling a lot better and during that day recovered completely, but I became gradually worse. Next day, with my

[1] Yet our first diagnosis was the correct one: we both did have heart-trouble. A year and a half later, just a few days after having written this manuscript, I was again stricken by the same pains but this time I was not at sea and thus could get a doctor to come to me. The cause was soon determined as a chronic heart infection with occasional crises. This finally explained all the fevers, 'influenzas', 'malaria' and general poor health I had had these past few years and which I had wrongly blamed on the tropical climate. This time I was to stay six months in bed, four of them in hospital, before recuperating.

pulse at 120, I was in agony and could not move at all, barely being able to breathe. I seriously thought that I was dying, and Simonne told me later that she had been terrified.

The next day my eyesight was back to normal and it was a little easier to breathe, so despite the pains which were still as sharp I became cheerful, as I felt the crisis was over and I would soon be well. The weather had also moderated and was, according to Simonne, who looked out of the hatch, only about Force 4 or 5. She would have been unable to set the ship on course, but I felt confident that next day I would be well and could continue the sail. But I was rejoicing too early, for during that night I had a relapse and felt worse than before, if that was at all possible. I lay then for three more days in such agony as to almost lose my mind from the terrible pains which never eased a moment, either by day or night. Simonne nursed me and hung up the white light every night.

Finally, five days after having hove-to the ship I felt well enough to get out of bed, take a few sun sights and set the course towards Rhodes again, helped by Simonne, who did most of the work, as I had no strength whatsoever; each movement gave me greater pains and in addition I was so dizzy that I had to hold on even when sitting for fear of falling over. We were going very slowly, as it had seemed altogether too much work for us to shake out the reefs. It was another two days before I felt able to hoist the full mainsail, still helped by Simonne, who hung on the halyard with all her weight.

The next day, the ninth day after our departure from Egypt, we sighted land ahead of us. A rapidly freshening south-easterly wind gave us a good speed, but as the glass was falling at an alarming rate we worried about whether or not we would be able to enter port. According to the *Pilot* it was very dangerous and at times impossible to enter the harbour of Rhodes in strong south-easterly winds. Of all the winds of the compass we had to have the one and only one with which the harbour could not be entered!

We decided to keep on the same course, hoping for the wind not to increase any further or to turn from another direction. If it really proved too dangerous to enter, we could then probably sail around the island and anchor in its lee. I was, however, not very anxious to try this last solution, because even if I thought I would be able to let the anchor fall over the side I knew that should the wind turn while we were at anchor and change our sheltered beach to a lee shore, we would be unable to get the anchor back on board and to do the necessary manoeuvre to get away from an anchorage which had become dangerous. Could we just get inside the port, then our worries would be over and we could get doctors, medicine, fresh food and new stores, because not knowing which of our food had caused us to be sick we hardly dared eat any of it.

To our great despair the wind kept on increasing, and by the time we were outside the harbour it was blowing a moderate gale, but when we looked at the entrance through the binoculars we could not see any breakers of importance, so disregarding the *Pilot*, which often had proved to be too pessimistic, we decided to chance it. The mainsheet was hauled in a bit by our united efforts, as I knew I would be unable to get it in fast as we turned into the basin, and it was safest to do it ahead of time. While I then steered with one hand, using the other to hold on to the rail, as I was still so dizzy that I thought I might fall over the side, Simonne went forward and undid the lashings of the small anchor which then hung freely under the bowsprit ready to let go if she undid the anchor warp.

I sighted for the middle of the outer harbour and once there laid the tiller over to get the ship to enter the inner harbour, between the two foundations on which the Hercules of Rhodes had straddled in antiquity. We passed through a vicious boiling sea, but it only lasted a few seconds, then the water became wonderfully calm and we were partially protected from the wind. Nevertheless it still blew hard enough to make us enter at a terrifying speed. Right in the middle of the tiny port I luffed the ship and signalled to Simonne to release the anchor while I crawled to the mast and undid the halyards. The sails only came partially down in the strong wind, but I did not care: it was enough to prevent the ship from forging ahead. I stumbled back to the main hatch and practically collapsed in bed, from where I was not to move for almost a fortnight.

As through a fog I could hear a powerful voice from shore ordering us immediately to hoist anchor and come alongside, as we were hindering the traffic, and I could hear Simonne's frantic voice that her captain was sick and that she could not get the anchor up and that we needed a doctor. The voice from shore shouted back that we would get the doctor when we came alongside and not until then.

A couple of hours later a launch came alongside with a very furious harbourmaster, but when he saw how sick I was he not only calmed down immediately but could not have been more helpful and kind. He had thought that it was the quarantine doctor that we had wanted, and apologised for having misunderstood the situation, as he otherwise would have brought a doctor immediately. As it was, he personally hauled up the anchor with the help of his sailor and towed us to a good and safe berth where he tied up the ship even more securely than I could have done myself. He then told his sailor to rush to get the doctor, while he furled the sails in a neater roll than it had been possible for Simonne to do, and then asked for additional gaskets to secure the sails and make it impossible for even the strongest wind to unfurl them.

The doctor was soon there. As he entered the cabin and before he had spotted me in the low bunk, he faced Simonne, and after just one glance at her stretched out his hand and wrung her eyelid so violently that I thought he would tear it off, and then exclaimed in very good French:

'But my dear friend, where have you been? What have you done to yourself? You look as if you don't have a drop of blood in your body!'

But Simonne still wanted no medical examination and insisted that she was perfectly fit and that I was the sick one if he would just turn around and look at me where I lay. So I was ordered rest and some medicine, but I knew that the crisis had been over several days earlier and that all I needed was indeed just rest.

That night the wind increased to such a pitch as to blow gravel and small stones from the dock all over our deck and even down the hatch and into the saloon. I was thankful for the safe harbour and the conscientious job the harbourmaster had done in tying us to the dock.

A few days later it became obvious that Simonne was getting ill again from her Red Sea troubles, and she finally had to see a doctor, who put her immediately on the operating-table. Thus the memory we have of our first fortnight in Greece is mostly of sickness and doctors, but we finally both recovered our health and were able to appreciate the wonderful islands in which we had arrived.

14

From Grecian Isles to France

WE were to love Greece and its many islands. The people were extremely nice to us and there was none of the cheating we experienced in the Arab countries. Prices were low and we always got the right change back. The merchandise was of the best quality and the market, which was just a hundred yards from where we were moored, was both convenient and very well stocked. Despite the language barrier we knew that we were back in Europe and felt almost at home.

Many tourists, including some Norwegians, were in the island, and when they saw *Dorothea*'s flag they often called over to ask if I 'had really sailed all the way from home in that little sailing boat'. Some of them wanted to know whether I had sailed through the French canals or the 'long' way around Gibraltar. One couple to whom I answered that I had taken neither of those routes, but had come by way of Panama and Suez, burst out laughing; I would not be surprised if they still think that I was joking.

We were the only yacht there at first, except for a couple of laid-up auxiliaries with just a paid hand on board, but as the warm weather arrived so did the yachts. Among them was the *Lua-Lua*, a home-made steel yacht from South Africa which had sailed up the Red Sea a few weeks after us and was on its way to be sold in the South of France.

And then to our great pleasure we saw one day the *Svea* power into port and anchor next to us. In the days that followed we went regularly to restaurants together and, as we felt almost like natives by this time, we showed them the town and acted as their guides. But to them Rhodes was just another stop and they soon made ready to sail to the next island. To us the charming little port had almost become like a home, but when they suggested that we should also leave so we could sail in company, we became aware of the time passing and that if we wanted to see something more of the Mediterranean before Simonne's leave of absence ended we should indeed sail soon.

So on the last day of April we sailed out of the friendly little port, headed for Symi, a small island with a beautiful anchorage in front of a

300-year-old monastery which the priest told us had taken twenty years to build. Today a building of that size would probably be built in three years, but it would never last three hundred; and yet from the condition of this monastery the passing years had hardly left a trace and there was no reason why it should not last another three hundred years.

From Symi we sailed to Kos, then to Kalymnos, making a stop in tiny Pseremos on the way; then to Leros, where our paths parted, as *Svea* wanted to sail down to Crete, while we wanted to see the ancient town in Delos and then visit Athens, where Simonne had set her heart on seeing the Acropolis.

Perhaps the island that made the greatest impression on me was tiny Delos. I had been interested in seeing the ruins, but I also knew that it was uninhabited now except for a few keepers, and I honestly thought that one afternoon would be enough to satisfy us and we then would sail over to famous Mykenos and there spend a few days. Ruins and museums had to me always been interesting, but also a bit boring if one saw too much of them. I had vivid memories of all the endless hours I had spent being dragged around various museums by my mother while a child in Paris.

But Delos was different. Here were no endless collections of broken pottery secure behind glass doors away from their natural surroundings. Here was, in fact, a whole town! Mostly in ruins, it is true, but some of the houses were in such good condition that they could have been used today, and been quite comfortable even by our twentieth-century standards. One house in particular caught our fancy: as we entered the gate we came to a large beautiful patio into which the rooms faced. The roof of the house was open over this patio, but there were no windows or any openings in the outer walls. This arrangement must have given far more privacy than we are used to in our houses today, while still giving adequate air and light to all the rooms in the house, with the added advantage of dampening the street noises.

The rooms next to the patio were brightly lit from the sunlight, but the inner rooms were, in fact, too dim, until I realised that these were the bedrooms and they had been wiser than we are today when they purposely made them dark: don't we sleep better in a dark room? Isn't it much more intimate? Also the best way to avoid the nuisance of flies is to keep a room dark. The walls were very thick, made of stones and covered with a sort of plaster which in some places was still in the original condition. The floors were decorated with delicate mosaics whose beautiful colours were still delightful after 2,500 years.

There is no water on the island, yet many thousands of people had lived there. They had solved the water problem by building several large cisterns in which rain-water collected during the rainy season. In addition to the public cisterns, one of which was filled by the water running down the slopes of the amphitheatre, each house had its own private cistern, generally dug under the patio and filled by the rain-water from the roof. They had access to their cisterns through beautiful marble 'wells'.

In one tiny room I noticed a small hole in a two-foot high seat, which was, in fact, a W.C., more than two thousand years old! Its 'plumbing' was a stone canal carefully enclosed which led under the house and was connected to the sewer canals under the streets. Its covering was now in a bad state of repair, but it allowed me to see where it led and to confirm for myself that it was really going all the way down to the sea. To flush it they simply must have thrown a bucket of water in the hole, basically the same as our system today. We have not invented as many things as we lay claim to, but admittedly we did not see any signs of television, although they did have theatres, complete even to the ticket-seller's box by the entrance.

From Delos we sailed to Wouliagmeni, a small harbour especially built for yachts and extremely nicely arranged. Each yacht had her own mooring forward with her stern to the quay, so it was easy to get ashore, and sufficient room was allowed between each yacht, so there was no need to put out any fenders. Ashore there were a small restaurant, showers, a cleaner and a laundry. A short bus ride took us into Athens, where Simonne had her wishes fulfilled by seeing the Acropolis, but it was a disappointment to me after having seen Delos, for between the buildings of a modern city and the myriads of tourists the spell was broken and to me the Acropolis was just a large pile of old stones; I missed the beautiful Delos, where we had been all alone surrounded by the blue water.

Cruising in Greece is not only interesting historically but it is a wonderful playground for yachtsmen. Some say that its sudden gales make sailing miserable, but what does an occasional gale matter when there are myriads of islands never far away where a safe harbour can be found until the wind moderates? The sun is warm and so is the water, the harbours are plentiful and most of them enchanting, people are friendly and living is cheap. What more can a yachtsman ask for?

On the seventh day at sea after having left Wouliagmeni we expected to see Malta and make port before nightfall, but despite having had beautiful sunny weather and a nearly flat sea the whole way so far, it had rained all that day and visibility was very limited. The wind had become very fresh from the east and gave us good speed towards port, but it also made Malta a lee shore, which was not too cheerful a thought with the barometer falling steadily, seas building up rapidly and no chance to shoot the sun in order to verify our position.

According to our D.R. transferred from the previous day's sights we should have been within five miles of the port, yet we could not see any land and there were only two more hours of daylight! According to the Bible it was on this shore that St. Paul was shipwrecked *en route* to Rome, which was no comfort. I considered heaving-to for the night, hoping to be able to check the sun next day, when we finally saw land dead ahead and quite close: the D.R. had been accurate, the visibility had just been poor, for normally we should see land much farther away than five miles, except such very low land as a South Pacific atoll. Less than an hour later we were securely anchored in the inner harbour, after having entered it at a great speed, pushed by the fresh wind.

We were to stay eighteen days in Malta and we enjoyed every minute of it. We made several friends among the Maltese yachtsmen and they took us for automobile rides in their beautiful little country, showed us the best restaurants, invited us to their homes, and generally contributed to make our stay one of the most pleasant we have ever had anywhere.

Historically Malta is very interesting, but what really fascinated me was the underground temple which was discovered by accident just a few years ago when a house-owner had decided to drill under his house for a well. The temple, dating back to about 4000 B.C., was found in perfect condition, and consisted of several rooms, one of which must have been a burial place, as the remains of several thousand skeletons rested there. Some of the bones were still in sufficiently good condition to be identified and showing that the twentieth-century man is much taller than his long-forgotten fore-fathers.

What was to impress me so greatly was a small hole dug into the wall of the inner chamber: when a man talked in front of that hole in a quite natural voice a very strange and awe-inspiring reverberation would repeat his words in a multiple echo-like sound. If a woman talked into the hole with her higher-pitched voice, no echo or anything unusual happened. We can well imagine to what use the priests could put this phenomenon, but we must presume that, as unusual as this acoustic effect is, they must have discovered it by accident when having cut the hole for one reason or another. Even the greatest sound specialist today would be completely incapable of producing such an effect, so how could anyone 6,000 years ago have any control over such acoustics? Yet it is easy to prove that they did know how to produce this sound effect, because on Malta there are several other temples of similar design, except that they are above the ground, and though varying considerably in size, all of them have the same shaped hole in one of the rooms.

Until the underground temple was found that strange hole had made even the greatest historians wonder in vain what they could be for. No echo came out of them, but that is only natural, because those temples were all more or less in ruins. Not until the discovery of the underground temple, which was in perfect shape and whose acoustics had not been upset, did one realise the use of these holes, and we realised that at least some prehistoric people knew more about some subjects than modern man knows today.

From one of the rooms a narrow and dark staircase with irregular steps led down to a deep pit after the seventh and last step. Anyone unaware would just suppose that the eighth step was a little deeper among those other irregular steps and would not realise he was stepping into empty space until it was too late. The fall would probably break a limb, but in any case it would have been impossible to climb out, as the walls were cut in smooth rock and offered no handhold. What was the purpose of that pit? It was simply a trap for thieves who might have noticed the priest using that staircase when storing offerings. What the thieves could not guess was that in the dark the priest, having reached the seventh step, would turn sharply to the right, where a narrow ledge would lead to the treasure room. The remains of two skeletons were found in the bottom of the pit, and it can easily be imagined that their agonising cries would have discouraged any other thieves from following them.

Next day, after having said good-bye to our friends, we hoisted sails again—this time headed straight for Marseilles, where Simonne's family must have grown impatient to see her again after three years' separation.

The trip to Marseilles was to be done at our slowest average speed, because the winds, in addition to remaining extremely light, would constantly change direction, thus forcing me continually to readjust the sails and the pilot. After having woken on several occasions and seen that the boat had gone completely about and was pointing back towards Malta, I decided to heave-to every night from ten o'clock until next morning at five, when I would again set the course for Marseilles. We thus slept happily all through the night under the protection of an all-round white light to prevent steamers from running us down (presuming, of course, that they did keep a watch). It was a slow way of travelling, but it was pleasant and restful.

Along the coast of Sardinia we sailed so close to shore that we could do some 'sightseeing' right from our deck, using our powerful binoculars, so even if neither of us ever did set foot on that land we still both feel that we know the country quite well. North of Sardinia we passed through the Bonifacio Strait, hugging the coast of Corsica without stopping and finally setting the course straight for Marseilles. We made our landfall on the thirteenth day after our departure from Malta, and Simonne recognised it immediately as 'Les Deux Freres', as she had played there often as a child, little knowing that one day the mountain's two peaks would be the first sight she would see of her old country after a long sail from the tropics in a small sailing boat.

Soon we were securely moored inside the Vieux Port in Marseilles, and after being told that the authorities had more important things to do than waste time with yachtsmen, we simply took down our yellow flag and went ashore, wishing that it could always be that trouble-free. A taxi soon took us to Simonne's home, where she was greeted like a long-lost child, and in the days that followed a long stream of her friends came to visit us on board. They knew she had arrived, because the newspaper had an article about the home-coming of a Marseilles girl who had almost done the trip around the world in a small yacht and was the first woman to do so in an engineless boat.

Simonne's leave of absence from the French public schools would end by the middle of September, and we were informed that her application for a position in Marseilles had not been granted, and that she was to work in Cannes for at least one year. It was a disappointment for her, but I must admit that however much I liked Marseilles it was still a big noisy city and the idea of spending the winter in fabulous Cannes pleased me immensely. Her working week consisted of only seventeen hours and she would also have countless holidays in addition to three months' summer vacation, and almost a fortnight free both at Christmas and at Easter. We would have plenty of time together to enjoy the advantages of the French Riviera.

After a four weeks' stay in port we sailed for Cannes, but decided to stop in every little port on the way and travel the slow way for a change. We first stopped in the beautiful miniature 'fjord' of Sormiou, where we visited a friend of Simonne's who had a small summer cottage there. Then we sailed to the charming town of Cassis, then Bandol, where many foreign yachts seem to gather: then beautiful Porquerolles, where a well-designed cruising yacht with an exhausted-looking crew anchored next to us and informed us that we could have no idea about how exhausting long crossings could be: they had come all the way from Corsica without making any stops and had been all of twenty-six hours at sea without touching any port!

Then we made a short stop at Port Cros before sailing to crowded St. Tropez of world fame, then St. Raphael and finally to Cannes, where we were to meet many old friends.

Mermaid, with George Clisby, whom I had laid alongside in the tropical harbour of St. Croix in the West Indies, passed through Cannes a little after our arrival. She was on her way back to the tropics, after having sailed from there across the Atlantic shortly before I had set the course for the Pacific. Then passed the *Sea Fever* with the Alexanders, whom I had been moored close by in Los Angeles while there in the *Windflower*, and then again in Papeete with the *Dorothea*. And then in early spring came the *Svea* on her way to Spain and spent about a week in the port, moored next to us.

In addition to these long-distance yachts which we had met before we were soon to meet several local boats, including the 30-foot steel sloop *Ia-Ora-Na*, specially built for a world cruise, the tiny *Jean Marie*, which looked too small for crossing oceans except that she was sister ship to *4 Winds* in which Marcel Bordiaux sailed singlehanded around the world via Cape Horn, and finally the *Long Courrier*, where I spent many hours happily talking: these boats were fitting out for that long dream-cruise to Tahiti, to the West Indies, to Australia, or for a voyage 'all-the-way-around'. Some came asking me for advice and some came giving me advice.

One man told me that the waters I had been in so far had been easy; it was those yet ahead of me which would be hard, if indeed I could make it at all: the passage from France to Gibraltar was almost impossible to do under sail and then even if I succeeded in getting to the straits it would be absolutely impossible for a boat like *Dorothea* to get through it without a motor. I had, however, heard such warnings so many times before, no matter where I was sailing from, that I did not listen too much to it.

It is indeed rather strange that yachtsmen everywhere in the world always seem to consider their own waters and those immediately below their own horizons as the most difficult in the whole world. Everything else is easy according to them.

Before leaving England I was told that the hardest of the whole trip to Tahiti would be to get down to Spain. 'If you can just make Vigo and safely get across the Bay of Biscay, the rest will be a piece of cake.' I arrived at Vigo overjoyed because I had no more difficulties ahead of me, but what do I hear? 'Across the Bay of Biscay you might get wind, but you would have had lots of sea room. Now you have the difficult part ahead of you: the coast of Portugal is famous the world over for its violent storms and you won't get any sea room should it blow onshore, which is usual when stormy. But if you can just get clear of the south point of Portugal it will be easy, and once you have reached Casablanca you won't have any more troubles. Then it will be a piece of cake.'

It was disappointing to learn that I still had a difficult stretch to do, but after that I would be able to relax. Imagine my surprise when an old salt in Casa told me that I had better be careful on the way to the Canaries, because those waters have the most unpredictable storms in the world and in addition the coast was so low and visibility often so cut down by the desert sands blown across the sea as to make navigation most hazardous.

At Las Palmas the warnings did not stop: 'You might have been through stormy areas, but you have never had far to get to port. Now you have three thousand miles of open sea where no one can come to help you should you get in trouble.'

Well, there always seemed to be something. In the West Indies—'You might have had cold waters and gales and tides, but you have never seen a tropical storm, which will uproot trees and throw steamships several hundred yards inland.'

In Panama: 'You can heave-to in a storm and you can get a warning before a West Indian hurricane strikes, but on the way to the Galapagos you'll find no wind at all. The atmospheric conditions are such that sun sights are not accurate and the current will sweep you around in a large circle until the ship rots. It is very difficult to sail with an engine to the Galapagos. Without an engine it is as good as impossible.'

In the Galapagos twelve days later: 'You have been lucky, but be careful between the islands. These are dangerous waters with sudden heavy swells and strong currents. Last year alone three yachts were wrecked here.' In the Marquesas twenty-three days and three thousand miles later: 'You must have had a lucky wind to be able to enter this port. Sailing to the Tuamotus? You can't be serious! They are not called "the Dangerous Archipelago" without reason. With a powerful engine and a large crew it is dangerous—for you it would be suicide.'

Strangely enough we had no warnings during our stay in the Tuamotus. Perhaps the language barrier had something to do with it. However, they started afresh in Tahiti. There I was to learn that the first half of the trip around the world, that is, from England to Tahiti via Panama, is rather easy. It is the second half which is difficult.

In Papua they warned me about the Coral Sea with its unknown reefs and sudden rain squalls which cut out all visibility. In the Strait of Torres they told me that crossing the Arafura under sail was impossible for lack of wind. In Darwin they said that the Indian Ocean was the most dangerous in the world. At Christmas Island they were greatly concerned about my trying to cross the doldrums with its violent gales and long-lasting calms. In Aden everyone agreed that the Red Sea was in a class by itself. And so on.

So I was not too surprised that now also someone should warn me about the difficulties ahead. Neither should we completely disregard such warnings, because there is generally some truth in them, but we should not let them scare us away from places we would like to see, because the sea has always been sailed upon by men all over the globe, and a safe ship manned by a careful skipper should be able to sail in anyone's waters.

Cannes is an agreeable town and a fascinating one. Everything can be found almost side by side: the chauffeur-driven Rolls-Royce next to the beaten-up jalopy, the millionaire and the penniless hitch-hiker, the old and the very young, those who came for their health and those who come for having fun, those who come to spend money and those who come trying to grasp some of the money being thrown around. In addition to the fabulous city, the country around the town is priceless for those who like the beauty of nature.

Throughout our stay in Cannes I would go for a couple of hours' ride every morning on my bicycle, covering twenty-five to thirty miles on small, quiet back roads where there was hardly a sound except for a few birds singing. It was a nice contrast to the harbour, for although it was a beautiful one and a convenient one, it was a terribly noisy place: due to 'progress' every yacht today considers electricity to be a necessity and, of course, motors to make electricity. Therefore when in a port where several hundred yachts are jammed side by side there will be a continuous roar of engines going on all day. As soon as one motor finally stops, another will have taken over. In addition to that nerve-wrecking annoyance these motors would also discharge exhaust fumes which, if the wind was right, could blow the poisonous air into the neighbouring yacht, or when there was no wind at all would lie over the harbour as a blue-grey haze. And all this was for the benefit of 'comfort'!

How much nicer the harbour could have been and how much more pleasant to live there before we became the slaves of progress: fresh air for everyone, the beauty of flax and cotton sails gently flapping in the breeze as they were hoisted to be aired, and at night the cosy light of an old-fashioned oil lamp in the cabin and never any barking motors hammering on our nerves hour after hour.

During the winter I wrote most of the chapters of this book, several articles for weekly magazines, and in order to make some additional money we delivered an old 65-foot motor yacht to Barcelona, where the much-needed repairs would be cheaper than in France. My friends warned me about going to sea with a ship which was declared as 'not seaworthy' by the local surveyor, and I should have listened to them, but the money was tempting and then I wanted to see Barcelona. I thought that the dangers would be very small if I stayed close to shore, for if the situation should become desperate and should the ship threaten to sink, I could always run her on the beach in order to save our necks, even if it meant the destruction of the boat: but I soon was to discover that to call such a yacht 'not seaworthy' was an understatement: she was a wreck! Nothing worked and everything fell to pieces, door-handles came off when we tried to open a door—even the wheel fell off once when in a lurch I had tried to hang on to it, only to be thrown on the floor with the wheel in my lap! Water was leaking through the bottom at a frightening rate, witnessed by the high-pressure stream of water shooting out of the bilge pump. When it broke down altogether, it became only a matter of whether we could reach port before sinking or we would have to beach the yacht.

The water soon reached the motors, whose flywheels kicked up fantastic geysers of dirty bilge water all over the walls and the ceiling, making it impossible to enter the engine room without getting soaked from top to toe with the disgusting filthy water. I did not want to wreck the ship by running her ashore until the very last minute, so by continually delaying the beaching until 'the next bay' we finally entered port, but by then we had two feet of water above the floorboards and the yacht lay so deep in the water that the harbourmaster immediately called the fire squad to pump us out, as he did not want the wreck to sink right in his port.

When the water-level sank below the floors so we could walk on them the oil in the bilge water remained on the boards, making them as slippery as a skating rink and caused not a little swearing from the French firemen and some giggling from Simonne watching them all fall over as in an old Laurel and Hardy film. When the mechanic had installed a new pump and when we had made sure that it did pump out the water as fast and even faster than it leaked in, we felt seaworthy again, our standards having become very modest since getting on board that ship.

Leaving Marseilles, we were no longer able to keep within a couple of hundred yards of land, because the Rhone estuary has many shoals stretching a fair distance out to sea, but we were not too worried about it, as the water was as flat as a mirror and with our eleven knots' cruising speed we were making good progress. Our optimism was not to last too long, as we were soon to discover the truth in the statement that in the Mediterranean sudden gales can change a flat sea to a very rough one within minutes.

The ship was pounding into the sea, so I had to slow her down in order to reduce the danger of stoving in the bottom of the ship. First to eight knots, then six, then finally to only about two knots. It eased the pounding, but I was horrified to discover a wide-open slot between the deckhouse and the deck which closed up tight when the bow plunged into the next wave, only to reopen when the ship came on top of the following wave: the ship was working and bending in the sea like a snake! I expected her to break in two any minute.

Fortunately we finally got into smoother water close to shore and soon we made fast inside Sete harbour. I was tempted to call the owner and tell him to take his wreck to Barcelona himself if he dared, but then I dislike abandoning a job half-way through, and studying the chart I saw that from now on we could stay within a hundred yards of the coast the whole way to Barcelona. We would follow every little bay along its shores rather than ever cutting across them. It would make a slightly longer route, but if we always stayed that close to shore we would not be in any danger, for even in cold water we could swim a few hundred yards. So we continued the voyage, stopping overnight at Port Vendres and St. Felux de Guiniol, before finally arriving in Barcelona, greatly relieved to get off the miserable ship.

As I did not want Simonne to remember her Easter vacation solely as a miserable one, we decided to make a side-trip to sunny Palma de Majorca. The steamship went direct every evening, arriving at breakfast-time. In order not to spend all the benefit of the delivery job, I purchased third-class tickets, as even if cabins in that class were tiny, they were to us the greatest luxury after the motor yacht. Here the blankets were dry, it did not rain through the 'roof', and neither did it stink from the bilge water. It was nice and warm and we felt as if in Paradise, gently rocked by the ship's easy motion through the sea.

We spent a few wonderful days in Majorca, but when the day of returning arrived we were informed that the ship was full to the last place—that is except for the 'royal suite'. If we delayed the trip till next day, Simonne would not get back to school in time, so I had no choice but to buy tickets for that suite at a ridiculously high price, considering that the 'royal suite' travelled no faster than any other class. But Simonne was thrilled. She had never travelled in a royal suite before, and then women always like luxury.

Back in Cannes our friends seemed genuinely glad to see us again, as they had really been worried for our safety when they had read about all the storms, although one of them added that as they had not heard any more from us they had decided to draw lots among them to determine who should inherit *Dorothea*.

Spring had come during our absence; in fact, it could be called summer, so warm and nice was it after the cold of Easter, west of Marseilles. The weeks passed quickly and soon the date of departure was only ten days away. I then stopped working on the book and on all articles and concentrated on fitting out for the voyage to England. All my friends who knew that I had not done a thing to the boat ever since arriving in France laughed when I said that 'yes, of course I am leaving on the 4th of July as intended'.

Simplicity is the key to trouble-free maintenance on board yachts. It took me two days to paint the whole ship, including decks and cabin trunk. I have no varnish outside and I use only soft white paint which does not need any sandpapering. It does not look as flashy as varnish and high-gloss paint, but it is quite satisfactory. It took one afternoon to scrape off the bottom. I did not have to get the ship out of the water, because she is coppered: just swimming with goggles and a longshafted brush did the trick.

Then I bent on the sails which had been stowed down below during the winter and those of the ropes which looked tired I replaced. All the running rigging is rope and not flexible wire, so all splicing was quickly done and the whole rig was shipshape in a day, including putting a new coat of oil on the mast. The main halyard is double-ended (a luff tackle is on the one side for tightening the luff in strong winds). The single-ended tail gives a purchase of two to one, so sitting on the bosun's chair it is very easy for me to pull myself up to the top of the mast without having to bother the neighbours for help, as all the modern boats have to do with their winches.

For oiling the mast I just pulled myself to the top of the mast, made a slip-knot which went under my thighs and then started to smear the oil on the mast, slowly letting the rope slip until I came all the way down to deck. An oiled mast does not have the shine of a varnished one, but it will be better protected and have a much longer life, as well as only requiring half an hour's work twice a year instead of countless hours of sandpapering and many coats of expensive varnish several times a year. Another couple of days with various small odd jobs and the ship was ready, except for getting the stores on board.

I still had four days left and could think of nothing more to do on the ship, so I went visiting my friends, who seemed a bit surprised when I said that the fitting-out was finished. Of course, had I had a motor to overhaul, electricity to check for a leak or other trouble, a toilet to repair, radios to get working again, skin fittings to replace, not to speak of the many other modern appliances which are purchased for comfort but which continually require maintenance and extra work, then I certainly would not have been ready in this short time. Sailing vessels without motors are said to lose a lot of time waiting for favourable winds, but I think far more time is lost by modern boats equipped with too many of today's complications.

On 3rd July I got all the food, water and paraffin on board and stowed everything securely. On the 4th it was blowing a fresh easterly wind, which overjoyed me, and I said to Simonne that we would have a following wind to the Balearic Islands. While Simonne took all our clothes out of the hanging-lockers to stow them flat in lockers instead, as the constant motion of a small boat at sea will badly chafe and damage any clothes in a hanging closet, I went to the Port Office to pay my dues and clear for England, our next port.

While waiting for my papers and watching over the sea I was disappointed to see that the wind was dying down and being replaced by a south-westerly wind which I could see approaching rapidly as it came closer. When I came back to the ship an hour later I saw Simonne in a heated discussion with some local fishermen:

'Tell them that this wind will be a following wind for us! They say that if we sail towards Majorca this is a wind dead into our nose,' she shouted to me as soon as she saw me.

She had not noticed that the wind had turned and I was deeply flattered that she had such great confidence in what I said that for not one minute did she consider the local fishermen could be right.

At noon the sails were up and we let go the moorings in a very stiff breeze which indeed was dead into our nose. Many of our friends had piled into a launch and were following us out of the harbour, while many sirens, foghorns and whistles were sounding as farewell greeting. We had 2,100 miles ahead of us to fulfil the trip around the world.

15

Returning Home

THE wind was to head us the whole way. Beating against the stiff south-westerly towards Gibraltar, I consoled myself that once through Gib that wind would become a wonderful reach for us, as we would then turn north towards England, but by the time we arrived by Cap St. Vincent and turned right, a cold blast of north wind forced us to beat all the rest of the way.

The only exception to these headwinds was in the Straits of Gibraltar, when a sudden easterly gale sprang up with such violence that we had to take down every stitch of canvas, and still the boat kept going at almost hull speed under bare rigging. It blew so hard that we could not keep our faces towards the wind, as it would have choked us. It only lasted a short time, but long enough to shoot us through the Straits against the powerful current which almost always flows into the Mediterranean from the Atlantic and can make it so hard for a sailing vessel to get out of the inside sea. In addition to helping us through that difficult spot, the gale also blew away the fog which had surrounded us at the entrance to the Straits.

Tuesday, 21st July, was a big day for me, because on that day we crossed my south-bound track of five years ago which still was on the chart. I had sailed completely around the world in my own sailing boat, fulfilling my teenage dream. Simonne made a cake for the occasion, even though it was only *Dorothea*'s and my celebration, since she had only joined up in Martinique.

From the lower point of Portugal we stayed well reefed down for about ten days, fighting our way closehauled against huge seas constantly washing over the decks. Everything had to be closed and we could never venture on deck without getting into our oilskins and seaboots. We could no longer just go on deck letting our skin be soaked by the spray, as we had done in the tropics.

When we reached the latitude of about the middle of the Bay of Biscay the barometer slowly began to rise and the wind moderated so I could shake out the reefs and at least on the after part of the ship get on deck without the oilskins. The motion of the ship moderated as the waves became smaller, making life on board much more pleasant.

During the night of 3rd August, about two hundred miles south of England, we hit something which made the ship tremble. Rushing on

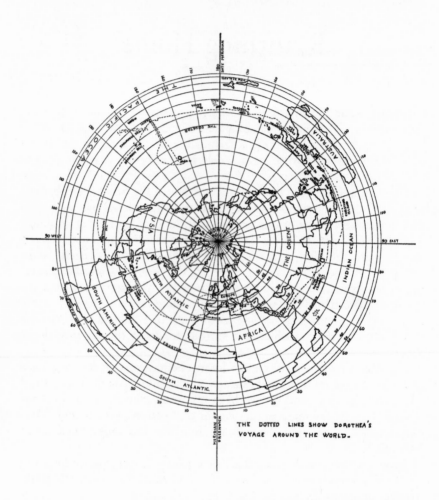

THE DOTTED LINES SHOW DOROTHEA'S
VOYAGE AROUND THE WORLD.

deck, I could see nothing in the pitch darkness surrounding us. A quick look in the bilges revealed that the collision had not caused any leak, as they were still dry. A boat is not like a car, which throws a powerful beam of light ahead to see the way: a boat will plunge through the seas during black nights, seeing absolutely nothing either behind or in front. The ship will only trust that as long as nothing is to be seen the sea is clear.

Had other ships been around we would have seen their position lights and if land had been close we should have seen lights either from light-houses or simply from illuminated houses, cars and streets. Uninhabited shores often have no lights at all and one has to be careful when approaching such shores, but at least we know from the chart where to expect them. One danger one cannot watch for at all is wreckage floating on the sea. The chance of hitting some odd wreckage is not very great, but it is nevertheless a very serious hazard for a small wooden boat. When we reached land we saw the damage: just above the waterline a 5 in. scar about $\frac{3}{8}$ in. deep had been gouged out of the tough pitch-pine planking! I shuddered at the thought of the damage had I been in one of those modern ultra-light displacement plywood boats. Chances are that it would have been not a 5 in. scar, but just a 5 in. hole!

On the 4th I shaved off the thirty-two-day-old beard and we cleaned up the boat thoroughly, as I knew that England could not be far away, even though I had not had any sights for two days due to the light fog hiding the horizon as well as the sun. Ships' sirens were sounding regularly all around us, making us feel rather uncomfortable, as we rather doubted if they would hear the little horn I was answering them with. It felt more like a toy than anything else and I wondered once more why foghorns and navigation lights get smaller and smaller with the decreasing size of yachts. It looks, of course, nicer when in port to have small lights on a small boat, but when at sea it is just as important to be seen and heard in even the smallest boat.

During the night the sirens gradually were only to be heard from our right side, which I took as a sign that we were between the shipping lane and the coast of England. I was sounding the lead frequently, so I would not run ashore and wreck the ship, but I felt that we were still a few miles from the coast and were in no danger.

Next morning a most welcome south-westerly wind sprang up and soon cleared all the fog. All of a sudden we saw land about four miles away with small brick houses and cars running along winding roads. I soon recognised where we were and a couple of hours later we entered Brixham, the harbour from which I had sailed away five years ago almost to the day, and which to me still looked like one of the most charming places in the world, even after having seen so many others. We anchored in front of the crowded yacht club, flying the flags of all the countries we had visited since *Dorothea* last had been in the port. The friendly harbour-master soon came alongside in a small launch which was well protected by fenders and all formalities were soon done.

As we got into the dinghy to row ashore our eyes caught sight of the ugly scar which probably would have sunk a lesser vessel. Simonne looked apprehensively at the damage and then declared thoughtfully: 'Sometimes I wonder if this business of sailing the seas in a small boat is not a bit risky?'

Walking ashore, I was thrilled to recognise all the small stores in the winding narrow streets where I had done so much fitting out for the voyage and I was glad to see that Simonne also liked the little town. Not much had changed during my absence, except for a few new stores, but the increase in the number of cars was astonishing and filled me with awe: where are they all going to be put if they keep on increasing any further? Many people recognised me and remembered me from the time they had seen me fitting out. Reporters interviewed us on tape-recorders and I appeared on several television shows as well as on the radio. The British are indeed very interested in long-distance sailing, for nowhere else in the world had anyone shown any interest whatsoever in our voyage except for an occasional small newspaper article.

After a few pleasant days in Brixham we sailed to Birdham, as I wanted to bring *Dorothea* back to her home port. We arrived in front of the bar guarding the entrance to the port of Chichester on 13th August early in the morning, but had to anchor outside the entrance for a few hours in order to wait for the tide to come back and give us sufficient depth of water for crossing the bar.

It was blowing a fresh headwind when we finally tacked through the entrance channel, I forward sounding the lead continually and Simonne by the tiller laying the ship over to the new tack each time the lead announced just a foot of water under the keel and I signalled to her to turn.

After safely having entered the main harbour we had an exciting slalom run among the hundreds of yachts moored in the several-mile-long river which leads towards Birdham, but finally we could let the hook go in the little creek outside Birdham's tiny yacht harbour. What strange feelings I had when setting foot on that land from the dinghy and being back after so many miles! At the office they assigned me a berth and gave me my mail.

In the following days the ship was continually receiving my many friends who had seen in the papers or heard on the radio that I was back. They had not forgotten me. We were invited to dinners, to have hot baths in full-size bathtubs and we were taken for long car drives in the beautiful English countryside. We had such a marvellous time that we just wished that there were many more hours than twenty-four in each day, so we would not have to decline so many of the kind invitations offered us.

One of the first on board to welcome us was Captain Taylor, the man who sold me the *Dorothea*. It must have been strange for him to see his boat again, thinking about all the places she had been while he had remained in the same office in London.

Mrs. Hawkins, the daughter of Dr. Segar, the man who had owned *Dorothea* before Captain Taylor and who had kept her until his death, also came on board, bringing her husband and her six-year-old son. They seemed thrilled at the thought of the many countries she had been to, but when the little boy understood that the ship had belonged to them before he wept and begged his parents to buy the boat back. When his mother tried to reason with him and explained that they did not have the money to buy any boat for the moment, he immediately offered all of the £7 he had in his piggy bank, hope shining through his tear-filled eyes.

I also had a visit from the original owner and his wife, Mr. and Mrs. Laurence Irving, an extremely charming couple who perhaps were the most excited of them all to come on board and to hear that their old boat had really been all around the world. Before driving us to Chichester for a nice lunch they spent several hours on board and both seemed as happy as children having re-found a long lost toy. Among the many questions he asked me if I had noticed the little piece of dark wood notched into the mast below the deck? I had, in fact, often wondered what it could have been and never thought that I would ever hear the reason, but now with apologies to Simonne he explained that it was a sliver of the timber of Nelson's flagship at Trafalgar. He also said that he felt sure that I must often have wondered why the yacht had been called *Dorothea*, and explained that when his mother had died he had used a part of his inheritance to build the ship and had named the new vessel after her in remembrance. His mother was Dorothea Baird, the famous actress who at the end of the last century had won the hearts of so many playgoers that she has become immortal in the theatre world.

*   *   *

What happens to a man who has spent many years of his life completely independent and free, a man who has not had to bend to social rules, a man who has not had any employer to breathe down his neck, nor any employee to watch, a man who did not have to worry about taxes, landlords, tenants, neighbours, and a man who has never had to return to work every Monday morning?

I was thrilled to be back in Europe and to see my many friends, but I knew that when the novelty had worn off I would miss the free life I had had and nostalgia for the tropics and for the trade winds would sweep over me. I knew that I would never be happy in the modern world with its thousands of laws and restrictions. Sooner or later the desire to sail back to the tropics would be irresistible.

Dorothea had proven her worth, but during the long voyage I had little by little designed my own dream ship based on the experience I had gained. It is now my desire to build a new yacht to that design with my own hands, and when the new ship is ready, the compass course will again be set south to the tropics, where I belong.

Post Scriptum

Just a year after this manuscript was written, on passage back to the tropics, we made a stop in Gibraltar and there, in a simple and quiet ceremony, 'for better or for worse' Simonne became my wife.

Glossary

Abeam: at right angles to the centreline of a boat.

Baggywrinkle: padding made out of old ropes to prevent chafe.

Bar: a shallow patch extending across many harbour entrances.

Beam: greatest width of a boat.

Beat, to: the process of gaining towards the direction from which the wind blows by sailing a zigzag course toward the wind.

Bermudian rig (also called *Marconi rig*): a rig where a tall triangular sail is set aft of the mast.

Block: pulley.

Blowing out: a sail blown to pieces by a strong wind.

Bobstay: a stay holding the bowsprit down.

Bulkhead: partition separating a vessel into several compartments.

Bulwarks: a low wall surrounding the deck, generally only a few inches high on small yachts.

Catamaran: a twin-hulled vessel.

Celestial navigation: a method of calculating a vessel's position on the chart by measuring the angle of celestial bodies.

Chafe: wear due to continuous rubbing of various parts of the ship against each other. Very common problem in sailing vessels.

Chronometer: special extra-accurate watch.

Clew: the rear lower corner of a sail.

Closehauled: sailing as close to the wind as possible. (Racing boats in smooth water can sail as close as forty degrees from the wind-direction, but cruising boats at sea can rarely do better than fifty-five degrees, and sometimes a lot less.)

Coachroof: a part of the deck which is raised in small crafts for increasing headroom inside.

Come about (also called *to tack*): to head the boat into the wind and then steer on the equivalent course on the opposite side of the wind when beating to windward (see *Beat, to*).

Cross-trees (also called *Spreaders*): cross-bars used to spread the load of the rigging and lessen strains.

Cutter: a vessel rigged with only one mast, but having two sails forward of the mast (see *Sloop*).

Dead before: with the wind exactly aft of the vessel.

Dead reckoning: finding a ship's position on the chart by using the compass, the log (or estimated numbers of miles) and taking into account the effect of wind and current.

Double-ender: a vessel pointed at both ends, and with the rudder fastened on the extreme after end.

Down-haul: a rope for hauling down a sail.

Draught: the depth of water needed for a vessel to float.

Fenders: touch cushions to protect a ship's side.

Flush-decked: a vessel without a coachroof.

Forecastle: the forward compartment of a vessel.

Force (Wind Force 8): a system of designating the wind's force called the Beaufort Scale and graduated from Zero (complete calm) to Force 12 (full hurricane).

Fore-and-aft sail: sails rigged along the centreline of the ship and receiving the wind on either side of the sails depending on the ship's heading.

Forestay (also called *Jibstay*): the stay on which the foresail or jib is attached and which serves to hold the mast forward.

Freeboard: the distance from the water to deck.

Full main: a mainsail which is not reefed (see *Reef*).

Gaff: the spar supporting the upper part of a gaff mainsail.

Genoa: a large staysail overlapping the mast considerably, which started on racing boats, but has now also become popular among some cruising men despite its unhandiness.

Gimbals: arrangement of suspending a vessel's stove or table so it will always remain level no matter how much the ship bounces about.

Guy: forward line to hold a spar from slamming at sea.

Halyard: ropes or wires used for hoisting a sail.

Head: nautical term for a toilet on board a vessel.

Headsail: all sails forward of the mast.

Heave-to: to slow down a vessel by making one or more sails counteract the other. Some ships can be made to remain almost stationary using this technique.

Jib: a triangular sail set at the foremost end of a vessel.

Jibe: turning a ship so the wind will strike the vessel from the opposite side by turning downwind as opposed to tacking when the vessel is turned toward the wind. Jibing is considered by many as a dangerous manoeuvre, but it is only dangerous when the crew is taken unawares. The jibe is then called 'accidental jibing' as opposed to 'controlled jibing'. It is the most difficult manoeuvre of them all on fore-and-afters.

Ketch: a two-masted vessel with the aft mast the smaller and stepped forward of the aft waterline.

Knot: a nautical speed measure equalling one nautical mile in one hour. (The expression 'knot an hour' is incorrect.)

Knock down: violently heeled over and out of control.

Leeward: downwind.

Lee shore: a shore downwind to a vessel.

Leeway: the drift a boat is sliding sideways from the course she is pointing due to the pressure of the wind.

Log: an instrument which registers the distance covered through the water.

Main sheet: the rope which controls the mainsail.

Mast track (also called the *Railway*): a track running the whole length of the mast on Bermudian-rigged vessels for holding the mainsail.

Mizzenmast: the aft mast of a ketch and of a yawl.

Moored: when a vessel has anchored on two anchors so she cannot swing in the large circle single-anchored vessels do. Also when attached to a permanent oversize anchor or cement blocks in harbour, where very little length of cable is required, thus again reducing the swinging circle.

Noon sight: measuring the angle of the sun at noon for determining the latitude.

Octant: predecessor of the sextant.

Out-haul: a line used to haul out a sail to the extremity of a spar.

Overhang: that part of a vessel which overhangs the water measured from the waterline of the hull.

Pilot (*book*): a guide-book made for seamen describing the oceans and the coasts of the world.

Port side: the left side of a vessel when looking towards the bow.

Pooped, to be: to be buried below a wave, when running ahead of big seas.

Preventers: extra ropes used to prevent slamming of spars at sea.

Pulpit: protective railing fixed to bow.

Quarantine: a ship arriving in port from a foreign country must prove that she carries no contagious diseases before anyone on board is permitted to land. An old law dating from the time of the pest and other diseases which were brought to new countries by the ships. Today, when the aeroplanes make it impossible to prevent disease spreading from one country to another, the quarantine formalities have little value and are only a most boring formality.

Quartering winds: a wind blowing from aft at about a forty-five-degree angle to the centreline of the boat.

Reaching: sailing with the wind on the beam and until forty-five degrees aft of the beam.

Reef, to: reducing the amount of canvas carried normally.

Rigging: the fixed wires holding the mast upright are called the 'standing rigging', while the ropes or wires used for controlling the sails are called 'running rigging'.

Roller reefing: a device much favoured by some yachtsmen for reefing a mainsail. By rolling the sail around the boom.

Runners: the stays holding the mast aft and which has to be quickly released each time a boat comes about.

Samson post: strong, vertical timber passing through the foredeck for making fast mooring ropes.

Schooner: fore-and-aft vessel with generally two masts, but could have more, in which the forward mast is no taller than the others. (See ketch and yawl.)

Sea anchor: a stout open-mouthed bag used in stormy weather by small ships in an effort to slow down the boat, trailing the bag at the end of a heavy rope or of the anchor chain.

Sextant: an instrument used by seamen for measuring angles.

Shackle: a connecting link easily removed by unscrewing a pin.

Shear-line (or simply *Shear*): the curved fore-and-aft profile of a ship's deck.

Sheet: not any form of a sail, but a rope controlling the sails.

Short-ended: a vessel with short overhang.

Shoal: shallow water.

Shrouds: the permanent wires (could also be ropes) supporting the mast on either side.

Sight: an angle of a heavenly body measured through the sextant.

Sloop: a single-masted fore-and-aft vessel with only one sail forward of the mast (see *Cutter*).

Starboard: the right side of a vessel when facing forward.

Stay: a fore-and-aft wire supporting a mast.

Staysail: a sail that sets on a stay and can run up and down it.

Steerage way: a certain minimum speed necessary before the rudder will have control over the ship's direction.

Storm jib: a very small jib made out of extra heavy canvas and used instead of the normal jibs in very heavy weather.

Straight stem: a stem which is vertical above the waterline.

Tack, to: see, *beat, to*, and *come about, to*.

Tackle: a rope running through pulleys in order to gain a mechanical increase in power.

Thames measurement: a system of designating a boat's size taking into account only the beam and the length from stem to sternpost. Only used in Britain.

Topping lift: a rope or wire from the end of the boom to up the mast to prevent the boom from hitting the deck when lowering the sail. Also used when reefing the sail, and by some skippers used to relieve the sail from the weight of the boom, thus saving some wear.

Topsides: the side of a boat between the water and the deck.

Transom: the planking of the aft of a square-sterned vessel.

Trimaran: a triple-hulled vessel.

Trim: adjust the sail for best possible speed.

Trysail: a small sail of very strong canvas used instead of the mainsail in very heavy weather.

Warps: heavy ropes for towing or mooring.

Warp, to: to warp a vessel is to manoeuvre a vessel into her berth by handling ropes to temporarily laid anchors, to shore or to other stationary vessels. An almost forgotten art in the modern age of motors, but still of capital importance to the engineless sailing vessel.

Weather helm: the tendency of a sailing vessel to try to turn into the wind unless the helmsman holds the helm up.

Wind, hard on the wind: when sailing as close to the wind as possible.

Windage: the total resistance to the wind by a vessel's topsides, superstructure and rigging.

Working: the slight movement of a ship's various parts which will cause it to leak. Very common in old craft, especially if they have been lightly built.

Working sail: the sails ordinarily used under average force wind.

Yawl: a twin-masted vessel with the aft mast considerably smaller than the main mast and the smaller mast aft of the aft waterline, its sail thus considerably overhanging the stern.

Index